Ageing with
Smartphones in Irelan

For Ciaran & Warly

Hope you enjoy it

Doug

Ageing with Smartphones in Ireland

When life becomes craft

Pauline Garvey and Daniel Miller

First published in 2021 by
UCL Press
University College London
Gower Street
London WC1E 6BT

Available to download free: www.uclpress.co.uk

ISBN: 978-1-78735-968-0 (Hbk)
ISBN: 978-1-78735-967-3 (Pbk)
ISBN: 978-1-78735-966-6 (PDF)
ISBN: 978-1-78735-969-7 (epub)
ISBN: 978-1-78735-970-3 (mobi)
DOI: https://doi.org/10.14324/111.9781787359666

Contents

List of figures

List of abbreviations

ARG   Active Retirement group

ASSA   Anthropology of Smartphones and Smart Ageing (a project based at UCL Anthropology and in which both Daniel Miller and Pauline Garvey participate)

BBC   British Broadcasting Corporation

CSO   Central Statistics Office (Ireland)

DEXA   Dual-energy X-ray absorptiometry for assessing bone density

DIY   Do-it-yourself

DNA   Deoxyribonucleic acid: the hereditary material in humans and other organisms

EU   European Union

GDPR   General Data Protection Regulation

GAA   Gaelic Athletic Association

GP   General Practitioner (a term for a medical doctor in countries such as the UK, Ireland, Australia and New Zealand)

HR   Human Resources

HRT   Hormone Replacement Therapy

ILH   Irish Life Health – a health insurance company in Ireland

IT   Information Technology

LAMP   Local Asset Mapping Project, based in St James's Hospital in Dublin

ME   Myalgic encephalomyelitis (also called CFD, or Chronic Fatigue Syndrome): a condition that causes extreme tiredness and a range of other symptoms.

OECD   Organisation for Economic Co-operation and Development

PhD   Doctor of Philosophy degree

PMT   Premenstrual tension

SPHE   Social, personal and health education (classes offered by the Irish national curriculum)

TILDA   The Irish Longitudinal Study on Ageing

Series Foreword

This book series is based on a project called 'The Anthropology of Smartphones and Smart Ageing', or ASSA. This project focused on the experiences of ageing among a demographic who generally do not regard themselves as either young or elderly. We were particularly interested in the use and consequence of smartphones for this age group, as these devices are today a global and increasingly ubiquitous technology that had previously been associated with youth. We also wanted to consider how the smartphone has impacted upon the health of people in this age group and to see whether we could contribute to this field by reporting on the ways in which people have adopted smartphones as a means of improving their welfare.

The project consists of 11 researchers working in 10 fieldsites across 9 countries as follows: Alfonso Otaegui (Santiago, Chile); Charlotte Hawkins (Kampala, Uganda); Daniel Miller (Cuan, Ireland); Laila Abed Rabho and Maya de Vries (al-Quds [East Jerusalem]); Laura Haapio-Kirk (Kōchi and Kyoto, Japan); Marília Duque (Bento, São Paulo, Brazil); Patrick Awondo (Yaoundé, Cameroon); Pauline Garvey (Dublin, Ireland); Shireen Walton (NoLo, Milan, Italy) and Xinyuan Wang (Shanghai, China). Several of the names used for these fieldsites are pseudonyms.

Most of the researchers were based at the Department of Anthropology, University College London. The exceptions are Alfonso Otaegui at the Pontificia Universidad Católica de Chile, Pauline Garvey at Maynooth University, the National University of Ireland, Maynooth, Marília Duque at Escola Superior de Propaganda e Marketing (ESPM) in São Paulo, Laila Abed Rabho, an independent scholar, and Maya de Vries, based at the Hebrew University of Jerusalem. The ethnographic research was conducted simultaneously, other than that of Al-Quds which started and ended later.

This series comprises a comparative book about the use and consequences of smartphones called *The Global Smartphone*. In addition we intend to publish an edited collection presenting our work in the area of mHealth. There will also be nine monographs representing our ethnographic research, with the two Irish fieldsites combined within a single volume. These ethnographic monographs will all have the same chapter headings with the exception of chapter 7 – a repetition that will enable readers to consider our work comparatively.

The project has been highly collaborative and comparative from the beginning. We have been blogging since its inception at https:// blogs.ucl.ac.uk/assa/, where further information about the project may be found. Our main project website can be found at https://www.ucl. ac.uk/anthropology/assa/. The core of this website is translated into the languages of our fieldsites. The comparative book and several of the monographs will also appear in translation. As far as possible, all our work is available without cost, under a Creative Commons licence. The narrative is intended to be accessible to a wide audience, with detailed information on academic discussion and references being supplied in the endnotes.

We have included films within the digital version of this book; almost all are less than three minutes long. We hope they will help to convey more of our fieldsites and allow you to hear directly from some of our research participants. If you are reading this in eBook format, simply click on each film to watch them on our website. If you are reading a hard copy of this book, the URLs for each film are provided in each caption so you can view them when you have internet access.

Acknowledgements

Our first and foremost thanks go to the hundreds of people who became our research participants. Many of them had their own prior experience of research and were themselves mostly interested in understanding the topics of ageing and smartphones. As a result we did not so much 'study' people as collaborate with them in jointly trying to appreciate how things have changed and assessing their contemporary experience of ageing. We cannot name them, however, since the project is based on anonymity. But we hope they realise just how much their time, patience and interest in our project was appreciated by us both.

We worked as part of the ASSA team, other members of which were continually reading and commenting upon our research drafts. We are therefore greatly indebted to the entire team. We would also particularly like to thank Georgiana Murariu, who kept us organised during the writing process and edited the volume, Catherine Bradley, who copy edited the volume, and the staff of UCL Press. Nor would this project have been possible without the support of our partners and families.

We wish to acknowledge the support of Maynooth University and in particular the generous advice of Professor David Prendergast, who also helped with the short films we made with our research participants. Grateful thanks also go to Daniel Balteanu, Digital Media Specialist for Maynooth University, as well as the research participants and anthropology students who participated in the film-making. We would also like to acknowledge Joseph Timoney from the Department of Computer Science, Maynooth University and Daniel Paul O'Neill for their kind assistance in developing a Social Prescribing website that features in this book. Thanks also to Catherine Hayes, Fiona Murphy and to all those who contributed in countless other ways to the production of this volume, including individuals from the various organisations, from those who gave us time and invaluable information to those who helped with transcription. Lastly, we are grateful to those who read drafts of this manuscript, including Tom Inglis and Anne Holohan, as well as research participants from Cuan and Thornhill, including Bob, Maria, Ray, Ruth, Bill, Eithne and Anne. We also wish to thank the anonymous reviewers who offered insightful comments on the draft manuscript. The project was funded by the European Research Grant ERC-2016-ADG – SmartPhoneSmartAging – 740472.

1
Introduction

Summary of conclusions

You might expect that a book about ageing must be about people getting older. In some measure that is indeed the case, but the full title is 'Ageing with Smartphones'. When older people master the smartphone, they have incorporated a technology that up until recently was largely associated with young people. Consequently, this may make them feel younger themselves. The smartphone is pivotal, but is not alone in this process. The evidence from our fieldwork suggests a series of analogous movements as older people embrace the idea of wellness or the politics and aspirations of an environmentalist movement whose spokesperson, Greta Thunberg, was then aged only 16. This volume, therefore, is actually about how people paradoxically become younger as they grow older: how they acquire certain capacities as they lose others. This makes for a more unusual approach to ageing. However, the evidence will suggest that we need to appreciate and understand both of these trajectories if we are fully to engage with the experience of a large segment of the Irish population today.

The two fieldsites, here represented by pseudonyms – Thornhill in Dublin city and Cuan in Dublin county – are dominated by relatively affluent middle-class retirees, many of whom worked in the professions, banking or the civil service. The first conclusion of this volume is that for this population there has been a considerable change in a further aspect of the experience of ageing. Historically, ageing reflected conventional categories. People became elderly, conforming to stereotypical images such as the grandparent seated on a rocking chair with grandchildren at the knee. People today increasingly refute any such categories of age, however, and have separated ageing from frailty. As long as they remain healthy, they prefer to see themselves as simply representing continuity. Even those in their nineties may not see themselves as elderly per se until they become significantly frail. This has resulted in a more egalitarian relationship between the generations and a more active older population.

Over the course of our research, we have found that the organisations dealing with ageing populations do not always recognise the extent of these changes, which also varies by social class. There are, however, other ruptures or step changes in life that feature in this volume. For example, the impact of menopause is discussed in chapter 6, while chapter 2 focuses on retirement. In several of the other ASSA fieldsites many people emphasise an identity based on continuity with their prior work status. This is much less a feature within our Dublin fieldsites.[1]

A volume on ageing in Ireland will also differ from others because of the particular history of this nation. It has to reflect the radical shift experienced by many Irish people whose lives originated in poverty. Generally our research participants little anticipated the relative comfort they now find in retirement. This may partly explain the subtitle of our volume: 'When life becomes craft'. Most of our research participants focus upon one specific life project, that of crafting their own lives. This becomes clear in chapter 3, which focuses upon the myriad activities in which they are engaged. Crafting tends to be a social rather than an individual pursuit, however – even though one of its primary aims is to maintain the fitness and wellbeing of the body. The volume provides an account of the sheer range of activities undertaken by retired people in these fieldsites and also shows how these are crafted into daily routines.

Chapter 4 is devoted to the most important activity of all: comprising their engagement with social relations, including family, friends and neighbours. One of the central conclusions of our project is that grandparents have become a kind of new 'sandwich generation'. They may find that for a few years they are intensely involved again as daughters and sons, assisting frail parents in their nineties. At the same time they may not have completed their responsibilities to their own children who, unlike themselves, may not be able to afford housing. Grandparenting also often turns out to be the resolution of the history of our prior experience of kinship. It consists not just of the relationship to grandchildren, but often re-develops the relationships to children, partners and the wider family. The smartphone has, in effect, reversed the historical shift from extended to nuclear families. It enables people to re-engage with the extended family, but keeps it at a distance, so this is not felt as oppressive.

Chapter 5 focuses specifically on smartphones. These have swiftly become an unprecedently intimate device that may reflect back both individual personality and wider Irish values. There is a curious discrepancy between a discourse that is generally very negative about the impact of smartphones, as devices that create screen addiction, encourage surveillance and the wasting of time, set against a relatively positive appraisal of the specific capacities of various smartphone apps, for example in seeking information, locating places and organising one's life. Our experience in teaching smartphone use to older people revealed how age can exacerbate an important digital divide, leading to the disenfranchisement of those who fail to master the technology. Knowledge gained over decades may now appear worthless: a well-honed sense of direction is less impressive when you have Google Maps available. At the same time smartphones become particularly helpful as people lose mobility; they have contributed to the sense of retained youth for those who have become comfortable with their use.

Chapter 6 focuses upon the changing experience of health and wellbeing. Among the middle class, complementary health practices have expanded to rival those of traditional biomedical health. We suggest this is partly because, for older people, the experience of illness expands from isolated and specific ailments to a sense that various forms of ill health, stress and difficulty are simultaneous and related. So a more holistic conception of health issues aligns directly with their own experience as older people. Menopause can also be an important nudge towards a more holistic sense of the interrelation between physical, emotional and social concerns. Older people also regard health as part of this shift to crafting, joining walking groups and yoga or Pilates classes and developing a commitment to a more general ideal of wellbeing related to diet and fitness, as well as a current fashion for mindfulness. The chapter also investigates the rise of 'googling' for health information, suggesting that this may exacerbate differences in education or class: well-informed people used their smartphone as a research tool to become better informed, while those less well informed may become more misinformed.

Chapter 7 examines the issue of downsizing and the surprising degree to which people who might have been expected to downsize may actually choose to move to properties with as many bedrooms as the house they moved from. Alternatively, they do not 'rightsize' at all because the types of accommodation they need are not being built in their localities. Our evidence suggests that moving house is most commonly seen as a way of becoming more modern or streamlined, creating a new domestic environment that reflects a new stage in life. In addition, for some older people, divesting themselves of their possessions has become one of several ways to associate themselves with ecological concerns and current ethical issues. Much of this crafting comes together under the general umbrella of sustainability, since it involves both their efforts towards individual wellbeing and their ethical concerns for the planet. All these strategies help older people to align themselves with the most contemporary 'green' issues of the day, alongside young people. As a result, activities that would have once been viewed as an acknowledgement of ageing now contribute to older people's reassociation with the concerns of people of all ages. Such activities, set alongside the smartphone, help them in effect to feel younger rather than older.

The penultimate chapter brings some of these themes together through a consideration of life purpose. This begins with acknowledging further dramatic changes that have taken place in Ireland. Most of our research participants were born at a time when Catholicism was immensely powerful within the family, in government and in providing an answer to questions of life purpose. It does not seem that secularisation, including a decline in belief in the afterlife, has been replaced by any clear substitute. The shift has rather been towards the crafting of life discussed in the previous chapters, a process that includes a more general ethical responsibility to the wellbeing of individuals and the planet. Some older people may link this to forms of alternative spirituality that they first encountered when they were teenagers in the 1960s.

Equally important has been the moral imperative towards wellbeing and sustainability. A good example of this has been the growth in interest in the Camino de Santiago pilgrimage trail in northern Spain, an activity that blends the secular interest in walking and keeping fit with a sense of spirituality bequeathed from religion. Overall, then, a project that started out trying to investigate how people become older has instead accumulated considerable evidence for how people become 'younger' in later life. Within this re-orientation, arguably the single main contribution has come from their adoption of the smartphone.

Ireland: a historical and contemporary portrait

Introduction to Ireland

The Republic of Ireland, with a population of almost 5 million, shares the island with Northern Ireland, a part of the United Kingdom with a population of around 1.8 million. Ireland declared independence from the United Kingdom in 1919 and this was acknowledged in 1921. The capital city of Dublin has a regional population of around 2 million, with Dublin city standing at around 600,000. One of our two fieldsites lies within the city itself; the other is in the region within an hour's travel from Dublin. Ireland became a member of the European Union (then called the European Economic Community or EEC) in 1973.

The lifetime of most of our research participants has been an economic rollercoaster. Younger people find it hard to comprehend the social and economic transformation that Ireland has undergone within living memory. At the time of independence, 58 per cent of employed men worked in agriculture;[2] up until the 1950s this agriculture-oriented economy was constantly on the 'verge of collapse', resulting in both mass unemployment and mass emigration.[3]

Many of our participants were born into rural locations; even the present-day Dublin suburbs were countryside when they were young. They talk of collecting milk from the local dairy or working on the farm as a child. One man describes tasks like making the porridge in the morning and stew in the afternoon as the source of valuable skills that stood him in good stead in later life. Another recalls having to milk the cows before school each morning and remembers being 'overworked as a child'. Whereas some recall childhood memories fondly, others comment bitterly on the deprivation – 'I know poverty, I know what it smells like, I know what it tastes like' – or on the socially conservative environment of their youth.

Emigration too has been a hallmark of twentieth-century Ireland, creating a diaspora that is widely dispersed around the world.[4] From 1922, Irish Independence saw a steady replacement of colonial authority with that of the Catholic church. Religious orders ran the health and educational systems and had a strong grip over government, creating something of a theocracy. Very many research participants commented on the deeply conservative beliefs held by their parents, if not themselves. Not infrequently differences of opinion about religion led to rifts within families that spanned decades and left lasting scars.

For older people, the transformation in these underlying religious beliefs and social norms over their lifetimes was as dramatic as that of the economic transformation. First gradually, then more quickly, life changed and most of our research participants saw a marked improvement in their standard of living and disposable income. Urban centres, particularly residential construction in Dublin suburbs, sprawled. As sociologist Tom Inglis argues, in one generation Ireland has transformed from being an isolated Catholic rural society revolving around agriculture to being a liberal-individualist, secular, urban society revolving around business, commerce and high-tech transnational corporations.[5] In the past 20 years the pace of change has been dramatic. In the early 2000s Ireland was identified as having an open global economy. The authority of the Church did not so much decline as abruptly collapse from the 1980s onwards following the key scandals of sexual abuse and the ill-treatment of unmarried mothers and children.[6] This development reached perhaps its apogee during fieldwork in 2018 with the convincing vote to repeal the constitutional ban on abortion. The scale of such change is also evident in issues such as homosexuality, illegal in Ireland in 1993. Just 22 years later, in 2015, Ireland represented the first country to legalise same-sex marriage by popular vote and was hailed as the 'vanguard' of social progression by *The New York Times*.[7]

However, also seared into the consciousness of our participants was the depth of the economic crisis after 2008. The recession, sparked by the economic freefall of the global banking system, led to a bailout by the International Monetary Fund and EU.[8] The period was characterised by high levels of unemployment, mass emigration, a collapse in domestic construction and austerity measures imposed by the European Central Bank.[9] Among the other casualties of the crash were retirees who had invested their retirement packages or savings in the expectation of a decent income in the future, only to experience massive losses. By 2017, when the fieldwork began, the recession had largely passed, but many scars remained. Austerity had led to increasing levels of inequality and the percentage of the population at risk of relative poverty (if not absolute poverty) had risen to 21 per cent. Economic growth for 2017, however, was among the highest in the EU (at 7.3 per cent), due chiefly to the activities of the IT sector. Domestic activity was up 4.9 per cent and there was strong employment growth, while property prices in 2016 soared to rates of increase that mirrored the earlier 'Celtic Tiger' economic boom.

A long history of emigration had been halted by the attractions of Ireland as a site of immigration during its 'Celtic Tiger' period. With recession this was again reversed, only for the tide to turn once more as Ireland recovered its economic prosperity, such that by 2013 there were renewed invitations for emigrants to return.[10] One example was The Gathering, which was launched by the Irish Tourism Board. The Gathering encouraged Irish people to invite the Irish diaspora to return to Ireland to participate in 5000 events across the country.[11] Here we see evidence of the Irish economic and social rollercoaster in action.

Fieldwork coincided with a new confidence, although the shadow of the recession is still present in many people's lives.[12] In the post-recession era Ireland became the fastest growing economy in Europe, while still dealing with the legacy of recession. Whereas a century ago ideals of rural life were closely associated with an authentic Irish identity and nationalist sentiment, today by contrast Dublin, as a European city, stands at the forefront of new continental sensibilities.[13]

The period of fieldwork was one that reinforced this positive sense of European identity, set against a dramatic decline of the international reputation of the former colonial power of Britain. This was particularly true during the height of what were regarded as the somewhat farcical Brexit debates, a very common topic of conversation.[14] These also created renewed anxiety about the future of the Northern Irish border and the potential economic slump of a no-deal Brexit. Additionally, fundamental state services such as housing had been cut during austerity, while health and welfare provision were still quite fragile. The word 'crisis' was a common adjective to describe both health and housing.

Housing represents a particularly potent cypher for the state-citizen contract in Ireland,[15] with economic boom and bust measured in the popular imagination in bricks and mortar. The fact that Ireland saw the highest percentage increase in property prices during 2017 of any developed country, at 12.3 per cent (5.6 per cent in 2018), seemed reminiscent of the unsustainable pre-recession property boom. Income inequality is average for OECD countries. It would be more unequal, however, if Ireland's redistribution of taxes from household income had not been so effective in reducing inequality, as a recent study shows.[16]

By contrast, Irish politics is relatively stable with nearly a century of fairly predictable alternations between two parties that had origins in a bitter civil war: Fianna Fáil and Fine Gael. These are generally regarded as now two sides of a centrist coin. Our two fieldsites, being mainly middle-class, would be strongly reflective of this largely liberal consensus. A further conspicuous factor is the sheer size of the Irish diaspora, which dwarfs the local population. A more recent emigration to the UK in the 1950s, and again in the 1980s, succeeded the better known migration to the US from the seventeenth century onwards.[17] By contrast, immigration was relatively sparse within our fieldsites owing to high property prices. However, women from Eastern Europe and Brazil were increasingly evident within the local labour force, particularly in catering and childcare.

Today there is a generally positive sense of Irish identity at home and abroad. A growing sense of European identity has been boosted by the sense of European support for the Irish position during the Brexit negotiations. There is a keen interest in foreign travel, with the Irish generally finding that they are regarded as genial and egalitarian. At the same time many people either retained or were developing interests in icons of specifically Irish culture. These included Gaelic athletic sports (GAA) such as hurling, or traditional music. Many of our research participants took pride in the fact that Irish music and literature punches well above its weight, represented by figures ranging from the novelist Sebastian Barry to Fontaines D.C. (a post-punk band from Dublin), alongside a generally positive – albeit romantic and often crudely stereotypical – American-Irish identity disseminated through film and television.

Anthropology in Ireland

Historically, anthropological studies in Ireland focused on rural communities, family structure, inheritance and religion. The early classics such as *The Irish Countryman* (1937) and *Family and Community in Ireland* (1940) traced rural farming communities in transition,[18] although other works such as *Saints, Scholars and Schizophrenics* by Nancy Scheper-Hughes have since been criticised for representing Ireland as a 'culture in demise, a social system characterised by pathogenic tendencies'.[19] With the late twentieth century, however,[20] there has grown a sizeable body of work that focuses on contemporary Irish life.[21] This scholarship is both rich and varied. It has ethnographically explored the dark underbelly of urban life, in areas such as addiction,[22] migration, marginality and precarity,[23] as well as expressions of creativity, language[24] and music.[25]

This volume continues these more recent trajectories, situating itself in the mainstream of contemporary Irish urban experience. We have deliberately chosen to engage more with the mainstream than the margins, focusing on everyday life for the majority rather than populations that require policy interventions, which are often the grounds for social science research. We appreciate the specificity of our fieldsites and participants, but also believe that the core of our findings could be extended beyond Dublin. In contrast to historical studies, we find our participants in cafés rather than in pubs, discussing WhatsApp rather than religion. Although this volume does represent an ethnography of ageing in Ireland, we are concerned with historical precedent only where there is evidence for continuity and we trace evolving ideas surrounding belief or affluence insofar as they are relevant for our participants. For example, being middle class but born into conditions of poverty may make this feel more like achievement than an entitlement – something that may in turn prove relevant to practices of sustainability or ideals of generalised equality.

A key priority for our participants was the use of their smartphone to communicate with family members and friends; we spent a good deal of time discussing the roles and responsibilities that arise from grandparenthood or intergenerational living. Irish family structures have undergone profound changes in recent decades and are characterised by a particular blend of tradition and modernity.[26] Historically, the family has occupied a core position in the social structure and religious ethos of Ireland. The strong presence of Catholicism played a formative role in ideals and practices surrounding the family, particularly for women. In their role as wives and mothers, women were one icon of the new Irish Free State and religious nationalism. Inglis argues that placing women at the centre of a state ideology based on moral superiority served to discourage them from participation in the public sphere of work or political life. For example, through the introduction of a marriage bar in the 1930s and its enforcement until 1971, women in the civil service were legally obliged to give up work on getting married. Both church and state thus encouraged women to concentrate on rearing children and caring for families.[27] However, the clerical scandals in the 1990s and 2000s have undermined the Church's credibility, while shifts in economic profiles and a dramatic rise in living standards have both had a profound effect on modernisation processes.[28] A reversal of past attitudes to same-sex marriage, divorce and co-habitation have led to newly established norms.[29] What is distinctive about Ireland is not these liberal values per se, but the fact that they developed both later and faster than in many other regions of Europe.[30]

While there has been a growth in secular values and some forms of individualism,[31] the two-parent nuclear family is still the most typical environment in which children grow up in Ireland.[32] Divorce rates remain low (6 per cent) when compared to trends in other European countries. Many Irish parents rely on grandparents for regular childcare and there is an emphasis on extended family relationships. While most countries in Europe are concerned with increasing older populations and low birth rates, Ireland's population is relatively young and fertility rates are among the highest in Europe[33] at around 1.9 children per woman.[34] Intergenerational ties are strong[35] and The Irish Longitudinal Study on Ageing (TILDA) has found that a high proportion of householders live near their parents – one of the reasons why grandparenting is a major topic for this volume.

The focus on ageing

Along with gender, age is one of the primary parameters by which societies throughout history have structured and governed themselves.[36] Through countless gerontocracies, older men have historically ruled much of the world. Yet since the 1960s this hegemony has been undermined by the increasing value placed on youth culture, facilitated by the association of new technologies with youth. In Ireland the 'baby-boomer' generation who were the first to create this positive association with youth cultures have now themselves aged.[37] Today we see unprecedented icons of aged rock stars who continue to embody 'youth' values. As a result, there is a new ambivalence and uncertainty about what age is and what it may mean. The demographic sector we studied are unclear whether to claim the traditional authority of seniority or the status of youth.

This project began with the observation that academics who study ageing will tend to focus upon periods of life defined by age, either youth or the elderly. This might lead to a neglect of people who are in between. This is reflected in rather indeterminate, contested (and often relational)[38] labels for this period of life; life-cycle has become 'life course',[39] old age becomes 'third age' and, along with the mid-life crisis, we have 'life reimagined'[40] or indeed 'smart ageing'.[41] In many wealthier societies, age has also extended class discrepancies as those between the ages of 45 and 70 become the most asset-rich segment of the entire population; they represent a class that has settled its children and can now capitalise upon the new choices of consumer culture. Yet at the same time these ageing populations may face problems of isolation and loneliness linked to a loss of respect for the authority of seniority, though this may be alleviated by contact through new media.

As people become older, they may also find that, as Hazan noted,[42] 'The aged are conceived as a mass of needs bound together by the stigma of age'. As their children move on and they experience mandatory retirement alongside the decline of religion, identities and life purposes may become less defined as previously dominant role-based conceptualisations of personhood have declined. The next chapter will show how our expectations became challenged by our evidence. Research on ageing in Ireland with particular attention to the role of digital technology builds on extensive work such as the Global Ageing Experience Programme in Intel's Digital Health Group,[43] as well as research undertaken within academia.[44] Our research results have also been continually assessed against the findings of TILDA, The Irish Longitudinal Study on Ageing.[45]

Introduction to our fieldsites

Both of our fieldsites are predominantly middle class, as is most of Ireland.[46] By 2002 more than one-third of employment was professional or managerial.[47] In the most recent census, Cuan is only slightly above the average national income. These relatively sedate areas with low levels of crime are again fairly typical of contemporary Ireland, as are the high standards of local education.

Cuan

For some periods in its history Cuan (a pseudonym) was an important fishing port, but this peaked in the eighteenth century. Towards the late nineteenth century the boats were used to trade items such as coal. The surrounding area is good for agriculture, but was dominated by English landowners under a tenants-at-will ruling that meant life was extremely fragile. Generally the area was poor, as was most of Ireland, but it was perhaps a bit less food-poor, and consequently less affected by the famine than the west of Ireland. The historical records emphasise the heroism of those who supported Republican calls – for example, in the 1916 uprising – and streets are named after associated martyrs. Less discussed were the splits, even within families, represented by that period and the subsequent civil war, a probable catalyst for the emigration of those who ultimately supported the losing side. This turbulence was combined with the destructive impact of the First World War.

The population before the modern expansion was around 2,800. When most of the research participants were born, Cuan had become mainly known as a holiday destination; local people often rented out their homes for the summer and lived in a smaller dwelling during that period, often set up within their own gardens. Cuan was known for its holiday camps, ballrooms and lively music scene. This proved highly significant when the first private estates were built, since many of the people who chose to purchase these houses knew of Cuan because they, or their parents, had taken holidays there. (The holiday industry itself pretty much collapsed in the 1970s when people in Ireland started taking cheap holidays abroad.) Despite this, if you mention Cuan in Dublin or elsewhere, it is seen as an undistinguished place, off the beaten track. People know little about the town and it does not feature in the main tourist books.

There was never much by way of industry in Cuan. Its class identity was mainly a result of geography. People saw themselves as higher class than the more proletarian town on one side and lower than the more upmarket towns on the other side that continued to draw holiday makers from Dublin. With respect to internal class divisions within Cuan, there have been two major state housing projects, the first built conspicuously outside what would have been the town boundaries at that time. Private housing really took off in the 1970s, during which time the population doubled. From that time onwards there has been an almost continuous building of new estates, which remains the case today. The result is a major expansion of the population, to around 10,000 at the time of fieldwork. Much of the state housing has been sold off, with less than 200 such homes remaining. It is common for adult children in Cuan to leave in their twenties, but return in their thirties when they want to have families since their memory of their own childhood is generally positive. Many people from the new estates commute to Dublin and around 700 individuals in Cuan stay at home to mind their family. A feature of note is the degree to which community activities tend to be dominated by the 'blow-ins' – the population not born in Cuan who come from all over Ireland, attracted by the housing estates and proximity to Dublin. They are now the majority population. People today remain very conscious of whether someone is Cuan-born or a blow-in.

Why pick Cuan as a fieldsite? One reason was that it enabled Danny, who researched Cuan, to remain not too far away from Thornhill, Pauline's fieldsite. A second reason was that Cuan has a particularly active 'Age-Friendly' organisation and the main demographic shift evident from the censuses of 2005 through to 2016 is an increase in the proportion of older people. More than 10 per cent of the population are over 65, with many representing those who arrived in the 1970s. A third reason was that a town of 10,000 individuals seemed big enough to preserve the anonymity of our participants, but small enough that an ethnographer would frequently bump into the same people, making it easier to get to know and feel part of the local community.

Cuan is well served with restaurants and pubs, generally more upmarket than those in the surrounding villages and towns unless one goes closer towards Dublin, which can be reached within an hour. Otherwise the high street is fairly typical of Ireland. It has one large and one more local supermarket, a garage, two banks and a good number of hairdressers and pharmacies. The most striking discrepancy is between how people within Cuan and outside Cuan describe the town. Those living there generally have an extremely positive view of Cuan, both as an ideal place to bring up children and also for retirement. They take pride in community activities, such as the Irish Tidy Towns competition.

However, as noted above, little of this intense local pride is reflected in the way people outside of Cuan refer to the place: the majority see it as nondescript and evince surprise that Danny would choose to live there. Politically, this is a fairly liberal area. Its votes reflect those of much of Ireland, fluctuating between Fine Gael, Fianna Fáil and Labour, though with a marked increase in Green and Sinn Féin votes in recent years.

Today there are four main types of housing in Cuan. The first is the old town, representing around one-third of the whole. This is extremely mixed, including some very large fine period housing and equally large new houses built by wealthier people to exploit the views over the beach. It also includes much smaller housing and is the area with the most bungalows – often the original cottages, some of which still have thatched roofs. The second type consists of big estates, built from the 1970s through to the 1990s. These are mainly very decent three- and four-bedroom houses, with little variation (Fig. 1.1).

The third type is social housing, mainly the Vartry estate, comprising smaller, mainly three-bedroom houses. Around half of the 330 houses are now privately owned, as is almost the whole of an earlier social housing estate. Many of these were originally rented to less well-off local people. While the Vartry estate represents the primary area of

Figure 1.1 Example of the older housing estates in Cuan. Photo by Daniel Miller.

Figure 1.2   Film: *Bob*. Available at http://bit.ly/assabob.

state housing, it is certainly not homogeneous. It includes some families who the state regards as highly dysfunctional. If a crime is committed in the town, it is generally assumed the perpetrator was from either outside Cuan or from the Vartry estate. Cuan also has a group of older men, who might once have been fishermen and labourers; they spend much of the day in one of the core pubs watching the fate of their betting slips.

At the same time, all the children of Cuan go to the same secondary school and education has been a significant instrument of equalisation. Even for the older population there are new opportunities, and it is likely that the majority of people on the estate seek to make use of these. An example is Bob, who appears in the film above (Fig. 1.2): no one would ever have expected that this former butcher and school caretaker could, on retirement, become an accomplished poet – but he did. The number of people in Cuan involved in creative writing was astonishing and represented a very wide range of backgrounds. Bob is thus both unique yet also, in some ways, typical.

The fourth and final type of housing is the big new Brittas estates, again consisting mainly of three- or four-bedroom properties (Fig. 1.3).

Apart from in the old town, there are very few flats, bungalows or one- or two-bedroom properties. House prices went wild during the 'Celtic Tiger' boom. Many people bought properties to let and lost considerable sums in the subsequent crash.

One silver lining of the financial crash was that more children of local people could afford to buy into the new estates. About one-third of the Brittas estate has been bought by people from Cuan, mainly children who have returned to bring up their families here. Most of the rest are from this region of Ireland, though there are some middle-class migrants from all over Ireland, as well as others from abroad. Cuan housing is

Figure 1.3   Example of the new estates in Cuan. Photo by Daniel Miller.

more expensive than most of the towns and villages nearby, but less expensive than middle-class Dublin and some of the towns between Cuan and Dublin. A three-bedroom property sells for around €350,000, a four-bedroom for €450,000 and a house with a sea view for €550,000. Less than one-quarter of properties are rented. Over 90 per cent are houses, rather than apartments. The population is fairly homogeneous as only around 8 per cent are foreign-born, the largest group being British (often of Irish descent), followed by people from Eastern European countries often working in the town. Income levels tend to be a bit above the national average, but lower than in Thornhill. Overall the sense is of a middle-class town with a central pocket of social housing.

Thornhill

Thornhill (also a pseudonym) represents one of the closer suburbs to Dublin city (Fig. 1.4). Fishing represented its core centre of gravity in the eighteenth century, but by the nineteenth it had developed as something of a holiday resort for affluent city dwellers, who sallied out from the city on a local tram service that followed the coast northwards. From a location that was rural and dominated with large estates, farms and dairies, large residential areas were gradually added, especially between 1920 and 1960. With the sea marking the eastern edge and a large private estate marking its western fringes, however, there was a limit to the space that could be developed. In addition, one or two prominent families ensured that no large-scale estates or manufacturing were built. There were strenuous efforts, for example,

Figure 1.4   Film: *An Irish town*. Available at http://bit.ly/anirishtown.

to avoid the construction of large estates of social housing that one finds in nearby areas. Instead smaller estates, red-brick, semi-detached and terraced houses were built, starting in the 1920 and 1930s. These tended to be on the lands of previous dairy farms, though some farms remained in place until the 1970s and 1980s, where participants were sent to collect milk when they were young. An example of this type of housing is pictured below (Fig. 1.5). Thornhill was still considered countryside in the 1930s, retaining some large houses and estates as well as former bungalows built for returning officers in the British army after the First World War.

Although Thornhill lacks a single 'village centre', it contains a small clutch of shops, including restaurants, a bakery, cafés, a supermarket and estate agents, pharmacies and an off-licence; these make it feel like something of a centre. Thornhill has good public amenities, such as large playing fields for rugby and cricket. It also has a large building that houses the Gaelic Athletic Association sports, which heaves with hundreds of children during training at weekends and weekday evenings (Fig. 1.6). There is also a large park, previously privately owned but now run by Dublin City Council, and the sea is not far away. A good deal of research for this book involved meeting people along the seafront.

Thornhill is well served by churches. Historically it has had a strong Protestant community, with the Church of Ireland parish being one of the most populated Anglican parishes in the country up to the 1950s. Other Christian denominations were equally well represented and the area included a Presbyterian and Methodist church alongside the Catholic churches and those of the Church of Ireland. Relations between these Christian communities have always been good and mixed marriages were part of life even in the early twentieth century. The religious orders

Figure 1.5 Typical housing in Thornhill. Photo by Pauline Garvey.

associated with these churches are heavily involved in the running of local Catholic and Protestant schools, with the local priest and vicar respectively sitting on the schools' boards of management. Commonly found close to the churches are spacious parish halls; these host diverse activities for children and seniors as well as occasionally running the local Meals on Wheels.

At the time of research, Thornhill had a core population of about 17,000 people. It is designated as middle class/affluent according to the

Figure 1.6   Thornhill is well provisioned in terms of sports pitches. Parents usually volunteer to help with training. Photo by Pauline Garvey.

national deprivation index. Estate agents describe the town as primarily populated by professionals, including those in management and banking. Housing is similar to other Dublin suburbs which are primarily owner-occupied (68 per cent). Although people think of the main divisions in Dublin as lying along a north–south axis, the Dublin Housing Observatory website illustrates that the real social and economic divide is actually between east and west: a more affluent area to the east, stretching along the coast, and a higher incidence of social housing, overcrowding and bedsit accommodation to the west. Thornhill feels a world apart from areas of considerable disadvantage, just 5 km away.

The socio-economic profile of the area has changed since the 'Celtic Tiger' era of the 1990s–2000s. With the rise of inflation, many of the children of its middle-income residents have had to settle in less expensive areas. Residents talk of three Thornhills. There is the area occupied by long-time residents who grew up there. They describe going to the local convent school and the farms that were then just a short walk away; some recollect the basic amenities in the houses, with outdoor toilets characteristic of what was a down-at-heel working-class area. In the 1990s many left for larger, more comfortable homes, and their cottages were occupied by the professionals who were increasingly moving into the area. Lastly there are the recently settled populations, the 'blow-ins', who were in the main more affluent and attracted by the area's amenities and its proximity to Dublin. There is little social and ethnic diversity in Thornhill, unlike proximate areas in Dublin's inner city. Within Thornhill the exceptions would be a strong representation of female childcare workers who came from around the city and from further afield, particularly Brazil.

Relevant here is the wider growth of Dublin's suburbia, the subject of recent studies by Corcoran and her colleagues.[48] Suburbia retains its sentimental attachment to rural living. Generally Irish people do not consider themselves to be urbanites and it was not until 1971 that the majority of Irish people lived in settlements with more than 1,500 inhabitants.[49] Ideals of community and nationalism reflected these origins in rural life.[50] Nevertheless, despite the extensive immigration of new residents or 'blow-ins', there is strong commitment to locality in Cuan and Thornhill. Even if residents were 'unlikely to share an identity created solely through their interactions in the place where they live',[51] they nevertheless developed strong affiliations with their local neighbourhoods (Fig. 1.7). There are local networks of social support and

Figure 1.7   Every spring one Thornhill Catholic church hosts a meal for all the people who volunteer with them during the year. Photo by Pauline Garvey.

either established or, for the blow-ins, subsequent development of family networks. People generally felt good about where they lived and were emotionally invested in its history, heritage and distinctiveness.[52] While Irish society has undergone dramatic transitions in recent decades, 'there is little evidence to suggest that being more globalised has a dramatic effect on how close people feel to their town, city or country'.[53] As will be shown in later chapters, Facebook has emerged as an important site for community interaction and information; during fieldwork WhatsApp also developed as an important site for still more local affiliation around individual streets or housing estates. These were further invigorated during the Covid-19 pandemic when streets and localities created or resurrected these WhatsApp groups. People who had previously shown little interest in participating in something associated with a residents' group found that these connections became more immediate and relevant.

Field methods

Ethnography consists primarily of participant observation – that is, simply living within our fieldsites, getting to know people and taking part in local activities. Unlike most disciplines, anthropologists do not aim to adhere strictly to their original intentions with regard to methodology, nor to remain consistent. The point is rather to change and refine methods as the work proceeds and understanding of the local community grows. While Pauline, who is Irish, was brought up with this knowledge of the local community, Danny, who is English, gradually learned the appropriate ways of getting to know people. He came to realise that when two strangers meet they tend first to establish who they know in common; only then do they relax in each other's company. This meant that methods used in previous studies, such as door to door introductions, would not have been appropriate here. Participation is privileged over interviews or surveys. It is easier to have an honest and relaxed conversation when on a five-hour hike as a fellow hiker or sitting with a Guinness in a pub for an evening.

Danny started by volunteering for the local theatre to make tea, hanging around the two local cafés where groups tended to meet up and then joining more and more groups. The ones he most frequently attended included the Active Retirement group for playing bingo, the Men's Shed,[54] the ukulele group, various traditional music sessions as part of the audience and a session that he participated in through reading

Figure 1.8 Fieldwork techniques – remembering to bring a gift whenever one was invited to visit someone in their home. Fruit bracks were particularly appreciated. Photo by Daniel Miller.

lyrics and poetry (since he cannot sing to save his life), local walks, a set dancing class, a book reading club, a film club, talks at the sailing club, the local historical society and attending mass at the Catholic church. After a while Danny started to receive more invitations, at which point he followed Pauline's advice to take a brack when visiting someone at home (Fig. 1.8). Brack, a kind of sweet fruit bread, was particularly appreciated by our older participants, carrying for some memories of childhood treats and rural living.

Although most of the fieldwork was in the core area of old Cuan, he made a concerted effort to include those living on the newest estates at the far end of the town – as well as low-income households living in social housing and recent migrants from Eastern Europe – in order to bring breadth to the ethnography. For example, Danny and Pauline distributed 300 leaflets in a social housing estate offering free weekly lessons in smartphones and computing in the local community centre. Danny lived in Cuan throughout the ethnography, though he often spent weekends in London with his family. Since the end of fieldwork, he has tried to reverse this pattern, spending some weekends in Cuan. He had no car and hardly ever went out of Cuan to Dublin or other towns. He also tried to attend one-off events and groups, which ranged from celebrations of International Women's Day, the 'Darkness into Light' walk for supporting those affected by suicide, a traditional music festival and meetings of groups such as the community association or protests against unwelcome local developments. At a guess Danny probably spoke at some time or other to at least one-quarter of those aged over 65 in Cuan.

Both Pauline and Danny volunteered to work with Age Action Ireland in tutoring older people on how to improve their computing and smartphone skills. Pauline then contacted a local secondary school that was offering a similar service and found that people were much more interested in learning how to use smartphones than computers. As a result, Pauline worked with several large and small Active Retirement groups in Thornhill; here she explained the nature of the research and offered to give smartphone assistance to their members. In addition, Pauline joined a raft of locally-based volunteer activities that would bring her into contact with people. Over 16 months these included everything from litter picks to helping out in the activities of organisations such as the Scouts, the schools and fundraising activities arranged by the Catholic Church and Church of Ireland. These tended to be short-term activities, but were bolstered with longer-term, in-depth weekly meetings with retired participants, in situations ranging from evening meetings of the local history society to morning craft groups and church-based social occasions (Fig. 1.9). Through helping out with cake sales and Christmas events, Pauline was included in preparations for other church-based activities; she thus gradually got to know some of the people who dedicate their time and energies to providing a social outlet for other members. Some of these groups were composed of older people who either had no smartphone or were fearful of them. Such meetings were informative in revealing the extent of the ambivalence that some people continue to feel about these technologies, and the degree to which they feel themselves to be digitally excluded.

By contrast, groups run by local retirees such as music groups or sports groups tended to attract people with a very different perspective; many relied on their smartphones to organise their hectic lives. Walking groups and traditional music lessons are two examples that brought Pauline into the orbit of people representing a broad spectrum of ages, and whose age was somewhat irrelevant to participation. In general, Pauline, being younger, worked with more people in their forties, fifties and sixties while Danny concentrated more on people in their sixties and seventies, though with considerable overlap.

Because so many of the research participants are relatively affluent, free from obligations and still healthy, their responses may seem to paint a rather rosy portrait. In a later volume Danny will discuss in more detail the low-income families living in social housing in Cuan – a group that

Figure 1.9 Craft and coffee weekly meetings. Photo by Pauline Garvey.

also works as a community, but in a different way. He will also focus on more problematic issues such as the incidence of depression. This is one reason why there is less about low-income families or depression in the present volume. But the main reason is that the middle-class population which dominates the examples given in this book does represent the clear majority of those whose lives we were engaged with in both these two fieldsites, and seems to represent the mainstream of contemporary Ireland.

The protocols for the project as a whole included an initial commitment to carry out around 25 recorded interviews. These were to be concerned with each of our three primary areas of smartphone use: ageing, life purpose and health, considered either separately or in combination. A key element in the smartphone interviews was to ask people to open up their smartphones, record every single app present on the screens and discuss whether these were used and, if so, how. Generally anthropological interviews tend to follow the lead of the participant and their interests rather than follow a strict questionnaire. Interviews were recorded with well over 200 different research participants. There was some limited background surveying, mainly to establish typicality,

Figure 1.10   Film: *Ethnography in practice*. Available at http://bit.ly/ethnoinpractice.

since we put more trust in our qualitative work. In addition, it is helpful to interview people with specialist knowledge. These may encompass pharmacists, hairdressers, vets, the police, retired GPs, nuns and complementary health practitioners. Each can provide perspectives that might not be available in day-to-day fieldwork. For example, some men who were struggling with issues around retirement would only open up to psychotherapists, so it was only through interviewing the latter that we might gain access to the depth of those problems. Much of chapter 7 on downsizing is informed by estate agents. We also made an effort to try and find people who did not join groups of any kind but might agree to meet up with us in local cafés or locations of their choosing. A further sense of how we conduct fieldwork is given by the film *Ethnography in practice* (Fig. 1.10).

Ethics and people

The issue of ethics has been transformed for anthropologists in recent years by the development of ethics committees and bureaucratic compliance. The danger with this trend is the temptation to think that one is behaving ethically primarily because one is compliant with the procedures mandated by these processes, such as following the data protection requirements of GDPR or making sure people read information sheets and sign consent forms. These processes homogenise ethics as something that applies equally to all. This is quite different from an anthropological view of ethics.

For us, ethics has more to do with taking individual responsibility for learning what would cause harm to people. We assume that this will differ across different populations and demands a sensitivity to the specificity of each population. For example, it quickly became clear to us that many research participants in Ireland were not comfortable with being photographed, unlike those in the other fieldsites within this project. In our craft and coffee groups or in Active Retirement gatherings it felt intrusive to pull out our phones and snap photos. We therefore took relatively few photographs of people and always ensured that we had their permission when we did.

Discretion is of particular importance to anthropological work, since we are constantly exposed to information about people whom we also know. It is important not just to respect anonymity in publishing, but also to ensure that we are not the conduits for local gossip. Mostly our participants appear in anonymised form. We may change details about them that are not relevant to the points we are making, in order to ensure that they are not recognised. If people who appeared visually wanted to keep their own names we respected that choice, using an additional consent form to register that preference. In these days of googling, it would not be hard for a reader to work out the actual places in which we lived. But we would ask readers to respect our pseudonyms, as these assist in our concern to protect the anonymity of individuals.

Notes

1. This was particularly the case for Cuan. ASSA refers to the Anthropology of Smartphones and Smart Ageing project. See https://www.ucl.ac.uk/anthroplogy/assa for more details.
2. Share et al. 2007.
3. O'Riain 2014, 32.
4. One example is the Global Irish Civic Forum, which encourages the Irish diaspora abroad to come to Dublin to discuss their work and engage with government. See Ireland Department of Foreign Affairs and Trade 2017. Its website can be accessed here: https://www.dfa.ie/global-irish/support-overseas/global-irish-civic-forum/.
5. Inglis 2007, 7.
6. See Keenan 2014, 99–109.
7. Hakim and Dalby 2015.
8. State pensions (contributory) are relatively generous at €248 per week, compared to the UK where they are £159. Some of this is explained by the high cost of living in Ireland compared to other countries in the EU. See *The Economist*, 2019.
9. See O'Riain 2014, 1–31.
10. See Fáilte Ireland 2020. For more details of the 2013 initiative to encourage the Irish diaspora to visit Ireland, see the website: https://www.discoverireland.ie/The-Gathering-Ireland.
11. https://www.failteireland.ie/FailteIreland/media/WebsiteStructure/Documents/eZine/TheGathering_FinalReport_JimMiley_December2013.pdf.
12. Murphy 2017, 158–74.

13. Horgan 2004, 44.
14. See Miller 2020.
15. See Norris 2017, 37–59 and Norris 2020.
16. A 2020 study by the Economic and Social Research Institute found that Ireland's tax system does more to reduce inequality than any other country in Europe. 'While the distribution of household income in Ireland is the most unequal in the EU before taxes and benefits, the study finds that Ireland's highly progressive tax system substantially offsets this, bringing inequality in take-home income very close to the EU average'. See Economic and Social Research Institute, 2020. See also *The Economist*, 2019.
17. See Hickman 2014, 133–44.
18. See Arensberg 1937, Arensberg and Kimball 2001 [1940]. See Byrne and O'Mahony 2013, 9 and Wilson 1984 for discussion. See also Brody 1973, Fox 1978, Taylor 1996.
19. For discussion of Scheper-Hughes 2001 [1979] and others, see Peace 1989, 89–111 and Egan and Murphy 2015, 134–41. See also Scheper-Hughes 2000.
20. More recent studies include Taylor 1995, Peace 2001. See also Wulff 2007.
21. Curtin et al. 1996. See Wilson and Donnan 2006, 17–42 for discussion.
22. Saris 2008, Saris and Bartley 2002.
23. Maguire and Murphy 2015, Murphy 2019, Curtin et al. 1996, Maguire and Murphy 2016, Heffernan et al. 2017.
24. Ó Crualaoich 2003, Ó Giolláin 2000, Ó Laoire 2005, Coleman 2004. Also see Wulff 2017.
25. Wulff 2015.
26. Forsberg and Timonen 2018.
27. Inglis 1998. This can be seen in the 1937 Irish Free State Constitution, which 'endeavours to ensure that mothers shall not be obliged by economic necessity to engage in labour to the neglect of their duties in the home' (Article 41, Paragraph 2). See Wills 2001, 33–57 for discussion.
28. Breen and Reynolds 2011, 195–212.
29. See Garry, J., Hardman, N. and Payne, D. 2006, in Forsberg and Timonen 2018.
30. Forsberg and Timonen 2018.
31. Most of the trends described above are typically interpreted as aspects of growing individualism. See Gray et al. 2016, 101. In one of his scholarly works Tom Inglis (2007) charts a rapid and profound transition in Ireland. He documents a series of shifts during the late twentieth century in which Irish society moved from being dominated by values related to Catholicism, such as humility, piety and self-denial, to being a liberal-individualist consumer culture in which self-indulgence was, generally, valorised over self-denial. Ideas surrounding the person, self-realisation and the body took centre stage in this transition and former taboos surrounding sex were challenged in politics, the media and popular culture. The prime movers in this transition were, he argues, the media and the market, under whose influence a Pandora's Box of unspoken topics was broached on the airwaves and in print media. See Inglis 2007.
32. Connolly 2015a, Introduction, Connolly 2015b, 10–38.
33. Gray et al. 2016, 56.
34. Hannan in Connolly 2015a, 39–54.
35. Gray et al. 2016, 167–77, Arber and Timonen 2012. See Forsberg and Timonen 2018.
36. Spencer 1990, Aguilar 2007.
37. Hodkinson and Bennett 1999, 1–6. See also Blaikie 1999.
38. See Degnen 2007.
39. See Hunt 2005.
40. See Hagerty 2016.
41. Hockey and James 2002, Keith et al. 2005, Cohen 1994, Featherstone and Wernick 1995.
42. Hazan 1994, 21, Hazan 1980.
43. Which has resulted in several publications that are relevant to this topic, including Prendergast and Garattini 2015, Garattini et al. 2012, Drazin 2018.
44. See King-O'Riain 2015, 256–73.
45. See The Irish Longitudinal Study on Ageing (TILDA) 2020. The TILDA website can be found at: https://tilda.tcd.ie/.
46. Ireland experienced the biggest expansion in the middle-class cohort of any EU country between 1991 and 2010, according to the US-based Pew Research Center. The share of middle-income adults rose from 60 per cent to 69 per cent of the entire adult population over that period. See Walsh 2017 and Kochhar 2017.

47. Share et al. 2007.
48. Peillon and Corcoran 2002, Corcoran and Share 2008, Corcoran et al. 2007, Corcoran et al. 2010 and Corcoran 2010.
49. Horgan 2004, 44.
50. Horgan 2004, 44.
51. Corcoran et al. 2010, 270.
52. Corcoran et al. 2010, quoted in Inglis and Donnelly 2011, 134.
53. Inglis and Donnelly (2011) argue that globalisation does not impede attachment to the local. Instead they believe that local attachment and identity not only become adapted to globalisation, but that these also complement and sustain each other.
54. The Men's Shed movement was started in Australia in the 1980s as a means to give occupation to older men that could enhance their health and welfare. There are now over 450 Men's Sheds in Ireland.

2
Ageing and retirement

Introduction

The topic of this book is prescient because the population aged 65 and over in Ireland is growing: it is projected to double between 2011 and 2041,[1] with the over eighties increasing by 250 per cent.[2] Until recently, Ireland was economically fortunate in having a relatively high proportion of people of working age, but this will soon decline.[3] Ireland is also the site of a large-scale study aimed at understanding the experience of ageing as well as gathering information on the social, economic and health information of those aged 55 and over. The Irish Longitudinal Study on Ageing (TILDA), based at Trinity College Dublin, began interviews with 8,504 participants mostly aged between 50 and 64 in 2009 and is ongoing. Each wave of the study investigates various aspects of ageing. As a snapshot, the 2011 report noted that 62 per cent had at least secondary education, 22 per cent had lived abroad for at least six months and 62 per cent of men and 46 per cent of women were working. The average weekly income was €767, but state pensions made up two-thirds of income for those over 65.[4]

One finding that is striking is that the self-reported average quality of life does not decrease linearly with age. It peaks at 68, after which it gradually declines, but only declines to that of 50-year-olds when people reach 80.[5] Though any measure of 'quality of life' requires careful interpretation, it implies that for our research participants becoming older corresponds to the most fulfilling period of their entire lives.[6] Much of this volume will document our observations on how people have crafted their life during this period from aged 50 to 90 and what we can learn from this. After reading this book, the statistics may look more plausible and the sentiment is one that was echoed by our participants.

Chapter 3 will explore the activities this age group are involved in, while chapter 4 considers another finding from TILDA: that a sense of fulfilment is closely related to sociality, including extensive social networks and positive supportive friendships. TILDA found that women are twice as likely (31 per cent) to report such friendships as men (16 per cent). Chapter 6 examines health where, despite a well-publicised crisis in the Irish health system, a recent study found that 'Ireland has the highest self-perceived health status in the EU, with 82.9% of people rating their health as good or very good', although this figure declines with lower incomes.[7]

TILDA's findings have proved illuminating and valuable to our research. However, an ethnography provides very different kinds of evidence that are vital if we are to understand, explain and learn from the experiences of this age group. Our ethnography will also be concerned with the sheer variety of experience; it may include broader differences around, for example, gender, but will also reflect a sense of the diversity and ingenuity represented by each individual we came to know through living in these communities for more than 16 months. *Ageing with Smartphones in Ireland* explores the unprecedented and the trends, but will also acknowledge those who remain wedded to tradition. As noted in chapter 1, the bulk of our participants could be described as middle class and were settled in comfortable residential suburbs, which doubtless contributed to a positive quality of life.

Ageing and frailty: the subjective experience

The original intention of this study was to examine mid-life from the perspective of the changing experience of age itself. Our starting point was that most studies of age focus on populations defined by age, that is either young people or the elderly.[8] This bias results in the neglect of those who considered themselves to be neither young nor elderly. Before the research, we imagined this meant that our focus would be on those aged between 45 and 70. We imagined that we would thereby perhaps be working towards a new conception of middle age or mid-life. By the end of our research, however, we had an entirely different view of our topic. We were especially mistaken when it came to the upper age limit. People we met in their seventies and eighties commonly reject the idea that they are elderly. They may remain engaged in physical activities ranging from dancing to hiking in addition to wider activities such as writing or community work. Commonly they say things such as 'I feel 40. My body has aged but I haven't' or

> Despite my age – 70 – I still don't regard myself as being old. As they say – you still feel the same on the inside! Presumably, I am viewed by others as elderly and I am sometimes even offered a seat on the train by well-mannered young lads.

As argued in a recent book called *The 100-Year Life*, while longevity is conventionally understood as implying we are older for longer, the convention is in fact being overturned: we are staying younger for longer.[9] Of course, maturity comes with some physical limitations. One may not be able to party all night, for example, but we met people who cycle or play sports well into their seventies.

These sentiments suggest a radical departure from the conventions of using biological age as the definition of who a person is.[10] Our evidence is that age measured from birth has been replaced by a distinction between biological age and physical frailty.[11] From their fifties onwards, it is not uncommon for individuals to have had a serious illness. They will certainly know others who have. Recovery time becomes extended, sometimes even from minor ailments. Frailty is separated from age, however, because 'age' never happened in the way that people expect.[12] For 75-year-old Fiona, for example, chronological age is less important than the realisation that there are things she can no longer do. At one point she realised that she had lost her confidence to drive at night, though she is not sure whether that is due to diminishing eyesight or a stiff neck. When asked how she felt about this, she replied 'mournful, yes, you are, yes, you are, yes'. But she also pointed out that people may dislike driving at night at any age and for any number of reasons.

Participants commonly told us of how they expected to feel 'old' when they turned 60, but this did not happen. They had the same experience at 70, and then again at 80. As we had defined the participants in our project as those who did not yet see themselves as elderly, it followed that these people needed to be included within the parameters of our study. Sometimes this even meant including people in their nineties. This, in turn, meant the project was now dealing with a very extensive period of life. With the rise of higher education and training, people often do not start salaried work until around 25, which gives them a working life of around 35 years. If they then retire at 60 and live to 95, their retirement life is of equal length to their working life.

If biological age has no clear breaks, then retirement, the one step change that people do experience, becomes particularly important. The research for this book included working people, but often those are also thinking about retirement. Retired, however, by no means meant inactive. There is a general sense that keeping physically active helps retain a sense of youthfulness.[13] Brendan gives us some sense of this. During his nine years of retirement from teaching science, he has not just joined activities, but has also established some. The most successful has been the ukulele club, which for him was always about more than just the music. When the committee was trying to restrain the extremely active ukulele WhatsApp group, such as limiting postings to required organisational issues or information, everyone knew that Brendan could not resist posting jokes or WhatsApp messages about his holidays. As the founder of the group, however, he would be cut some slack.

Now in his seventies, Brendan's sense of responsibility extends to keeping himself fit and healthy. Attending weekly t'ai chi sessions helps to maintain the suppleness and strength he needs both for walking and his active life in the community. At other times, he might go to Dublin to watch a sports match, and there are many chats with neighbours in his cul-de-sac. Brendan has become a Tidy Towns volunteer, responsible for picking up litter in a designated patch of roads, and he also volunteers for a charity in a less affluent town. For some years he taught a science class in Central Africa and is always looking for some new challenge, currently represented by his art class. He enjoys his fair share of holidays and travel to new places. Recently he and his wife spent two days at the Hermitage Museum in St Petersburg, appreciating one of the world's premier art collections. He and his wife also enjoy walking the Camino de Santiago, a pilgrim route in northern Spain. Despite his scepticism of formal religion, Brendan speaks of walking the Camino in ways that foreground his commitment to spirituality and deeply felt experiences. Yet for all his interest in spirituality and art, the thing that Brendan brings to all his activities is a sense of fun, even a bit of mischievousness.

If our observations suggest that many people do not automatically become elderly as traditionally understood, it is still common for them to anticipate that they will. Martin, for example, retired at age 60 because he had already planned to undertake a PhD in art after a long career in the civil service. Early retirement made sense because he felt 60 is 'close enough to 40', whereas 70 is 'too old' to undertake a major project. Now he is in his late sixties, but still very active in organising local music groups where he is present several days a week. Another man dreads turning 70 because 'people die in their seventies'. He still feels youthful

Figure 2.1   A meme circulated by a Thornhill participant offers a humorous look at age-related conditions. Photo by Pauline Garvey.

in his sixties, but anticipates a decline as he moves into the next decade. Anticipation of becoming elderly therefore has consequences, even when little actually changes at the next decennial birthday.

What does eventually happen is frailty, which may come in many different forms and is often a source of dread (Fig. 2.1). Commonly people claim that what they fear is not death, but the manner of dying. By far the most significant source of anxiety is dementia. These fears are often based on personal experience and are not unreasonable: as life expectancy grows, so does the percentage of people with dementia. There are currently approximately 55,000 people with dementia in Ireland, but the number affected by the condition is more like 500,000 when all the family members are included.[14]

Ageing is not just a subjective experience: much of it consists of changes in how other people view us and treat us. At present some welcome it when young people give up a seat on the train for them, while others do not appreciate this sign of age. So, far from wanting to protect their pursuits, older people are putting considerable effort into persuading young people to take up activities such as golf and bridge, precisely to demolish the age associations of those activities. In previous generations, to be elderly might have meant becoming a senior person, sometimes iconic patriarchal or matriarchal figures. They might have been associated with the wisdom thought to develop with age. Historically, in periods of less frenetic innovation, older people knew more about the tasks of life gained from experience, such as farming or traditional knowledge.[15] They were literally the keepers of 'old wives' tales'. Today, to an unprecedented degree, the most significant knowledge pertains to technologies mostly associated with the young – a shift that inverts traditional values, threatening entrenched positive connotations for ageing.

Some older people still make claims to traditional wisdom. For example, one resident of Cuan opined:[16]

> Yes, there is a strong feeling of having 'seen it all before'. There is an inclination to think one sees the 'answers' to many social questions and problems more clearly than younger people. As in a sign posted in the window of a pub in Dingle, County Kerry which read: 'Warning, retiree inside who knows everything and has all the time in the world to tell you about it'. When I meet with my seven retired friends on Thursday mornings, we have over 500 years of experience between us. This, needless to say, is not cumulative and doesn't make us any wiser than anyone else, but when we come to a consensus on various issues (as we sometimes do), it must have some value.

In some of the other ASSA fieldsites, the evidence suggested a very significant sense of loss of both seniority and wisdom. The evidence from Dublin was more complex. It seemed that here the effect is to include older people within a more general egalitarian ethos that simply judges each individual according to their merits. Many of the walking, music and other groups within which retired people participate are open to people of all ages. On their committees, interventions by older people were treated in much the same way as those of the young. Respect was accorded to the quality of the contribution irrespective of whose contribution it was. There is certainly a loss of both respect for seniority per se and the belief that an older person is always assumed to be wiser as a result of their greater experience. But in this context that meant a stronger alignment with contemporary liberal and egalitarian ideals, which was generally regarded as positive.

As King Lear unfortunately failed to recognise, respect may also be closely related to changes in the distribution of power and control over assets. The most recent significant shift is a dramatic rise in adult children co-habiting with their parents. In 2018 78 per cent of those aged between 16 and 29 were living at home with their parents,[17] compared to the EU-28 average of 67 per cent. With the housing crisis, it is becoming much less clear that young adults will be able to establish their own homes even when they have children. On the other hand, an egalitarian ethos prevails in intergenerational relationships: it is far less common to threaten disinheritance, show patronage or favouritism or expect a specific son or daughter to take on the role of looking after elderly parents than might have been the case for previous generations.

To conclude this section, although we are not studying the young as defined by chronological age, we were struck by the story of a Thornhill taxi driver. He complained about having to go to Las Vegas because his teenage daughter had become obsessed with seeing Cher who was 72, not quite as old as Mick Jagger or Paul McCartney. A key moment in popular culture came in 2008, when a group of people with Zimmer frames ('The Zimmers') YouTubed themselves singing The Who's 'My Generation', which includes the line 'I hope I die before I get old'. For The Beatles, 'When I'm Sixty-Four' was already elderly. In retrospect, it seems that it was The Who that got things right – but not in the way that they anticipated. For them, it was the young who hoped to die before they got old. Yet the good news from the evidence presented here suggests that now we can pretty much all expect to die before we 'get old', though we are likely to become frail and ill as a prelude to dying.[18]

Complications: class and invisibility

So far the emphasis has been on a somewhat radical shift from more traditional trajectories of ageing, but this is certainly an overgeneralisation which needs to be tempered. Firstly, there were many people who, given their age, were brought up within a period when 'elderly' still remained a clearly designated category and many retain that perception of themselves. Our ethnography suggests that the self-designated elderly might include most 90-year-olds, perhaps half of the 80-year-olds and a few of those in their seventies and sixties. Much depends upon education, class and background. The majority of our research participants were middle class, with the better education, higher incomes and general prosperity that reflected national economic trends. However, they had often been born into relative poverty, within large families and with parents who struggled to cope with limited economic prospects. Participants whose origins had been harsh tended to view their relative middle-class affluence as an achievement more than an entitlement. They were also more likely to insist that they were not yet elderly.

One distinction that tended to reflect wider class and educational distinctions was whether older people played bridge or bingo. Cuan hosted a weekly meeting of sometimes 70 people, almost entirely female, called the 'Active Retirement group'. The name is something of a misnomer because these groups were generally *less* active than other retirees. Mostly they met to play bingo, but there were some other activities reminiscent of the past such as tea dances. Bingo had been an extremely extensive traditional activity and the Catholic church used to provide buses to take people to various bingo clubs; the game in Ireland has also been associated with more general social solidarity and camaraderie.[19] While there is some overlap in both activities, there were broad distinctions between the groups who enjoyed playing bingo, a game of pure chance, and those devoted to the highly competitive game of bridge, often regarded as a good form of 'brain training', to retain mental agility.

In Cuan those playing bridge were able to raise a very significant amount of money to purchase their own building for amalgamating various disparate bridge clubs; many thought nothing of travelling abroad to attend a particular bridge tournament. So the distinction between the two games corresponds quite well to differences in financial resources and social expectations. Bridge groups also attracted some younger players as well as retirees, and were therefore more mixed in term of age and activity. In contrast and speaking broadly, more of our research participants in the Active Retirement groups acknowledged a sense of being elderly. Of course, this identification was by no means universal. For the largest such group in Thornhill, some admitted they joined with some trepidation because they did not like to mix with 'old people'. A 75-year-old brought in an 83-year-old neighbour who commented on entering 'Just look at them!', then refused to join precisely because there were 'just old people there'. So even these bastions of age segregation are threatened by a growing preference for groups undefined by age.

There are also instances of people who simply fall out of sociality completely and become lonely and isolated as a result. An example of this is Mark, who complained about becoming invisible as soon as he retired. Aged 71, he took early retirement from a demanding job that required long evenings at work and a lot of travelling. The work was very enjoyable and he loved it, climbing his way up from the lower ranks to one of the most senior and becoming someone that everyone wanted to get advice from. The work took its toll, however, and by 61 he was feeling drained, even as new staff or 'fresh blood' were recruited to his office. Instead of looking forward to the daily tasks of advising and taking decisions, Mark found he was nodding off while driving around the country; he used to have to stop for a quick nap before continuing. Consequently he decided to take early retirement after 37 years at work. In the decade that followed, Mark has developed few routines save taking a leisurely breakfast and a long walk. The slow pace is in marked contrast to when he worked from 7.30 a.m. long into the evening, but now he says he delights in having no demands on his time. The daily walk helps him to control his weight. Otherwise, he says he does not enjoy group activities and feels that, in comparison with his working life, he has become somewhat invisible. People look at him as if they are thinking, 'what would he know, he is only an "ould fella"'. Even in his interactions with his mechanic recently, Mark's suggestions about his car were easily discounted, even though they turned out to be correct. 'People used to always ask my advice and now they never do,' he complained.

Many older participants feel this increasing invisibility as an affront. If in and of themselves they do not feel they have aged, it is frustrating to see the way in which other people react to changes in their external appearance. Again, responses varied. For example, there are women in their fifties who find it liberating not to have to care what men think about them, and report feeling more confident and less cowed by male friends or colleagues. They may cultivate a more feminist sense of self-crafting rather than dressing for others. It helps that the clothing which once designated age has largely ceased to do so: black or jeans are just fine at any stage of life. They are more concerned with keeping fit and not putting on weight. Again, it is easy to overgeneralise. Many women talk about the effects of the ageing process on their bodies in disappointed tones, noting the surprising growth of facial hair and how they now try to avoid all mirrors or photographs. For some, the ageing of appearance is not something they feel they will ever be reconciled to.[20]

Retirement

The overall emphasis so far in this discussion of ageing is on unexpected continuity, as people fail to become elderly until they are met with frailty. This continuity only makes retirement stand out more starkly as an experience of rupture.[21] There is no single retirement age in Ireland, although 65 is generally regarded as the norm. A 2014 report suggests that most people retire before they feel entirely ready to.[22] This also reflects the rise in life expectancy, which for a retiree at 65 is now 84 for females, 80 for males.[23] In 2011 the government decided to raise the age at which the state pension becomes payable to 67 in 2021 and 68 in 2028. Over the last two decades, the number of older people staying in the workforce has roughly doubled.[24] Also in recent decades there has been a marked increase in organisations focused upon older people,[25] with several organisations developing courses on preparing for and managing retirement funded by employers. The Retirement Planning Council of Ireland recommends people 'ease into retirement'. It devotes much attention to how to use skills and develop new routines, with advice on 'deciding who you are now' and 'resisting bringing your work self home'; there is also an emphasis on setting boundaries and growing a social network. The Council strongly recommends that individuals nearing retirement should phase their exit from work in order to find 'a sudden stop' less stressful.[26] The transition from full-time work to retirement is said to require detailed planning and commitment. Mostly such courses formalise activities that people are often already engaging with, but re-frame them as retirement-friendly activities.

Such activities can start years in advance. One woman recommends starting retirement preparation on becoming an empty-nester; others start even earlier. Sive noted how, on her 50th birthday, she started 'thinking about the future'. For Sive this did not mean her financial planning but taking up a musical instrument. Her husband Peter is now struggling with his tin whistle lessons. After trying to self-tutor through YouTube, he realised that to progress beyond a beginner's level he needed to join a local but thriving traditional music group. The couple's goal is to be able to play proficiently for pub sessions or even busking on the street by the time they retire from work.

Dublin-based organisations include a variety of Active Retirement associations, sports, arts and culture groups. Some are orientated to providing a social outlet while others organise traditional leisure activities, education and training. There are also advocacy groups such as Active Retirement Ireland, Age and Opportunity and Age Action Ireland, which promote greater participation of older people in society in fields such as art or sports and provides national advocacy on behalf of older people. These are complemented by various Age-Friendly schemes and initiatives provided by the county councils. The Age-Friendly programme now has representatives from over 30 organisations and businesses who are working to improve the delivery of key services to older people.[27] From an ethnographic perspective, however, these vary greatly. As already noted, the Active Retirement group may follow a more traditional expectation of age, but even here older people are becoming more conscious of their experience and potential contribution. One woman complained that they always had outside speakers come into the community centre to talk to them while they drank tea. 'Why not invite us to give talks about areas that we know about and have lived?'

Ideals of 'successful' and 'active' ageing have come to dominate policy discourses on ageing worldwide. Originating in Europe and the United States, discussions of the Third Age distinguish between healthy, active and engaged older persons in this third stage of life and those in need of care.[28] However, these ideals of 'Successful Ageing' as a targeted pursuit were generally rejected by our participants, with people tending to resist the kind of moral pressure or judgement of failure that this term implies. Successful Ageing as a paradigm also tends to bring continuity from ideals of entrepreneurial success, bringing work goals into retirement, a concept that was also largely rejected. Quite simply, our research participants had little knowledge of or interest in Successful Ageing.

In this respect our ethnography proved a marked contrast with some of the other simultaneous ethnographies. In our Brazilian fieldsite, for example, Duque found that most people wanted to retain very clear links with their previous work lives, while in Kampala, Uganda most people could simply not afford to give up work. Although some of the groups of men who meet weekly at a café will tend to be those who previously worked in the civil service or in teaching, one could spend a year meeting regularly with a retired person, as in the Men's Shed, and never know what their previous job had been. The prior distinction between who had once been senior management and who had been a manual worker is thereby suppressed.

Not everyone lets go of the attitudes inherited from work quite so easily. One man from Thornhill took a course in retirement counselling, hoping that his new expertise might contribute to a modest retirement income stream through teaching people successful retirement. He put up adverts all around Thornhill but did not get a single student, much to his chagrin. Most people did not see ageing or retirement in instrumental terms. Instead, for them, one of the key pleasures of retirement was the ability now to distance themselves from this kind of goal orientation or judgements on their activities. As with Mark, who we met above, people delight in a leisurely lifestyle in stark contrast to their former patterns of work.

For those in public service, which was a common occupation, there was often a transition period during which they provided some consultancy for their ministry, or some teaching if they were in education, or one more audit. Typically this might continue for around four years, after which all their attention was redirected to the voluntary sector. Others decided after a while to go back to work, either due to financial need or boredom, though this might be in quite a different role from their previous employment. For example, we met a former worker in administration who then took a job as a school librarian, emerging from her interest in English literature. It paid very little, but she found it rewarding. In retrospect, most people would have preferred to have retired gradually, and she agreed:

> In my view, the ideal is to retire in stages, in other words, to wind down gradually over a period of years, by either reducing one's daily working hours or number of days working per week, or a combination of both.

They also felt that the failure to provide them with an opportunity to transfer their accumulated knowledge to their successor showed both the stupidity of the system and a failure to acknowledge or value their contribution.

By far the most common factor mentioned concerning the timing of retirement was finance. The reason people do not retire, or retire later, often has nothing to do with the work itself but with their lack of financial security. They have enough for home and food, but perhaps not enough for more expensive aspirations such as travel. They do not want to retire until they know there is the money for at least annual holidays. They may weigh up their assets quite carefully. One asked their trade union to work out the optimum time to retire, which for him was 59. Another calculated that she could rent out an empty bedroom, the rent money from which would be specifically dedicated to travel. Almost everyone had paid off their mortgage on their house so, unless they were in state housing, they owned their house outright.

People working in some government services need to work 40 years to achieve the potential maximum pension, that of 50 per cent of their salary, and one person retired the day that goal was achieved. Others noted that the decrease in taxation combined with not having to pay for a commute or lunch elevated the effective value of pensions. Most of the retirees did not seem to have that much trouble living on their pension, though many had pensions from work in addition to the state pension. Couples also have fewer costs relative to pension income. As these examples suggest, the key criterion to a surprising degree is not the cost of living, but the prospect of spending time abroad on holiday.

The experience of retirement was very varied. Mostly it was compulsory, either having reached the age limit or having been made redundant during the recession, with that fate having loomed over them for several years. Increasingly, people speak of changes in work practice precipitating retirement. The rise of HR, compliance procedures and similar bureaucratic burdens have made work less attractive and more onerous, at which point an arduous commute no longer seems worth it. There is a wide spectrum of attitudes, providing a common topic for conversation. Aideen, due to turn 60 soon, is looking forward to retiring from the social welfare office where she is employed. Her husband is not so light on his feet and she wants to spend more time with him. Mostly, though, she wants to travel, and has decided that her sister would be a good companion, particularly for walking holidays that her husband might find too taxing. Her friend, who is in her late fifties, announces that she is 'all set up for retirement'.

> I love to write… and I paint, and I have all these activities, whereas my sister-in-law in the States has nothing set up; she has no hobbies. She often says to me, what am I going to do when I retire?

There are, however, some men – and less frequently women – for whom retirement is a disaster. They had lost the most significant component of their status and identity, the foundations of their self-respect, from one day to the next. A few of these still craved audiences and places where they would be listened to with customary respect. Yet after a time they might find new routes that proved surprisingly successful. They might think of writing the story of their lives and achievements, if only for the family to read. They could research and then give lectures to the history society or the sailing club.

But others failed, and here the spectre of loneliness was significant. Maria, aged 69, went from full-time employment to what she called 'nothingness', leading to a deep depression. Maria did not have many friends or family members living near to where she retired and no developed social networks. She felt that she had nowhere to go, nothing to do and deeply regretted retiring when she did. Pauline met Maria while participating in a computer course offered by a local secondary school to older people. Maria spent most of the time talking to the students while the screen saver ebbed and flowed. As with most people who felt digitally excluded, what she really wanted was not computer lessons but guidance on using her smartphone. Her partner agreed that she is completely cut off without access to WhatsApp and text messaging, and was clearly concerned at her decreasing social circles.

Another example is provided by 65-year-old Resa, who never particularly enjoyed her work in the insurance industry. Her husband died before she was 40, leaving her with three children, no mortgage protection and a load of bills she had not the least idea how she was going to pay. She did not even know how to put petrol in her car. What she did have was her anger. If it hadn't been for the kids she might have...[29] Resa took up cricket and later golf, hoping that these would lead to lasting friendships; when they did not, she lost interest. After her husband died, the local wives did not want her around – often with reason, as some husbands propositioned her. With the kids grown up and retirement, she struggles to see any particular purpose to life. Once a year Resa travels to France with a friend from Wexford. They sit and set targets – get fit, lose weight, drink less, but always over several glasses of wine. Resa has been drinking since she was a teenager; she jokes that at this point, her most reliable, if problematic companion, is a Chilean called Merlot. Wine is wonderful for helping her get to sleep, but terrible for waking her up again in the middle of the night. Sometimes retirement of any kind is not easy.

Those who could not pick themselves up from their 'fall' often consulted psychotherapists and counsellors, who therefore became our key participants for this group; some of whom specialise in the condition of depression following retirement. The loss of status may be exacerbated by diminished libido, physical attraction or sporting prowess. In chapter 6 we consider some of these transitions in more detail. In general women were more likely than men to have close friends in whom they could confide and share experiences. Men who continued to 'perform' their desire to impress others in public – for example, through banter – might find professional counsellors as the only safe place in which to expose the degree to which they had fallen apart.

These cases represent a minority experience. Most people viewed retirement as a positive opportunity (Fig. 2.2). As one participant put it:

> I was prepared because the year before I had talked about it with my wife and family and I knew, yes, this is what I want, and I knew that I had all my hobbies in place, so I was not really scared.

Figure 2.2 'Adventure before dementia' sticker on a camper van in Dublin. Photo by Pauline Garvey.

Retirement is also seen as beneficial to the health concerns people are developing. Removing the stresses of work allowed people to both be more relaxed and to increase their opportunities for exercise, which might include walking, running and yoga. One man who simply could not decide about retirement was completely converted to its virtues after reading a book by Ernie J. Zelinski called *The Joys of Not Working*.

Our expectations as researchers had been that retirement would constitute a significant step towards ageing. However, we were surprised by the degree to which it was seen rather as an opportunity to regain something of one's youth. Some refer to their seventies as a return to teenage years, shorn of the previous decades of employment and childcare. Suddenly all those activities, holidays and interests that they expect to enjoy are now available while, to their surprise, they are still fairly healthy and relatively affluent. Since they do not have the same issues of anxiety and social embarrassment of actual teenagers, this period may be exceptionally carefree – which would then correspond to the TILDA statistics about claims that this is the most fulfilling period of life.

Retiring together: couples

Gender differences are strongly inscribed before retirement through differential work experience. Many of our female respondents had started their employment at a low level, for example, in clerical work, but often reached a relatively senior level in administration or management. Some women aged 70 or older had been required to retire from work as soon as they married, a legal requirement at that time. For women in relatively low paid but demanding employment, such as healthcare, there is considerable opposition to any rise in the state pension age, as they are looking forward to retirement.[30] Also for many women patterns of work were more intermittent, with extended periods at home looking after children, and the home was already as significant a location as the workplace. For most of the men we worked with, by contrast, careers were relatively straightforward and retirement relatively clear-cut, leading to a quite radical shift in orientation and relocation from work to the home.

Otherwise there was a very wide spectrum in the responses of males to retirement, simply because work tended to play a stronger role in defining who men consider themselves to be. As noted above, we were surprised by the evidence that most men seemed to expect that, after an initial period of continued work responsibilities, they would entirely sever any connection with their previous work life. This is surprising because so many of these positive retirees were extremely successful in careers such as education, medicine and the civil service. They may have ended their careers as headteachers or running a sub-ministerial office. Yet in most cases, these men gracefully relinquished status and power as they became part of the community of retirees.

One of the other effects of growing life expectancy is that most people retire as one-half of a couple and may remain together for decades. They are probably far more present together than ever before, since they are neither busy working nor parenting. Such intense co-presence may result in strains, but it may also be the condition for a more profound partnership. A man reports that:

> Yes, it is an issue about coming back into the home. Because in the beginning, I was just retiring and taking things easy, but I was

getting under her feet. I haven't really realised the extent to which she in her own right had a full-time job looking after the home. Of course, when I was working, I would help out, and it's not that I took it for granted, but I wasn't really aware of the situation. But then you are at home and she's like saying – can you not just get into the next room? Then it really dawned on me I'm under her feet and I'm interfering with her job. I started to realise that I also needed to get away from her situation so that she can continue doing her job without having to look at me sitting in the chair.

A woman offers another perspective:

I came home and that's when I had this thought – what am I going to do with the rest of my days? And my husband was already retired for about six years. We live in a bungalow, so it was very difficult. They try and prepare you for this on retirement. They give you retirement training, two-day retirement programme and one of the things is, if the man's retiring, he should never ask the woman when she's going out the door – where are you going and when will you be back? She had a life while you were at work and you can't intrude on that. It was the reverse, you see. He had his own routine, and it was not easy now to fit in.

Finally we have an account from a couple for whom things worked out just fine:

My wife was still working at the time. I had her evening meal ready for her when she returned home! My wife retired recently, nine years later than me. Again, this was positive as we can now plan to do things together more easily. It has given my wife and me more time together and also enabled us to see more of our children and grandchild who are living abroad.

One important factor is that Irish sociality tends to be gender-separated. In the coffee shops it is still more common to see groups of all-male and all-female retirees having coffee together. A tendency to separate may help the couple negotiate the balance between spending time together as a couple and spending time with friends. A piece of advice given in retirement classes is to retain separate interests, so that a couple will always have something to talk about.

Ageing with smartphones

Ageing, or at least frailty, is associated with a loss of capacity, but today it can also be a time for gaining new skills. In the last few years retired people have been able to take up smartphones, something previously regarded as a youth technology. Mastering the smartphone then corresponds to the idea of re-engaging with youthfulness in itself, but the impact is certainly not just one of association. It is immensely practical, particularly as 97 per cent of the Irish population owns a smartphone.[31] In all the following chapters, whether on health or social relations or retirement activities, smartphones enter into retirement as devices that make finding out about possibilities, keeping organised and researching far easier. As will also become clear, learning to use the smartphone has become a key retirement activity. Much of *Ageing with Smartphones in Ireland* will be an exploration of the consequences of smartphones for both retirement and ageing. Certainly it contributes to many people feeling that this is their most carefree period of life, albeit one that is obviously much closer to the end of life.[32]

This chapter started with the example of Brendan, for whom smartphones are now an integral part of daily life. For his ukulele group, the only specific app he has is a ukulele tuner. However, the ukulele group dominates his WhatsApp since this is a very active group, with more than 70 members and multiple daily WhatsApp posts. Brendan may first download a song from YouTube and then change it into an MP3, which allows him to send it to a Bluetooth speaker, which he employs when practising with the ukulele group. Facebook is the main way he interacts with other ukulele groups around Ireland and beyond. He uses text and phone to make more detailed arrangements when they play at events or nursing homes, for example, which is quite common. He may then use maps to find the place in question, as well as the calendar to organise himself. Meanwhile Brendan's music app has thousands of songs stored. Many of these uses are relatively new, but they derive from his taking up the ukulele. This is just one of his activities, though, and we noted that smartphones were equally important in sharing his experience of the Camino.

Similarly Anne is a 75-year-old retired teacher; she first retired when she got married because of the marriage ban. When her children were grown up and she was in her fifties she went back to teach Spanish as part of an adult education course in a further education college, then gradually decreased her working hours before finally retiring completely at the age of 65. Anne was one of the few participants who looked up our profiles before meeting us. She makes the most of her smartphone, viewing it as a tool that helps to maximise her access to information. Based on her smartphone research, she had prepared succinct questions regarding our research. During our meeting, she would occasionally pause our chat while she looked up the species of bird that had just landed in the garden or ordered a book from an online system that the local library put in place for her book club. Members of her book club without access to this facility are constantly on the back foot, she told us. By the time they call into the library, all the copies of the specified book have been reserved.

For Anne, the smartphone is a constant source of new information; for Brendan, it makes his primary retirement activity easier and more effective. A device once considered something that would never be used by those over 40 has become commonplace for these people in their seventies. In this way, the smartphone has become perhaps the clearest outward sign of how they see themselves inside. The technology may be viewed as a reflection of the changing experience of age, but it is also a cause. Older people listen to 1970s rock music on Spotify when they themselves are in their seventies. They keep abreast of the latest news and fashions more easily, and generally remain more engaged with others and with the world. The smartphone is thereby instrumental in this shift to the sense of continuity with youth, confirming and giving a further boost to these changes in the experience of ageing. It will play a major role as this volume unfolds within what we propose is best seen as a movement towards the active 'crafting' of individual lives.

Conclusion

This chapter describes an Ireland in transition, which accounts for much of the diversity that has been encountered. On the one hand, there are some very clear conclusions understood as the direction of travel. It seems that the previous experience of becoming elderly, the grandparents of previous ages who were largely housebound and socially invisible,[33] is being replaced by a subjective experience of continuity. We may all die before we get to *feel* that we are old. Instead, what matters is eventual frailty and the decline towards death. With greater life expectancy, dementia has become more prominent in people's consciousness of frailty. At the same time there are those, often from lower-income households, who retain more traditional ideas about ageing, influenced by their memories of how different ageing had been in the past.[34]

There is also considerable variation in the experience of retirement. For some, it is experienced as a traumatic loss that may end in loneliness and depression. Yet people can increasingly develop more positive outlooks and an unprecedented experience of freedom. Instead of being invisible, they have the chance to create new configurations of activities and social lives that will be explored in detail in future chapters. The years of retirement may now rival work as a proportion of one's life.

There are many unexpected shifts in ageing,[35] including the way in which people may have to engage in an intense resumption of son/ daughter roles as they care for dying parents. Furthermore, as well as often being grandparents, our participants may be something of a new sandwich generation. Their children may not be able to afford housing, resulting in a new period of being relied upon that they had not anticipated. There are also changing expectations of support between the generations, which varies mainly in relation to class.[36] Retirement can thus include sudden shifts between unprecedentedly carefree times and other periods involving considerable commitment before, eventually, becoming the subject of those commitments by others.

Mostly, though, the emphasis in this chapter has been on understanding something that is largely without precedent: a much extended part of life during which people feel both relatively young and are no longer working. This chapter thereby sets up the foundation for all the chapters that follow. Much of this volume is an examination of how these same people respond to this situation through various attempts to craft life, rather than just living through it. Bob, in the first chapter, exemplifies this trajectory. It is only with retirement that life opens up other possibilities and he is able to make his final shift from butcher through school caretaker to poet. We will focus especially on the use of digital technologies. Liam in the next chapter with his VR goggles will be a case in point.

The characterisation of this period is difficult. In the literature on ageing, there is some resistance to the suggestion that we now live in a time of 'agelessness'.[37] No one is ageless. Our ethnographies would also point in a slightly different direction. People are well aware that they are older, and they certainly feel that the accumulated experience of life makes a significant difference. They are not actually teenagers again and the references to being young are mostly made through jokes. The emphasis is rather more on continuity, without a clear break from youth or middle-age, which is not the same as being ageless. The key experience was that there was no step change represented by successive decennial birthdays. Older people are still the same person at heart. But then suddenly life can change overnight with the emergence of some new frailty.

If the subjective experience of individual ageing has shifted, retirement itself is, if anything, more of a change than anticipated. Most people see it as a complete and radical break from their working life; often we could not tell what work some participants had spent decades engaged with. The final finding that we have tried to convey through the structure and style of this chapter is that, in this dynamic new age of Ireland, there may be simply more diversity of experience: all generalisations need the caveats and nuance represented by the particular experience of individuals.[38]

Notes

1. The projected increase from 2011 to 2041 is 160 per cent (that is, an increase in absolute numbers from 535,716 in 2011 to 1,396,585 in 2041). For more information see TILDA's website for the background to the study: https://tilda.tcd.ie/about/background/.
2. For the extent of change see Gray et al. 2016, 168–70. Ireland has had prior experience of an ageing population, at the end of the nineteenth century, mainly as a result of the famine. See Gilleard 2016.
3. See Wall and Horgan-Jones 2019.
4. See Barrett et al. 2011.
5. For more information see Wave 4 of the 'Wellbeing and Health in Ireland's over 50s 2009–2016' survey, Carey et al. 2018.
6. This does not necessarily imply that their younger lives were less fulfilling, but that working and family life are possibly thought about in different ways.
7. See Department of Health Ireland 2019.
8. Leibing and Cohen 2006, Buch 2015.
9. Gratton and Scott 2017.
10. For a more general discussion of shifts in people's experience of ageing viewed in context see Sokolovsky 2020.
11. For the problems associated with a focus upon frailty see Gilleard and Higgs 2011. The emphasis upon frailty also implies a greater concern with the body, both as corporeality and embodiment, for which see Gilleard and Higgs 2018.
12. See Condon 2011, who reports that older people in Ireland did not think about getting old until they experienced frailty.
13. Compare to Hurd Clarke et al. 2020.
14. See Health Service Executive (HSE) Ireland 2020a.
15. In the rural Ireland of the 1930s there remained a certain degree of veneration of older people. See Arensberg and Kimball 2001 [1940], 163.
16. For an ethnographic case study of how the wisdom of older people was viewed in Ireland see Edmondson 2005. Although already in 1928 the poet Yeats (then aged 60) noted of Ireland: 'That is no country for old men… An aged man is but a paltry thing, A tattered coat upon a stick…'. See Yeats 1968.
17. See Eurostat 2018.
18. The stance taken by books such as this one may create a problem for gerontological studies, since in a way it kicks some of the most problematic issues further down the road, 'othering' the frail and very old. But this book mainly concerns people younger than those studied within gerontology. See Higgs and Gilleard 2015.
19. Gallagher 2012. Perhaps unsurprisingly balcony bingo was one of the first activities that went 'viral' during the Covid 19 lockdown in 2020. See Pope and McGreevy 2020.

20. For a more general discussion of the disgust people feel in their own bodily decay see Nussbaum 2017. However, anthropologists have noted quite varied responses to the ageing of the body, for example Buch 2015.

21. Mandatory retirement tends to be at 65, with provisions for early retirement from 60 (or in some cases 55). Everyone is entitled to a state pension, though this is means-tested, from 66 (rising to 67 in 2021 and 68 in 2028). The current (2018) weekly pension is €232.00 plus €153.30 for spouse/partner under 66, with reduction based on current earnings, falling to zero for incomes over €257 per week. Other factors include whether a person is living alone or has an additional pension based on contributions during working life. The public service also has its own generous pension, though again this is means-tested. Another very extensive benefit for older people is free travel across the whole of Ireland on any bus or train. Those aged over 70 have free television, an energy allowance, a free driving licence and a reduction in health costs, again subject to means-testing. See The Pensions Authority 2020.

22. See Carvill 2014 in a report from the Retirement Planning Council of Ireland. This report also notes that 37 per cent of people expected to continue in some kind of work after retirement.

23. Life expectancy is currently 84 years for women and 80.4 years for men. See Department of Health 2019.

24. In 1998 just 48,000 people aged 60–64 and 34,300 people over 65 were still working. Today, according to the Central Statistics Office, some 112,000 60–64-year-olds are still working, and 66,000 people aged 65 and over are still in the workforce – roughly double in both age groups. However, a disproportionate number of the over-65s work in the sectors of agriculture, forestry and fishing. So this figure may in fact reflect self-employed farmers, rather than embracing late-in-life workers. See Reddan 2017.

25. For a typical example see European Innovation Partnership on Active and Healthy Ageing 2012.

26. For evidence in support of this see Wels 2020.

27. For a general appraisal of the global Age-Friendly movement see Stafford 2019.

28. Buch 2015.

29. Implied suicide.

30. Ní Léime and Street 2019.

31. Goodbody 2018.

32. There is also the wider impact of digital technologies, for which see Prendergast and Garattini 2015.

33. Specifically there is an acknowledgement that older widows may not conform to such stereotypes. See Chambers 2018.

34. There are important policy implications of these observations. In retrospect, people noted that they had often simply followed some work trajectory after education before they had really determined who and what they wanted to be. It seems typical that it is only at around the age of 40, when children have grown up, that women in particular – but often also men – seem to have found a path they want to follow. This may be something that would have been a salaried employment, such as teaching or car repairs, or may be what is seen as a leisure pursuit such as writing or music; this may also be a time when individuals have the confidence to start a business. If trajectories continue towards automation in manufacturing and services and salaried work declines still further, the period of retired life may grow to even exceed that of working life. This would open up radical new possibilities. Perhaps retirement at 65 could be replaced by two more equal phases, the first from the end of education and the second starting around 40, when people would be allowed to return to education or training and spend as much time in a second career as in their first? This seemed like the kind of change that many of our participants would welcome, but by no means all.

35. We acknowledge that we have not tried to cover the extensive relative literatures devoted to gerontology and also the life course, for example Settersten 2018. The focus on life course would pay more attention to the way in which an individual's life developed. But in a way the previous chapter covered this perspective, in that Ireland as a whole has gone through a clear trajectory, from poverty to wealth and religious control to relative secularism, that covers almost all the population's personal history.

36. This observation is found also in Scharf et al. 2013.

37. See especially commentary on Andrews 1999.

38. An ambition that is generally shared by novelists – see Zamorano Llena 2019.

3
Everyday life: activities and routines

To conceive of life as a form of craft, implied in the subtitle of this book 'When life becomes craft', implies that people are dealing with something malleable, a substance that can be sculpted and shaped. For this chapter, that malleable substance is time. As noted in the previous chapter, most of our research participants had lived lives where time was anything but malleable; it had been largely a constraint and an insufficiency. Between the demands of work and those of parenting, there was not usually enough time for the many things people felt had to be done with it.

When people retire and/or their children leave home, however, time takes on quite different qualities. It lies wide open, free of demands, waiting to be shaped. For many approaching retirement, a key question was how time itself should be filled? Would they prefer to be a busy bee or a relaxed slouch? We have a rich language associated with time which is invested with moral and normative connotations. Is relaxation time 'wasted' and 'frittered away'? Or is it 'me' time or 'well spent'? This chapter is partial, since time spent with other people is the subject of the next chapter.

In the film mentioned here (Fig. 3.1), Deirdre recalls being shocked by her own use of time. First, she lists a stream of activities in which she is involved, including looking after grandchildren, working for the local community association, making costumes for the local theatre group, planning her trips on the Camino pilgrimage route and chasing down ancestors on ancestor.com, sometimes until 3 a.m. But she then goes on to note that her iPhone has a feature that informs her of how many hours a day she has spent on her phone; during the recent past this was often six or seven hours, which she admits was devoted mainly to playing card games. Deirdre has a very good explanation for this, but from our point

Figure 3.1   Film: *Deirdre*. Available at http://bit.ly/DEirdre.

of view it shows the problem posed for this chapter. An individual retired person living on their own has 112 hours a week to account for. This time requires filling one way or another. The substance would include what people label as activities as well as their daily routines, their use of entertainment such as television shows, listening to the news and reading newspapers and books – all in addition to the social activities discussed in the next chapter.

When Pauline visited the Retirement Council of Ireland, Derek Bell, the Chief Operations Officer, made clear that in his experience people who are planning retirement think their primary concern will be financial. In fact, structuring and organising free time quickly emerges as just as important. This was confirmed by our research participants. Activities in our fieldsites have a social, moral and even existential significance. Not only do they represent a social outlet and opportunity for physical exercise, but they also provide a sense of foundational security in routinising and adding structure to the day.[1] The stuff people do as part of everyday life, such as preparing meals and listening to the radio, feels humdrum and ordinary. Activities, by contrast, are what people see as giving purpose to life; they make them feel they have 'something to do'. One reason for this feeling is that other people do not see us when we eat lunch at home or watch the television news, but going to a yoga class is publicly visible and acknowledged by others as 'social', even if we do not talk to anyone. That which is communal and recognised as an 'activity' seems to accrue an additional status over solitary pursuits.

In our fieldsites, some groups meet weekly to play cards, knit and chat while sharing coffee and cake. Other groups swim in the sea, attend church, go for bracing walks or gather to engage in litter picks. Many research participants refer to these activities as both building community and enhancing health. One Thornhill respondent, Josie, was approached by a local priest who asked her to set up a weekly coffee morning. Some of the local elderly parishioners were isolated, he said, and needed somewhere to go. He thought that they might prefer to attend something organised by a lay, active and popular member of the community. Josie was adamant that she would not just create a coffee morning. The participants had to *do* something while drinking coffee – ideally something practical and worthwhile that could accrue funds for charity. The subsequent group ended up knitting for the local hospice, for grandchildren, for church funds and a variety of other good causes. Not only did the activity give structure to the week, but the charitable outcome gave structure to the activity. It concentrated and distributed their efforts in such a way that the group was as much about helping others as amusing oneself. For others, activities such as these carry an explicit health objective. For example, one participant in a craft group shared a post called 'The Health Benefits of Knitting',[2] which argued that the repetitive action of knitting reduces the stress hormone cortisol. WhatsApp is integral to the creation and moderation of these groups. It has, then, an important bearing on the types of sociality that they engender, the frequency of online interactions or the banter that they facilitate. This facility for continuous online conversations is generally seen as something novel which may excite, delight or frustrate.

Social Prescribing

As part of our research, we helped to develop a health-related intervention called Social Prescribing, so-called because it is intended to allow counsellors, psychotherapists and others to prescribe activities, rather than immediately reaching for antidepressants, for people who are lonely, isolated or depressed.[3] Despite its relatively lively social scene, one Thornhill therapist commented that isolation is a real issue, with many older people seeing nobody from one day to the next. Retirement is particularly relevant because some people may have developed their entire social networks around work, only to find themselves anchorless when their working lives come to an end. To create a Social Prescribing website, which can also be accessed on smartphones or as hard copies, we first needed to make a comprehensive list of all available adult activities in our respective fieldsites. We had discovered that most such activities are only known about through word of mouth, which meant that people not well socially connected were those least likely to know about them. Word of mouth seems to gain much more traction for developing activities than more formal information such as community and church hall notices boards, though in Cuan the fortnightly news magazine certainly helped. Generally, however, easy-going informality is widely appreciated by people in Ireland, and social navigation often requires a personal recommendation to be taken on board.

In Thornhill, for example, activities often pivot around one designated person who both organises events and channels information to others. Walking groups or Active Retirement meetings may have Facebook pages, but these are not necessarily kept up to date. The local Men's Shed was co-organised by a man and woman who volunteered regularly in parish activities. Two other women baked apple tarts and scones for the men each week, and these women spread the word among their husbands. The men themselves recognised that the Men's Shed movement was more orientated to manual labour, but since they had led professional lives they replaced it with a 'men's group' centred on telling tales of their childhood, playing musical instruments or just chatting. All the participants knew the founding members and it was unlikely that people would have joined the group other than through personal connections. Similarly, although there is a Facebook page for Thornhill walking groups, actual up-to-date information is exchanged through texting between friends. In both fieldsites the term *locality* suggests not only a geographical term but also a sense of belonging to an area.[4]

As a more formal method of dissemination, Social Prescribing takes a holistic approach to health that embeds it in these social networks and cultural activities. In Ireland, the Health Service Executive webpage suggests that Social Prescribing should link people to a wide range of physical, cultural and social supports for maintaining health and wellbeing, such as social isolation, stress or anxiety. On a national level, according to TILDA research, 60 per cent of adults aged 54 years and over take part in active and social leisure activities at least once per week, while 47 per cent participate in at least one of these organised groups at least once per week.[5] Public activities are integral to the way people think about the place in which they live. In Thornhill, participants of all ages speak of the local resources available to them in the form of parks and walking routes, as well as their proximity to the city centre and local beaches. People in Cuan frequently exclaim that the town they live in is wonderful, precisely because of the number of activities available to them at this stage of life. They have good reason for this pride.

Early in our research we came across a project called Local Asset Mapping Project (LAMP), run through St James's Hospital in Dublin. This has a webpage which conjures the following scenario:

> Imagine visiting your doctor and as well as getting a prescription for a pill, you get an electronic prescription designed especially for you, with a list of all the local businesses and services around you that might improve your health – that is the vision of LAMP.[6]

This observation aligns with the TILDA project, whose findings suggest that quality of life is strongest for the age group being discussed here but only if social engagement is strong.[7] This caveat was also evident in our own research.

Subsequently we created (though have not yet been able to implement due to Covid-19) Social Prescribing sites for both Cuan and Thornhill, intending to make these available to local counselling and psychotherapy centres.[8] We also set up an additional site called 'Social Activities for Adults' which provides a list of activities, contact information for each activity and a map that pinpoints the location of the activity for use by the general public. These listings can be accessed on computers, smartphones or as hard copies for those unfamiliar with digital technologies; they are hosted on local community websites. We took a holistic approach based on a broad definition of wellness, including both complementary health and mainstream medical services. For example, activities in Thornhill include seven general practitioners, a state-run health centre and three private nursing homes; there are also seven centres offering Pilates, yoga, mindfulness and acupuncture. There was also a range of activities from dance classes and card games to gardening clubs and charitable activities such as Meals on Wheels, although during the Covid-19 pandemic many of these activities, and the implementation of our Social Prescribing websites, were suspended.

During fieldwork retired people in Cuan could attend the film society, talks at the sailing club or the historical association. They could play traditional Irish music at Sunday 'slow sessions' or listen to four other weekly sessions in the local pubs. There were two town choirs, the ukulele group and classes for set dancing, jive, Zumba and dance/ exercises. There were three art classes, a local history society and another lively historical group studying topics such as the First World War. There was an Irish conversational group and a very active local theatre group that staged at least three plays a year. People could go to a creative writing group based on sharing their writing or one where they were taught creative writing skills. They could join classes in Spanish or French, flower arranging or silk embroidery, or attend a computer course. There was also a poker club, a whist club, a chess club, three very active bridge clubs and additional bridge classes. Cuan had four gyms and at least four different book reading clubs. Options for outdoor activities include allotments, 'Sustainable Cuan', the Cuan Community Harvest and a walking group.

There was also a range of community activities dominated by wide participation in the Tidy Towns competition. Cuan boasts a community association, a supported housing project and an Age-Friendly committee. People volunteered for Citizens' Advice and various charitable events or organisations such as for raising funds for a hospice, the St Vincent de Paul charity or the charity shop dedicated to helping people with autism. Many local retired people volunteer for Meals on Wheels. There is an Active Retirement group, a Men's Shed and a group teaching English to migrants.

Cuan has many sports associations including hockey, volleyball, karate, football, badminton, tennis, sailing, bowling, cycling, Gaelic football, hurling, athletics and cricket. Indoor and outdoor bowling was dominated by people of this demographic, and people in their seventies or older might still be engaged in cycling. For the rest of the sports, it was more likely that older people would be involved either in coaching or some managerial role. They might also go swimming in the sea or enjoy other water-based activities such as rowing and especially sailing; many of them had boats. Social Prescribing focuses strongly upon local activities.

Of considerable importance to some, especially the eldest faction, remains daily mass and other church-related activities, including a parish book club and choir, a weekly Catholic Charismatic prayer meeting or alternative churches such as the Church of Ireland and Methodist. Finally, there has been considerable growth in 'wellness activities'. Cuan boasts seven different sites for yoga in addition to Pilates, t'ai chi and various forms of holistic therapy.

These activities involved older people in two ways. They may play bridge, act, cycle or pick up litter. But since many of these are voluntary activities, they may equally well be involved in helping to organise and manage those activities. For example, the theatre in Cuan will need around ten volunteers every night of a performance to deal with front of house tasks, prepare the wine and tea/coffee for the interval, sell raffle tickets and put out publicity around the town. Deirdre, for example, whose film appeared earlier in this chapter, makes the costumes. At the annual International Women's Day evening, much was made of the opportunities to volunteer around the town, a point often reiterated by local politicians. Typically an individual dedicated to a specific activity such as sailing or the community association might spend a couple of years acting as the chair or treasurer or similar managerial activities, then lapse back into lay membership. The need for activities will vary. A woman who had settled in Cuan from Germany noticed the difference at weekends. People from 'old Cuan', who had extensive networks or people whose family were coming to visit, would be busy. But some of the blow-ins who did not have families or whose families now lived abroad were often in need of some other kind of social activity, which she then became keen to help develop. Finally, in addition, people attend many activities in central Dublin, such as sports events, theatre and music. There are increasing attempts to provide specialist activities for older people within Dublin. One of the most important is the Bealtaine arts programme, and there has been some research on its contribution to people's sense of wellbeing and social interaction.[9]

What emerges from this comprehensive exercise, while intended for Social Prescribing, is evidence of the sheer volume of activities. Nor is this unique to the older inhabitants: a parallel compendium of activities for children might be just as long. From the initial encounter, people in Cuan referred constantly to the feeling that Cuan is buzzing with activity. It is a place where anyone with a half-decent idea can find others who will help turn that idea into an additional resource. The scale of activities as much as their content is central to the way people think about the place they live in, and the considerable local pride that implies there is no better place to live. People in Cuan often say that the only things missing are a swimming pool, a dedicated cinema and a hotel.

The individual's perspective

Researching for Social Prescribing led to the creation of this comprehensive account of activities. What matters for the individual, however, is how they engage with them. For some it is the variety that counts. For example, Maeve, aged 75, currently goes to mass regularly and is heavily involved in the church choir and another choir. She also attends a book club and an art class, plays bridge, swims and attends an aqua-aerobics class. She used to do more philanthropic activities including Meals on Wheels, Citizens' Advice and adult literacy classes, but she gave those up, in the latter case partly because of increasing bureaucracy. The rise in bureaucratic procedures such as health and safety or GDPR, as well as the cost of insurance, may have generally diminished the level of volunteering in the town.

Catherine similarly had a career in education. For some ten years after retirement she was so involved in voluntary work, she jokes, that she needed to make an appointment to see her husband. During this period she set up a home help service for the town, helped to set up a pre-school playgroup, assisted with the church collections, chaired the fundraising for the local school and was a census enumerator. The most time-consuming activity was helping to develop the local credit union. Catherine typifies the many retirees who had been in public service and who tended to volunteer with organisations that also represented public service rather than self-development.

By contrast, plenty of people are involved in far fewer activities. A prime example was Resa, introduced in chapter 2, who mainly watches sports on television, her only public activity being yoga. Some people prefer to walk alone each day and have little or nothing else outside the home. Physical activities such as yoga, Pilates or Zumba are relatively popular too, but they can be practised at home alone. Some indeed prefer them for this reason. By contrast, others eschew self-directed activities and instead dedicate their time to philanthropic activities such as teaching English to migrants and Meals on Wheels.

If some are involved in many activities while others prefer few or none, a third category of people may be involved almost entirely in a single activity but really go for it. The film about Bob in chapter 1 shows his clear dedication to poetry, which he treats, for all intents and purposes, as full-time paid employment. Bill, the subject of a film in chapter 8, is very involved in photography and has published a book of images from 1950s Dublin. He has also arranged a small exhibition in the local café and organises the local 'film evening' in his parish centre. One bachelor devotes almost all of his time to two activities, collecting postcards of the town – which may include going to specialist postcard fairs – and otherwise reading and writing on the history of local seafaring;[10] another resident avidly collects coins, a hobby that takes him far and wide in his search for rare specimens. Deirdre was one of several participants who spend an inordinate amount of time on family genealogy online. She has also taken DNA tests, enabling her to link with other relatives who have also taken these tests. Creative writing has an impressive role here too, with many published authors; but then many places in Ireland have produced authors and poets, particularly in recent years.[11]

Some participants speak of the effect of activities in expanding their social network and affecting their perspective on life. Emma retired from school teaching at 55 because she knew people who had died soon after retirement and she felt she had given enough to the job. In addition, it was difficult keeping up with her younger colleagues who were so much more active and on top of the new curriculum than she was. Retirement activities felt more 'real' to Emma, by which she meant they were not timetabled to the same degree and felt freely chosen. She took up Spanish simply because she enjoys travelling to Spain and once found herself with a sick son in an area where people did not speak much English. She even took up bridge and a book club, despite having little interest in either, because she decided she wanted to be more outgoing and more willing to try new things and take chances.

There were, however, two significant constraints preventing her from these aspirations to a more devil-may-care lifestyle. The first is financial, as cost-cutting limits any travelling or even going to the theatre. Emma did not appreciate the financial constraints that her pension would impose on her until it was too late. She also feels a real sense of loss with the ending of the intergenerational mix that she enjoyed as a schoolteacher. On the other hand, she feels she has the right attitude for retirement. Before retiring, she describes herself as more 'closed'. 'I wouldn't be here with you now,' she says as an example of her willingness to try new things. Even if these new activities do not produce fast friends, Emma is accumulating acquaintances that she feels add to her overall life experience.

For many people, the foundations for their retirement activities were laid much earlier.[12] Typically they may have been asked to volunteer to help with various school activities such as sports, parent-teacher liaison or putting on a play. Women seemed to be more involved in these social obligations and some found themselves volunteering even though they were already quite busy. One example is Sophie, who says:

> I started with the playgroup of the children ... so I was a secretary or whatever. Then at the primary school, I was the chair, and then when I grew out of that, and the kids grew out of that, I was saying oh they (the youth) need something else, with a bigger umbrella. So, coincidentally, a note from the Community Association came in the door.

For many men, there was also a quite natural transition from playing sports to realising one was getting a little old for playing and instead becoming a coach or assisting in some other way. Often they first coached their children and their peers. And while many people drop out of activities when they are burdened with work and parental responsibilities, there was still a common perspective that some form of volunteer work is the lifeblood of a vibrant community.

Observing activities

Activities may be something a town is proud of or part of an individual's weekly schedule. But they also have their own structure, atmosphere and consequences. This chapter selects just four of these, which we attended on many occasions over the 16 months of fieldwork.

The ukulele group

It is hard to exaggerate the sheer exuberance and cheerfulness of the ukulele group, which meets every Tuesday between 7.45 p.m. and 10 p.m. in a room at the GAA (Gaelic Athletic Association), one of the core social/ activity hubs of pretty much any Irish village or town. There is one bass ukulele; the rest are standard concert or soprano instruments. A typical meeting might comprise around 9 men and 23 women, who generally keep to their own side. There is a break around 9 p.m. when the tea is made and one of the members always brings homemade cakes or biscuits. There is also a treasurer who collects fees. Members pay fees which are used to employ a professional ukulele instructor, who might circulate a proposed new song on their active WhatsApp account and prepare the group for a concert. She tends to assume a fair bit of knowledge and, after initial familiarity, might introduce a particular strumming pattern or divide the group so that they can play harmonies or countermelodies.

The final third of the lesson is usually a free session where anyone is welcome to suggest which song to play next. Everybody has the same large songbook which has 200 songs. New members are seated next to more experienced players who are always solicitous, usually weaving in a joke or two to put the new arrivals at their ease and ensure there is no tone of seniority or authority. The repertoire is mainly classic pop songs such as 'Hotel California', 'Ain't no Sunshine', 'Bad Moon Rising' or Eric Clapton's 'Wonderful Tonight', but there may also be new pop songs such as 'Shotgun' by George Ezra or seasonal Christmas songs.

During the tea and cake break people form small groups to chat. There is seldom a pause between two songs without some banter – for example, when Brendan, one of the founders, sat next to a new female member – but there is not even the slightest frisson of sexual tension among the group, who range mainly from their forties to their seventies. No one looks as though they have dressed to draw attention and the atmosphere remains unpretentious and egalitarian. As in the Men's Shed, the teacher will tone down her authority by exaggerating how affronted she is by an interruption, for instance demanding of somebody in jocular fashion, 'Are you giving me lip again?' The more established members give regular charitable performances, which might be in a retirement home or part of a Christmas celebration. Thirty-five members of the group also went on tour to a town in Italy that one of them knew from holidays in the region, where they played five concerts.

An analysis of 100 posts on their very active WhatsApp group showed an average of five per day by 23 different people, of which 30 posts included emojis. Topics included not only apologies for absence and decisions about who was bringing the mugs and milk, but also recordings and sharing of possible songs. There were also posts from people currently on holiday, for example in Spain, India or a cruise on the Danube, or celebrating holidays such as Hallowe'en or Christmas.

In the film featured here (Fig. 3.2), Peig relates ukulele playing to her aspiration to 'live a disgraceful life'. At least if one judges by how often it is cited, Jenny Joseph's poem 'When I Grow Old, I Shall Wear Purple' has been quite an inspiration to many older people. At a workshop for older people held by an NGO, Peig performed a hilarious 20-minute dialogue, partly about the consequences of her online dating at the age of 80, including lines such as '... and I also painted my toenails – just in case'. In the play she mocks her fictional 'family', who have to hold frequent meetings to decide what to do about her, discussing her in her presence, as though she could not hear them. Much of her time has been an involvement in an extremely successful local community group that now provides around 30 different activities for older people at a cost of

Figure 3.2   Film: *A disgraceful life*. Available at http://bit.ly/ disgracefullife.

€5 a session. Yet for all that Peig, since the loss of her husband, can be extremely lonely. Happiest when she is the life and soul of a social setting, back home she may have nothing but the birds for company – although, of course, she does feed the birds. So ukulele has proved to be an inspired choice for her, as for so many others.

The Men's Shed

The ethos behind the Men's Shed was well expressed by one of its members as follows:

> It made sense to me that men, when they retired, were being isolated. Y'know this feeling of uselessness and also the feeling that they had no value anymore, but I could see, and everyone could see, that they had a lot of value in them. There was a lot of experience and expertise that they had and it wasn't being tapped. Here, there were a lot of people with good heads on them and some of them were made redundant and missing the camaraderie and all that.

The main weekly meeting of the Men's Shed takes place at 2.30 p.m. It generally concludes at 4 p.m., at which point members go to a café for tea or coffee, which is paid for through a €2 fee from all those present. There are usually between 12 and 18 people, sometimes including the representative of the local council. Besides this, some go on Thursday mornings to tend to the Men's Shed allotment and a few on a Friday morning to an area where they can play French boules. There will always be some practical project that requires at least a weekly or sometimes more frequent activity, such as help with painting railings, clearing up for Tidy Towns or repairing a historical artefact. They could also organise weekly classes; six members, for example, were attending a cookery class. As will appear in the film about Liam below, the Men's Shed sees itself as a hub for helping with community activities and its members can be involved in a Men's Shed activity almost every day of the week.

The Men's Shed movement was established in Australia, with a view to finding occupations for men largely employed in areas such as manual labour. By appearance, the Cuan Men's Shed could have come from such a background, since they mainly wear cheap shirts, sweaters and jeans. But in fact many of them have worked for the government or in senior managerial posts; their background is generally white-collar rather than blue-collar. However, most men who participate have a good sense of DIY and manual activities, even if they did work in the civil service – all of which turns out to be quite perfectly aligned with the contemporary Men's Shed.

During the last few months of fieldwork, weekly meetings were dominated by the desire to get an actual shed of their own where members can meet and carry out repair work. There is discussion about material issues such as the laying of a concrete base, the relative merits of steel and concrete and the provision of facilities such as water heating, lighting and more detailed issues such as potential condensation on the ceiling. The men present have a good deal of relevant background knowledge and might well have their own rather smaller sheds in their gardens. But what takes up most of the time of the weekly meetings are a quite different set of topics: namely the issues of regulation, insurance, health and safety, police clearance and many other bureaucratic issues. These relate not only to acquiring an actual shed, but also to the small-scale activities members are involved in around the town, each one of which may require insurance cover and various forms of data protection or clearance. As these topics surface, so does the very considerable expertise that these men have acquired as senior managers and professionals on exactly these issues of health and safety and regulation.

Curiously, it turned out that this shift in what is required to be a contemporary Irish Men's Shed movement was ideal for its actual members' combination of skills. Occasionally they may have talks from outsiders, which might include safety and security or, for example, the distribution of plastic cylinders given to them for free by the Lions Club for storing basic medical information for emergencies such as having to call an ambulance. Again, the members could all contribute.

For an example of a Men's Shed, see the film that was made in Maynooth, Co. Kildare (Fig. 3.3).

Figure 3.3 Film: *Maynooth Men's Shed*. Available at http://bit.ly/maynoothmensshed.

Thornhill Strollers

In Thornhill, where walking is a very popular pastime, there are several walking and running groups that meet in the local park or by the sea front. The groups can be mixed but, in common with other activities, tend to attract more women than men. While walking, they share experiences and worries regarding their family and friends, for example, comparing notes on how to look after elderly and frail parents. One woman commented that her sister had recently become separated from her husband and moved back in with their mother. Unfortunate, but a boon for both her mother and extended family, since now their mother was having a proper daily cooked meal when she had previously stopped bothering for herself. Another set of walkers shared the problem of elderly people who could not or would not use smartphones. One man said that having persuaded his mother to have such a phone, she now turns it off when not making calls in case it is costing her money. They had had a scare one time when she was not answering the door to her neighbour and did not answer her phone. He left work in a panic and called her house, only to find that she had been in the shower. One woman offered the example that her father feels unable to master digital technologies and therefore enjoys going to the bank in person to pay any bills. It got him out of the house, she explained, and he would go into town once a week and pay the bills with cash at his bank.

The Strollers have a Facebook page but prefer to communicate on WhatsApp if the weather is poor. Generally the Strollers meet on weekend mornings and on Wednesday evenings for a short beach walk. On some occasions the outing is cut short and they retreat to the local café for coffee and cake, chat and laughter, which is clearly an integral part of their get-togethers. All of this chat suggests that a more appropriate name might have been the Thornhill Walking and Talking Group. However, this opportunity to compare and share problems in everyday life did not detract from the group's assertion of the positive effect of the activity in itself. At the end of the walk they talk about the importance of getting out, the delight of living in a city and having an open landscape on your doorstep. Familiar with movements within health and wellness discourse, one individual spoke extensively about the importance of people feeling as though they are doing something to improve their health. Wild swimming, for example, is not only good for giving the immune system a jolt, she says, but for feeling well more generally. Here, as elsewhere, there is a general sense that walking and exercise can help stop one feeling old.[13]

Other forms of outdoor activity and travelling are seen as extensions of the same ethos. Participants often discuss further plans for upcoming trips. Part of these discussions involves sharing and exchanging recommendations regarding nice places to stay or eat when they travel. One woman comments on the ability of herself and her husband to 'down tools' at any moment and go away for a week. 'These are the years to do this stuff,' the group is told. 'You're not working but you're healthy and what's to stop you?'

Another commented:

I'm not retired but I do think I'm better off now than anytime before. And I do think it's important to join groups so that you have people around you, which will be especially important as you age. I think being in my sixties is great.

A link between this example and those in several other chapters is the rise of activities and shifts in orientation that reflects the spectrum of new green concerns such as sustainability and wellbeing. Walking sits alongside very popular activities such as yoga and Pilates, as well as various sports. In addition, there is also the continued development of allotments, whole sections of which may now be designated as organic.

Craft and coffee

Some of these activities are rather more sedate and suit an older demographic. On Wednesday mornings between 15 and 20 women attend mass and then come into a Thornhill parish centre for craft and coffee. Conversations with these women reveal that most are in their seventies and eighties, and that what seems to bond them is a firm commitment to their Catholicism. While they do not talk about belief as such, their attitudes to doctrine became evident during the Pope's visit in 2018 and, to a lesser extent, the abortion referendum. One of our participants had tried to organise a group of people who would visit the elderly, hoping maybe to bring them out for coffee now and again. It did not work out because once people start to think of themselves as frail they become nervous of answering the door to strangers and less inclined to venture out, even if only for a coffee. It was the link with the church that made this group possible.

For these women, led by Josie, introduced at the beginning of this chapter (p.52), it is profoundly important to stay busy. The parish centre is a small, comfortable building beside the church and two volunteers prepare the hall, setting the table and putting out chairs. The women arrive in ones and twos and stay for a couple of hours while knitting and catching up. They pay a small fee of €2 each which, for a cup of coffee and scone, is far cheaper than anything available commercially. The presence of the community or parish halls provides an additional advantage to people of low income because there are not many other places to go unless you are involved in sports (for example golf) or cultural activities (for example art classes), which all entail fees. One local man calculated that he and his wife spend approximately €200 a month in the local café – something not financially feasible for pensioners, he laughed. The trouble, he says, is that they have developed a routine of going out for mid-morning coffee which is hard to break.

The craft and coffee group display a strong sense of morality, centred on doing something useful and filling time with good works. One man described his wife as 'like a shark – they die if they stop moving'; others commented with pride that since retirement they have never been so busy. As one put it, 'I'd feel guilty if I wasn't doing anything'. Time, therefore, becomes problematic – not because it is scarce, but because it must be filled. Staying busy is crucial for these women in their seventies and eighties. One woman told us how she had knitted 100 small chickens because 'I just knit when I'm watching television'. While watching television is not 'doing nothing', the emphasis is on being productive with time, not letting it slip away. This point is considered so self-evident that some participants look askance when asked why it is a good thing to be active. The metaphors are significant. Time needs to be filled, otherwise it might be empty or wasted, which would leave them feeling adrift. So the craft lies not just in the knitting, but in the organising of their lives.

There could be said to be a pattern to retirement activities in these fieldsites. They may derive from a hobbyist enthusiasm, but many exist because someone felt a sense of responsibility for creating the site for people to meet with others and for enjoyment. But this issue of simply filling time is also crucial.

Filling time

This idea that activities need to be considered in relation to the way people understand time itself is evident from both the formation and response to the craft and coffee group. This can also be seen from the perspective of the individuals who take part in some activities. Maura, for example, goes to the gym twice a week and spends her afternoons with her father, who is now in a nursing home. She also decided that she needed something to keep her brain sharp and took up French lessons. Maura travels with this group to France every year and so, like many activities, it combines an education or fitness element with a social one. On Wednesday evenings she occasionally attends a bridge club. Maura laughs when she talks about the speed with which bridge players make their tricks and their irritation at her slowness while she tries to get to grips with the rules of the game. All these activities are aimed to keep her active, both physically and mentally. Reflecting on retirement, she acknowledges that 'I'm entering the final stage of my life' and wonders how much time she'll have left: will she enjoy the same longevity as her father, who is 97? She often states that the sixties is the very best time to make the most of life. Her friends have found it is only in their sixties and possibly seventies that they retain both decent health and relative freedom. The energy to travel or do whatever they like is set against the feeling that some clock is marking down the days.

In line with the findings of chapter 2, Maura describes her stage of life now as a sort of older person in between being adult and elderly; she jokes she is like a sort of older teenager. What might run out is not so much life itself, but the healthy time before frailty sets in. It is this concern that brings the pressing need to make the most of the time while it is present. Maura feels that she took early retirement from nursing at the moment when she still has both the resources and the time to make the most of her freedom. Her mornings were now her own. If she did not have caring responsibilities she would be completely free, although she says she is happy to tend to her father in his final years.

A significant change in the very concept of filling time has been the arrival of the smartphone. In *The Global Smartphone*, our team book in the series, the device is discussed in relation to its capacity for 'Perpetual Opportunism'. Older people are often nostalgic about times before the mobile phone, when people actually talked to each other on the rail commute. But in practice they are as likely as anyone to use the smartphone to fill in those gaps in time, which range from standing in a queue to taking the bus.

There is a balance here. The smartphone may make life less boring, but it can also prevent people from properly immersing themselves since it is a constant distraction. The smartphone has become the hub through which flow a series of ongoing activities, a conversation we continue to have with perhaps several people through the day at intervals through the constancy of checking WhatsApp messages and other notifications.

With a smartphone, a person can be scrolling through news or Facebook or researching something they may want to buy, partly so as not to feel embarrassed at appearing to be doing nothing at all. So the smartphone is the basis for rethinking, in part, both what we mean by activity and what we mean by routine.[14]

The smartphone will also play a major role for people such as Maura, precisely because she is involved in so many different activities. WhatsApp, in combination with Facebook, is now of major importance in organising those activities, from getting information on times and places to scheduling and working out the best way to travel to them. The same goes for the organisers of these activities, so that people responsible for something like a Men's Shed find it quite irritating when they are forced to organise through email because not every member is using WhatsApp.

The example of Maura (one that could have been many others) suggests firstly that there is a common idea that time is something that needs to be filled, ideally in a productive way. Secondly, though related, is the idea that time – or at least *healthy* time – is running out, though this worry is balanced by the sense of this being a particularly good period of life to be making the most of time. There is another factor to consider, however, which is the degree to which time should include routine.

Crafting routines

The point about routine is that it gives structure to days and weeks. There are some, including Emma mentioned above, who value the idea of spontaneity in retirement as an expression of freedom. But it is far more common to regard this emphasis upon regularity and routine as essential. Niamh outlined how, when she first retired, her days were quite unstructured until she realised that structure helped her to organise her days. She explains:

> In the beginning, it was lovely to sleep in and everyone wanted to meet me for lunch and coffee, but I soon realised I'd put on a stone if I continued the way I was going, so now I have a plan.

Pretty soon, her hectic schedule left us feeling exhausted just listening to it. Living in the area where she grew up and having a wide social circle of relatives is key to Niamh's organisation of her days. Here are the first three days of her week as she presents them.

Monday: To get me out of bed, out of bed at 8, I go to 10 a.m. mass, and then I get my half-hour walk in (local park) and then I'm ready for the day. Monday evening I took up bridge to keep the brain going.

Tuesday: I'm in the retirement club, even though people keep asking me why I joined it and I say because I'm retired – but they say it's for old people, and I say you should see the 90-year-olds doing the quizzes and then winning the quizzes. And I never had a thing about age. Alternatively Tuesday is art class and I never did art before, but I took it up.

Wednesday: I love swimming and my niece is free on Wednesday nights, so we go to a local pool. On Wednesday too I have choral society. I was a member of a choir for 40 years and we meet and rehearse on Wednesdays. I was a founding member and we do concerts and we go away and all that. Wednesdays also I meet a pal. We go to Slimming World and go to (the café) and have scones and cream and coffee and I never miss that.

For others the lack of routine is a problem. One participant detailed how her husband bought a taxi when he retired just to keep himself occupied at weekends. Others talk of how they occupy time on a day-to-day level. Aidan retired at 60 during the economic crash. He did not particularly want to, but during the financial crisis civil servants were offered a lump sum to retire; if he had not gone then, his pension would have been reduced by 7 per cent. In one way, Aidan says it was good to have the decision made for him rather than having to decide himself. On the other hand, he is often at a loose end. He helps with his grandchildren and complains that his daughter texts him as a shorthand for actually getting in touch and having a conversation. Aidan tends to be at home quite a bit looking after himself or the grandchildren.

The activity that gives a sense of routine to Aidan is his walking.

I walk frantically all the time, I walk a lot, I like it down here, you can get to the sea in a few minutes. I like walking around, clears the head.

Every morning he drops his adult son at the train station and then goes for a long walk on the beach, which he knows will take him 53 minutes. For Aidan and many others, it is this daily walk that seems to centre the day. Apart from these daily walks, he set up a group of six friends he knew from the time he was employed. They go for around five walks a year, each six hours long. So there is the daily walk and these special walks. In a similar way, the friendship bonds built over three decades with his work colleagues who come on the special walks are more significant for Aidan than recent acquaintances he has established near his home.

There are also men such as Vincent, who have no interest in getting involved in community or local activities. About the only thing that constitutes routine for Vincent are the phone calls he makes each weekend to his sister in the UK. Mostly, however, when people lack routine they regard that as a problem waiting to be solved, rather than a positive choice.

Smartphones and special times

If the last section establishes the importance of routine, this section provides evidence that this generation are just as concerned with having breaks from the everyday. Aidan has both his routine walks and his special walks, for example. But for most older people in Dublin, it is hard to exaggerate the importance of travel in their lives. Holidays are one of the most common of all conversation topics. Those in the middle class may have a property abroad, but others would easily travel to the UK for a weekend to watch horse racing in Liverpool or visit their children working there. Simply taking a short trip to another part of Ireland is also very popular. Travel is also a pursuit that shows just how far the smartphone has become integral to the pursuit of activities for all ages.

Generally, the activities described above involve a particular configuration of apps. Some are mainly used for holidays, especially Tripadvisor, and there are also specialist travel apps such as Booking. com or Expedia. A very common set of apps are the airline apps; these days most of our research participants seemed comfortable using them to check in both remotely and when at the airports, so Ryanair and Aer Lingus will be present on many of their phones. For languages, they use Google Translate and a local dictionary for immediate use, but many also use Duolingo for brushing up on their language skills before travel. They may even listen to radio from that region to help them regain their fluency before travel. Currency converter apps are also seen as very useful.

Holidays abroad are also a period when some regular apps become even more important, including location apps such as Google Maps. However, there may be initial resistance to using these apps among older people. Some may at first try to convert the app into the equivalent of traditional map reading, by finding the route and memorising it before leaving, rather than using it during the journey, or by printing out the details in advance. They might then acquiesce in letting Google Maps direct their driving and, finding themselves in Moscow or Lisbon, may discover that it can also help them when walking. Once fully integrated, an app may then start to reflect local cultural interests. When on holiday, or living in their own properties abroad, social media and webcams become essential for keeping in touch with family and exchanging photographs. Travellers may hope the weather app is less essential than in the very unpredictable conditions of Ireland. If this is a walking trip, then the step-counter comes into play as evidence that they are using the holiday to keep 'healthy'. The smartphone is also used for envisaged or alternative travel.

Liam represents a suitable culmination of a discussion that links new digital technologies with travel (Fig. 3.4). In this film, we discover that Liam uses a virtual reality app linked to his Oculus goggles for travelling to places in the US that he will probably never visit in person. He also enjoys a VR 'trip' around a space station. He may browse different parts of the world using Google Earth, but it can also be employed in planning a trip to a wedding in Italy or revisiting previous holiday destinations.

No one told Liam that he could use virtual reality to compensate for those places he might never go to now: he simply worked that out for himself. But, as the film conveys, he is a resourceful character. He just realised that at his age you are simply not going to get to see everywhere you might wish to visit. While there are other places – such as outer space, literally on the horizon – which will always be *over* the horizon for him. But now, thanks to technology, there was a means also to travel there.

Figure 3.4   Film: *Liam*. Available at http://bit.ly/VR_Liam.

Conclusion: crafting

One of the reasons that the term 'crafting' seems appropriate is because older people are not simply availing themselves of a given set of possibilities provided by an external source, for example commerce or the state. Mostly they are involved in activities which they have both helped to establish and maintain – and may be quite resistant to any attempt by an institution or authority to intervene. For example, when it was proposed that the Active Retirement group might benefit from some computer classes, members made it very clear that they saw this group as dedicated to bingo; it was not something to be hijacked for such pedagogic purposes. Similarly, the group that runs Tidy Towns has become increasingly concerned with the way they feel that they are being exploited as an arm of the state, precisely because they are hugely successful. Awards are now assessed more on environmental activities than on simply making the place look attractive, partly because the relevant government ministry has switched from tourism to the environment.

To a remarkable degree, activities have no implications for status. At least for those we studied, it was clear that running them is a burden that people often have to be leaned on to undertake; they do so in their turn as a responsibility, before returning to the status of a lay member.[15] Nor is there much status in content. Only a few of those who join the art class aim to produce exceptional art. For example, the ukulele group contains better or worse ukulele players, but the film about Peig (see Fig. 3.2, p.60) shows that is simply not the point. This is in marked contrast to past ethnographic fieldwork in many other regions, where even the lowest level activity is a source of competition and status.

This age group feels it is entirely competent to create and develop activities as an expression of their genuine desires and interests. They also benefit from the huge amount of sheer competence that is the collective legacy of their working experience. On several occasions Danny heard Cuan praised as the kind of place that if someone wanted to start some new activity, they would always find half a dozen others to help them in this endeavour.

Chapter 3 also makes a contribution to the book as a whole because the evidence for crafting activities contributes to the claim that it is life itself which is being crafted. In this chapter, the research into the range of activities available has been balanced by constant reference to the perspective of individuals. People craft their particular configuration of activities both to create a weekly routine and to introduce the stimulus of breaks from routine. But the overwhelming sense from the perspective of individuals is diversity. Some are incredibly busy across a dozen activities, some focus on one and others eschew collective activity. There is no set pattern: an individual can construct their own relationship to these possibilities. If they fail to do so, it is clearly not because they lack opportunities. It is usually because of a problem in their social relations, the topic of the next chapter. It is this diversity in lives that is evidence for how people craft life itself, rather than just activities.

For most people the thing being crafted is time. There are the normal domestic routines of mealtimes and sleep times. There is watching television and listening to the news. For many, regular walks are particularly important in anchoring the day and showing responsibility to the claims of wellbeing. Most people create weekly routines and then introduce special times, such as holidays, as a contrast. This is not a completely free exercise: there is a cost to failure, in terms of boredom and loneliness. When it comes to time itself, people have no choice. There is a vast block of time standing there – if they do not attempt to sculpt it, this can become an oppressive and intimidating monolith, a 'nothingness', as one participant called it. For most, however, harnessing and moulding the resource of time was the key to a full and fulfilling later life.[16]

Notes

1. Relevant here is Giddens 1991.
2. Brody 2016.
3. Husk et al. 2019, South et al. 2008. See Health Service Executive Ireland 2020b. For an international example see the UK NHS website: https://www.england.nhs.uk/personalisedcare/social-prescribing/. See also Campbell 2018. The implementation of our initiative is presently derailed because of Covid-19.
4. Corcoran et al. 2007, Corcoran et al. 2010. See also Corcoran 2010 and Gallagher 2012.
5. See https://tilda.tcd.ie for details.
6. See eHealth Ireland 2020 for details of the Local Asset Mapping Project at St James's Hospital.
7. See McGarrigle et al. 2017. See also Garvey 2018b.
8. With the help of students from the Department of Computer Sciences, Maynooth University, Maynooth, Kildare, Ireland, particularly Daniel O'Neill. The implementation of this plan was unfortunately disrupted by the Covid-19 pandemic, which ended most activities. We were no longer able to map the subsequent pattern, although we still hope to return to this initiative when possible.
9. The Bealtaine festival (meaning May in Irish Gaelic) was launched in 1995 and is one of Ireland's largest festivals. It also boasts that it represents 'the world's first national celebration of creativity in older age'. It takes place each May and aims to bring people of all ages together while highlighting the experience and creativity of older people and promoting the arts community. The festival is supported by the Arts Council of Ireland and run by Age and Opportunity. Read more about it here: http://bealtaine.ie/page/about_us/festival_history. See also O'Shea and NíLéime 2012.
10. Other examples include a woman who is also currently involved in writing and does some amateur drama, but was once rather too much involved with alcohol. At the age of 72 she is obsessed with cycling and goes out on her bike four times a week for what sounds like quite

gruelling hill climbing, covering distances of around 40 km. Cycling is also the main thing she watches on television. Similarly, it seems at first that another participant is involved in several activities, but in fact every one of them is about raising money for cognitive disability charities. Even though this includes recreational activities such as playing poker, all are really an expression of a single interest.

11. See Lee 2008, 13. See Wulff 2017 and also see Clark 2019.

12. See Carvill 2014. In a report written on behalf of the Retirement Planning Council of Ireland, the company suggests most people were already involved in organisations they expected to be active in during retirement and 60 per cent plan to become involved in voluntary activities.

13. Hurd Clarke et al. 2020.

14. Another major form of relaxation is simply watching television. Many people felt that the contemporary television serial is perhaps of a higher standard than ever before – quite an admission from people who normally claim things have deteriorated. Typical examples might include crime series such as 'Line of Duty' and various Scandinavian noir series, but also a variety of comedy or series in soap opera style. The main channels for these are either the BBC or Netflix. Mostly these are watched at home, though for rugby and some other sports a few people watch in pubs; Danny joined some others, mainly younger people, in watching the last series of 'Game of Thrones' in a pub. As elsewhere, a particularly prominent series can then provide a topic of conversation, but mostly television is about domestic and individual consumption of time.

15. There may be some for whom this is not true and which we did not research, such as golf clubs and rugby clubs.

16. In a later publication Danny intends to look more closely into issues of depression and of the constraints for low-income households that would not conform to the generalisations made in this chapter, which is focused on the majority middle-class population.

4
Ageing and social life

Introduction

The social life of older people can be considered as having two dimensions. The vertical one reaches its greatest length as age extends the intergenerational links of kinship. Even for those without children, there is usually a grandniece or nephew. The horizontal dimension consists of friends, neighbours and those who share the activities we have just described. We cannot hope to deal with every aspect of social life in a single chapter. Here our focus will be on those that pertain to this particular age group, involving topics such as grandparenting, caring for parents with dementia and domestic relations after retirement.

Working with people in their sixties and seventies means, at least in Ireland, dealing with two very different systems of kinship. People of this age were born in an era with little access to contraception, often in large families with many siblings, at a time that retained traces of an older Irish kinship system[1] – older, but probably not the ancient system of stem families much discussed by anthropologists. This stem system was based around age grades with a single male inheritor and the dispersal of other siblings. The stem family had much diminished in practice and would probably never have been as important in the Dublin area,[2] though it was not unknown. An 80-year-old explained how his brother, the eldest son, inherited the farm, which suited him since he really did not like farming; he and his siblings had to seek other paths in life. Another associated feature was that many families included priests or nuns in their number. By contrast, Ireland today is characterised by the same norm of small nuclear families as most of Europe and the global middle class. Given this background, do we understand our participants in terms of the kinship system they grew up with or the one within which they live today?

The life span of our participants has also seen a remarkable shift in the relationship between kinship and friendship. When our participants were born, social life was dominated by kinship. Siblings and cousins constituted a large social network: childhood memories and deep-lasting friendships were formed simply through growing up together. Kinship also dominated conceptually as close friends of parents were introduced as auntie this or uncle that, although they were not blood-related. Today the situation has largely reversed. We are more likely to introduce someone as my mother/sister – but also my best friend. Kinship has been replaced by friendship as the dominant idiom because kinship is based on obligation; we cannot choose our kin.[3] Today, the more authentic relationships, at least outside of kinship, are viewed as those incorporating choice. But with what consequences? Do people now care more about their friends than their family as companions?

The complement to this sensibility is the importance of love, usually understood as the acceptance of obligatory relationships and as something that entails sacrifice. Here kinship dominates because the purest expression of love remains a parent's attachment to his or her children, while modern partnership is torn between these two ideals. There is also still a concern with relationships constituted through blood; this is evidenced in the widespread passion for genealogy, for instance in time spent on ancestry.com.

There is a parallel shift in the movement from neighbours to friends. Traditionally the core non-kin relations were to those who lived close by, from whom one could borrow a cup of sugar or pop in to visit. But people do not choose their neighbours and often prefer to keep a 'friendly distance' from them, avoiding quarrels over borrowed garden tools or noisy pets. Friendship is taken from a wider pool, reflected in the name of the most popular dating app used by older women in our fieldsites: 'Plenty of Fish'. There are also continuities to Irish sociality. Almost inevitably, when two strangers meet, the first thing they do is establish who they know in common, in the expectation that, given the small size of the country, they will easily achieve this goal. Only when mutual contacts have been established can they relax in each other's company. This was just as true of our ethnography. It was only when Danny knew enough other people in Cuan to establish common acquaintances when meeting new people that attitudes shifted markedly, from suspicion of this Englishman to accepting him as part of local social life.

This chapter will examine a series of relationships in turn. One effect of sheer longevity is that the family is also more extended vertically. McGarrigle and Kenny,[4] for example, report that in 2013 women in the sandwich generation accounted for '31 per cent of all community dwelling older women aged 50–69 in Ireland'. Today one can be both a grandparent and at the same time the 'meat' of this new sandwich generation. In conclusion, therefore, the emphasis will be on balance (Fig. 4.1). How much sociality do older people actually want as against privacy, autonomy and time and space for themselves?

The chapter will also consider the role of the smartphone in social relations, which has given rise to ambivalence. In almost every interview we conducted, people have complained that 'everyone is glued to a screen', something not conducive to social interaction. Yet they also wax lyrical about the way WhatsApp had helped them to re-engage with more extended family across greater distances. According to one 2019 survey,

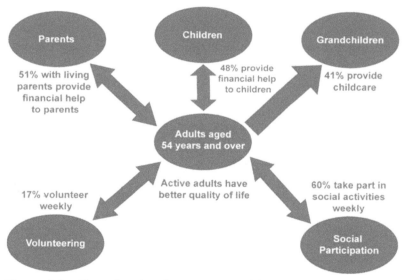

Figure 4.1 Chart showing the activities and familial obligations of older adults in Ireland. Source: McGarrigle et al. 2017. 'Health and wellbeing: Active ageing for older adults in Ireland. Evidence from The Irish Longitudinal Study on Ageing', p.18. Available online at: https://tilda.tcd.ie/publications/reports/pdf/w3-key-findings-report/TILDA%20Wave%203%20Key%20Findings%20report.pdf.

the number of smartphone users aged 55 years and older has increased by 34 per cent since 2012.[5] Smartphones have become integrated into the everyday social life of older people with remarkable speed, as several examples in chapter 3 attest to.

Relationships with partners

Overall in contemporary Ireland, after periods of extraordinary change, the evidence suggests that stable family relationships are generally the norm.[6] The nuclear family remains the primary social unit for most people,[7] though there is a growing plurality of family forms.[8] These might include civil partnerships, stepfamilies and other versions,[9] but, whatever the form, there remains a strong emphasis upon the moral duties represented by family ties. Our research confirmed that the majority of older adults with surviving parents have frequent contact with them. As Fig. 4.1 indicates, what we think of as the sandwich generation has moved up in age thanks to an overall increase in longevity. It is now the people who were our research participants who are more likely to be both looking after their parents and still have now-adult children living in their homes.

There has already been an extensive discussion of the impact of retirement upon couples in chapter 2. The examples described there showed how the increase in daily co-presence may produce tensions, leading in some instances to marriage breakdown (Fig. 4.2). Figures from the Central Statistics Office show a significant increase in the percentages of people who separate in the 40-plus age groups (CSO, 2016a), with the rate of separation peaking at age 48.[10]

The increased rate of separation comes as no surprise to Patricia, a practising psychotherapist. She works as a member of the Employee Assistance and Counselling Service, a free service for employees in state-funded hospitals and community health organisations. As she reports, a clear change over the last decade has been:

> A lot more men are coming to me, which is striking. Men are much more open now, a huge trend, for my parents never spoke about our problems, but since more women joined the workforce, men are more involved in the house and family, and men are much more in tune with their feelings.

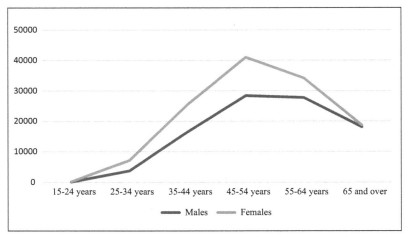

Figure 4.2 Graph showing the proportion of separated and divorced men and women by age group, 2016. Source: Central Statistics Office (CSO) Ireland, 'Census of Population 2016 – Profile 4 households and families', https://www.cso.ie/en/releasesandpublications/ep/p-cp4hf/cp4hf/ms/.

Retirement may mean the culmination of this trend, but is still for many a shocking revelation of the inequalities of domestic work. As Patricia explains:

> Before, like my father and my husband, men had no clue what was going on at home … now men are realising that they need to be participating in the home more, and more people are talking about their feelings and their stories, so it's ok to talk about your feelings … It has taken us years to get here.

The examples in chapter 2 concerned established couples. But with the rise in divorce and separation, this can also be a period when people are looking for new partners. This may be seen as one facet of the new possibilities of autonomy in post-menopausal years. As one woman said, it is a good time to reassess the second half of life and act accordingly. As previously noted, 'Plenty of Fish' is a popular dating app for older women, although users varied as to whether they were seeking a long-term partner or just company and friendship. They may be looking for casual relationships, having had enough of marriage, but they also often reported the experience of a different form of love that they describe as mature; this may well contribute to figures indicating a greater sense of fulfilment at this stage of life. There are some people, however, for whom looking for partners or enduring the absence of partners has all the angst and anguish of adolesence. One woman commented on the sheer gut-wrenching loneliness of her cousin and her desperation to find a partner, to the degree that she is terribly depressed and possibly suicidal. There could be a version of Sally Rooney's *Normal People*, but about people dating in their sixties.

The examples in chapter 2 also implied both the new constraints and new possibilities of freedom that arise for a couple in retirement. On the one hand, many of our participants are not just carers for children and parents, but often also carers for their partners. During the research we met several couples for whom maintaining the physical and emotional health of their partner was an ongoing challenge. Edward found that his wife had become exceptionally negative in outlook and distrusted new people or unexpected events. He thus prioritised a few fixed points of the week, such as playing golf, as 'me time', but dedicated much of the rest of the week to keeping her company. Not only did he worry about her potential to slip into depression, but he found he had to manage her attempts to control his movements and his social activities.

Relationships with parents

As noted in chapter 2, retirement is often initially envisioned as a period of endless leisure. The children have been raised and cared for, work is done, now it's 'me' time. However, there is a problem with this expectation. The age of retirement is, for many, likely to coincide with the period during which parents become frail. Conditions such as arthritis and dementia may develop as incremental disability over time, but they may also arise from a sudden fracture or illness. As a result, the newly retired suddenly find that they are cast back into the role of being children – but this time because it is *they* who are looking after their parents. Indeed, their parents may absorb their time and attention to a degree they have not experienced since the time when they had been looking after babies and young children. Our participants were rarely prepared for this burden, which is a neglected area in the discussion of retirement.

In Ireland, historical conditions also impact on these experiences. Many Irish adults live geographically close to their parents[11] and see them frequently.[12] In addition, half of those aged 50–64 with surviving parents provide help with household tasks, on average for 10 hours per week, while over one-quarter (28 per cent) assist their parents with personal care, on average for 14 hours a week. As the TILDA study found, this demonstrates the 'very high prevalence and intensity of involvement in the care of elderly adults by older adults' and challenges the portrayal of older adults as recipients of care rather than the givers of care.[13]

People recalled historical stereotypes that underscored the care of parents as an obligation. Some participants mentioned the so-called 'spinster' of previous generations, the youngest female child whose job it was to look after her parents as the latter became elderly. With an understanding that they would inherit the house, these women remained at home and unmarried until their elderly parents died. But, as one lawyer noted, in these days, as in the past, in many cases when the will is read out they find that this promise of the house is not fulfilled. One respondent, Mary, had never thought that such a situation would apply to her, but she has successively looked after her dying father and is now caring for her mother with dementia. Mary conceded that her siblings do seem to think that it is somehow her 'natural duty', since she is unmarried and without children. She can see there will be no reward in this life and she does not have much faith in the next one either.

As Mary found, when you have an elderly bedridden father or mother with dementia you can pretty much forget a social life or friendships. The state provided her with four and a half hours homecare per week – just about enough time to get the requisite shopping and visit the relevant institutions to ensure other services are being provided. Otherwise, all her father's care – shifting him to prevent bedsores, feeding and cleaning him – was up to her. Mary's days consisted mainly of these tasks as well as just keeping her father company while watching him deteriorate. It seemed unlikely that things could get worse. Until they did: for while her father was dying, her mother's dementia was progressing. Mary is horrified by the consequences. Looking after her mother at home led to constant anxiety. If her mother went out, would she return? Yet Mary loves her parents and could not imagine doing anything less for them. A description of visiting a parent with dementia in a care home will be provided in chapter 6.

Elderly parents do not have to be frail, however, or to require support. On retirement, some of our participants developed new routines regarding how often to visit and what needed to be done for their parents. With growing life expectancy, such duties may include taking the grandchildren to see their great-grandparents, ensuring one's parents do not feel neglected or unloved, taking their pets to the vet and a slew of other duties. This may also evolve into a more relaxed relationship with them than was possible historically, embodying these new norms of kinship as friendship. A 60-year-old may turn to her mother to ask advice about her husband in a manner she might not have done in earlier times.

A few years ago it was young people who had to keep a landline because their mothers did not use a smartphone. In the last five years, this has shifted a generation; now it is these 60-year-olds who need to retain their landline because it is their 90-year-old parents do not use smartphones, although some of this age group do. WhatsApp groups are particularly prominent in organising both routines of keeping in touch with parents as well as sharing out the care duties when they become frail. The most significant WhatsApp groups of all were those created to care for dying parents.

Relationships with siblings and wider kin

The question of sharing care for parents leads directly to the issue of sibling relations for people at this age. Siblings may be geographically close, but they are not always close in other respects. One source of familial strife that emerged with some frequency in fieldwork concerned sibling quarrels that erupted over care for parents, bereavement and disputes over money and inheritance.

Such quarrels were a common complaint in Thornhill. One woman complained that even though she had thyroid cancer, her brother expected her to carry the brunt of parental care 'because I lived closer to them'. Cora and her siblings feel they have to call in daily to the local nursing home or their mother will not be looked after properly. She and others complain of gender differences where brothers call the tune, but may do far less. In addition to such arguments, Helen felt that at the nub of her sibling's anger was the fact that she had the best relationship with her mother and that this was resented. She was the one that took her mother to the hospital and set up a WhatsApp group to communicate on her mother's medication and welfare. Helen was also the one who heard her mother complain that her other children did not visit her in hospital.

Helen consequently found herself disowned by her siblings. After their mother died, her father wanted to give money to Helen's daughter to help her purchase a house, but her sisters and brother objected strongly. She in turn 'blew up' with them over this matter, and the argument over property persisted until relationships completely broke down, leaving her excluded from the rest of her family. Helen was visibly upset in recounting a missed wedding and other family events. Last year she celebrated Christmas dinner with her husband and adult daughter, a situation in stark contrast to previous years when the whole extended family had come to her.

But you know what, I had to walk away. I was going to crack up. I just thought; let them have it, like feck it. I'd rather do without it.

The solution of Helen's daughter and husband was to purchase a dog for her, to help keep her company.

It is common, perhaps, to romanticise the large family in Ireland and this was often the default arena of initial friendships. From discussions with participants, however, the way people talk about their siblings can expose a darker undercurrent. For a start, large families were not always a choice: contraception was illegal in Ireland until 1980 and was only available with severe restrictions until 1985. Several of our older participants recounted growing up with scarce resources, in circumstances where any additional stress such as alcoholism or depression exacerbated an already difficult situation. Many of the memories around early sibling relations continue to influence adulthood, whether as close personal attachments or the glowing embers of bitter rivalries – often both. One source of competition between multiple siblings concerned access to parental attention; quite a few of our participants had read about 'attachment theory' from Winnicott or Bowlby and provided quite academic explanations of the causes of their issues. A woman recalls her own experiences and offers further insight:

> As a child, I remember I couldn't bear to be out of her [my mother's] sight, but I couldn't be too near her too. I used to be very troublesome and troubled and can remember instances where she was having babies all the time and miscarriages. If she was gone, I'd go mad, hysterical. So there was the anxious attachment, so I'm hoping that my daughter will have lovely secure attachments to her child, 'cos I know none of us get it 100 per cent right.

Some siblings who would rather not see each other nevertheless felt obliged to keep in contact in order for their children to have cousins and to grow up with close kin. Fiona had quite idyllic ideas of family when she returned pregnant to Thornhill after living in the UK. She anticipated meeting her siblings frequently and seeing their children grow up together. She quickly discovered, however, that the disputes and arguments that originated in her childhood left a legacy on their contemporary relationships. She describes her family as 'old style', meaning that her parents were loving but not demonstrably affectionate with their children or each other. Again and again, Fiona finds she is continually thrown together at large family gatherings with relatives she does not get on with. Now she uses WhatsApp as much as possible, in order to communicate with them but also keep them at a distance.

Similarly, Aisling had to remove her Facebook page because her sister, who is settled in the United States, kept posting aggressive and abusive messages on it. The public nature of some of these was particularly distressing: whereas Aisling can refuse to open an email, she could not prevent their differences being aired in public on Facebook. She also noted how glad she is that there was no social media when she was a teenager, believing that her poor relations with her sister would have had a much bigger audience than just their narrow circle of friends and family.

Complications also arise concerning wider kin. For some participants, the role of nephews and nieces takes the place of children, particularly for those who have no children of their own. Several women in Thornhill had established routines with nieces or cousins whom they met weekly. For the majority, the large extended family was a source of support and many referred to their extended networks as a source of pride. Smartphones allowed them to have close ongoing conversations which they would not otherwise have had. Because they were not just meeting on formal occasions, the tone of communication was more relaxed and informal. However, keeping in touch with siblings, nephews and nieces required ongoing management and could become a strain. Mike complained that at a family event at which his sister could not be present she nevertheless sent 60 photos of herself on holiday, something he found both irritating and excessive. Another woman, aged 50, commented on how WhatsApp allows her to 'check-in' with people without requiring the demands of a visit in person:

> We romanticise the small village and think the camaraderie must have been great, but I bet in reality it was a fecking nightmare.

Finally Niamh, aged 79, considers herself very self-sufficient since the death of her husband several years ago. She is adept at using her smartphone and feels affronted when shop assistants suggest she asks a grown daughter or son for help when she has a query: after all, as she observes, 'I had a computer at home before they were even born!' Niamh was one of the first locally to see the potential in smartphones for pursuing interests that would seem niche to Thornhill, such as her art group.

On the other hand, she soon experienced the drawback of smartphones when, to her dismay, a niece added her to an extended family WhatsApp group full of daily chat and endless jokes. After about a week Niamh removed herself, explaining to the nieces that she just 'didn't have time'. She feels that she has a rich life, listens to the radio and has her activities, but values her autonomy. At this point she has less patience for extended family. She no longer feels she has to 'put up' with boring small talk, preferring groups with common interests such as trad music. This freedom to be anti-social comes as a great relief, although she appreciates that the nieces were only trying to keep her company because of concerns that she might be lonely. However, Niamh does keep up with the WhatsApp group established by her children and grandchildren, since she greatly values her interactions with her nuclear family.

Grandparenting

Grandparenting can prompt retirement,[14] as several participants felt that it was now important to be potentially free to help at any time, especially in emergencies, rather than have to refuse because of work commitments.[15] When a grandchild is sick and needs a day off school, then the parent can remain at work. Bob, who appeared in the film in chapter 1 and previously worked as a school caretaker, notes:

> So I can pick up the phone and say I am available for help, whereas when I was working I had to check my calendar and see if I'm working late tomorrow; sometimes I had to work until late at night because the school was hired out to something and I would help as a caretaker. With the grandchildren, it's never really a problem now. I want to see them anyway, I never see enough of them really.

Sometimes it is the retirement activity that has to be given up, as Lilian explains: 'I was quite enjoying working at the Citizens Information Bureau, but felt I had to give it up to look after my granddaughter'. She has family responsibilities every day. Three grandchildren are at school and two of them come to her for lunch five days a week, while another comes once a week.

By contrast, for some of these participants in their seventies or early eighties, kinship has reached a natural conclusion. At 73 Emily has grandchildren ranging from 12 to 23, but mainly sees them at Christmas since the families now live at some distance. Eamonn, also 73, has had one year when he and his wife minded a grandchild one day a week, but subsequent involvement has been quite intermittent.

I helped my son when he couldn't get a babysitter, but actually there is no specific time we must be available at a certain point. It will just be a phone call saying there is a dental appointment or I've to take the kids off school early…. 'could ya?'…

Also, in this case, there would normally be two sets of grandparents, and they might not be the ones asked to help the daughter-in-law.

Some complained that their children made excessive childminding demands. Francis commented that:

Sometimes I felt they were taking me for a ride, to be honest. They'd start with 'this may not suit but…', but we'd always try and help them. I don't think young people could manage without the input of grandparents to be honest.

Expectations that grandparents will help with the difficult 'gap' period between the end of school and the end of the working day are common.[16] Nevertheless, for many in this age group, the degree of childcare is neither too heavy a burden nor too slight. Amanda feels that at this stage in her sixties life has become perfect:

And to be at this stage of my life, it's all coming together. I'm in a really good place, around my grandchildren and my husband. I have a very good partner. And my two kids around, you know I couldn't ask for…

Amanda has needed therapy and lacked confidence in the past, but now things have improved. She or her husband will do some of the dropping off, or collecting their granddaughter from nursery, but she will also look after her on some days between nursery ending at noon and her niece coming in to look after her at 3 p.m. Amanda has tender feelings towards the child, but not to the extent that it impinges upon her wider freedoms. The most common 'joke' that grandparents make is that they can always give the grandchildren back to the parents, or that they get all the joys of this engagement with few of the drawbacks.

This ideal of balance is always relative to the previous history of kinship. Very commonly, grandparenting is seen as an explicit complement to the earlier experience of parenting. Women who felt they did quite enough parenting may not be enticed by the prospect of being a grandmother to the same extent as their partner, who may feel, in retrospect, that he missed out on parenting and now has a second chance to enjoy the beauty, innocence, fun and love he sees in these toddlers. We thus met several men who were particularly enthusiastic about grandparenting. They were fathers at a time when feminism had limited impact on their lives and many report long commutes, often returning after the children had gone to bed. They see contemporary feminism as being as much a liberation of men, now licensed to be sentimental grandparents, as the establishment of gender equality.

Martin, for example, jokes that he will even turn off the football to read to his toddler granddaughter, something his own daughters wryly note would never have happened when they were young. He gladly concedes that his granddaughter has him 'wrapped around her little finger'. Another retired man now picks up three of their six grandchildren from school nearly every day, as well as sometimes having them for weekends or having holidays together, while also enjoying constant Skype contact with the other grandchildren living at a distance. This is not an obvious finding. We might have expected that people who are used to strong family commitments would want these to continue, while those with little experience of heavy-duty kinship would want to retain their freedom.[17]

The idea of grandparenting being the complement to the prior experience of parenting may be quite explicit. Alice felt she had been a good parent to her three children. However, having successfully discharged her responsibilities as a parent, she does not feel obliged to undertake extensive grandparenting. Her daughter is desperate to go back to work and can only afford to do so if her mother takes on her own child fulltime. This is something that Alice has steadfastly refused to do:

> I have never minded my grandchildren. Well, I did mind one for a year, but then the mother became pregnant and was looking to me to take over and I said no, no it's not going to happen, I would rather do my own job [cleaning in a shop]. She wanted to go back to work, but you would be getting the two children at 7 in the morning and you would have them to 7 in the evening: instead of being their granny, I would be their mammy. I was 60 at that stage and I am not going to become a mother at 60, simple as that. She is still not back at work; she will have to do what I did, which is wait till they go to school.

One of the key concomitants to understanding grandparenting is that it may be idealised as much because of the changes it creates in the relationship to one's children as in that to one's grandchildren. Suddenly, your children need you again. Instead of getting a phone call once a fortnight, they are in constant touch. Whatever the relationship to the grandchild, the crucial, overwhelming love often remains for one's own children. This re-engagement with one's own children is one of the reasons that grandparenting leads people to reflect upon their own parenting, regarding the latter in relation to the former.

Grainne goes further, remarking that it is only finally with her sixth grandchild that she can focus, using the currently fashionable idiom of 'mindfulness':

> I think my perception of their growth is much more acute than it would have been with the early ones as they've gone through the stages. This young lad, I feel that I marvel at him and watch the smile and everything else and the way he grows. I wouldn't have been as perceptive with the others I don't think.

Finally she is 'in the moment'. Perhaps the most consistent regret that contemporary grandparents express is that parenting all went too fast and they didn't take it in as it happened. Grainne noted that her husband had constantly to work late and subsequently felt guilty for his neglect of his children, something that he is expiating through his devotion to the grandchildren. For her, however, it works in the opposite direction. She loves her grandparenting, but knows that if it had become too much of a routine obligation to look after them she would not have such an unequivocally positive relationship with them. Such a commitment would have brought back some of the resentment she experienced as a mother in the form of endless self-sacrifice to her children.

Grandparenting can also renew tensions with children, however. Modern parents may want grandparents to be present but simultaneously resent any influence they try to have on the grandchildren. For some, such intervention by grandparents is seen as an unwelcome intrusion into a realm where parents may claim exclusive authority.

Having worked in an academic institution, though not an academic herself, Amanda is quite analytical about these complex intergenerational linkages. Again quoting attachment theory, her starting point is that she quite resented her children. She was just experiencing that sense of emancipation that came with feminism and 'I wanted to be out all the time'. But she can reconcile any such tensions when it comes to her grandchildren.

The one who I mind, I was telling you, she is the love of my life, my husband and I. She's three and a half at the moment. Even this morning when I got up and she comes in, we have a little ritual. I take her and hold her face and kiss her. It's just, it's amazing.

She is also explicit about this idea of grandparenting as the repair, in some sense, of parenting. When a grandson was born and she offered to look after him, the fact that her daughter was very happy for this to happen was taken as the ultimate valorisation of her own parenting. It showed her that her children did not resent her, or perhaps were never aware of her own resentment. She sees her daughter's agreement to this grandparenting arrangement as 'a fabulous compliment – that I want our son to get the love and attention that I got'. The point here is that if her children felt they had suffered from bad parenting, they would never have been this positive about giving their son to them for care.

Another less evident implication of grandparenting is that a similar process may develop for the relationship between spouses. While parenting almost inevitably creates tensions and frustrations that would tax any couple, the advent of grandparenting can be an expression of a new balance and love between partners. This possibility was most fully expressed in the way that each spouse tended to incorporate the other in their discussions with us. They often use plural pronouns. 'She is the love of our lives', confirmed as meaning for both grandparents. His giving up something to look after the grandchildren is also her giving up something. Discussions of grandparenting are most common expressions of the experience and attitudes of the couple, rather than the individual. The language and attitudes imply that grandparenting is very possibly the culmination of the gradual maturing and cementing of that couple's relationship, which achieves its final harmony through their common love of the grandchildren. It is a key moment when me and her/him has more firmly become *us*.

Finally, grandparenting may also resolve the tensions described above with the memory of being parented, if this is the age when people feel freer to re-think their past. They now admit to themselves that it was difficult fully to experience what they now call attachments at a time of poverty, with large families, struggles with income and sometimes alcohol and an uncompromising religiosity. Visiting a psychotherapist, these participants talk about not having received the love they craved. Often today the issue is cathartically resolved – not so much through therapy but rather through seeing these memories as being abrogated, in the sense that they as grandparents have become the precise opposite of their own experience. They see themselves giving love, attention and freedom as the systematic repudiation of what they recall as coldness, inattention and harsh discipline.

People often think that there are patterns of cycles that descend through generations, especially of what is now termed dysfunctionality. Using that discourse, they now see their grandparenting as an opportunity to break those cycles and replace them with entirely positive and supportive feelings – these good attachments. It does not always work out, however. Miriam is grieving deeply for her 16-year-old grandson who committed suicide: 'I remember holding his hand, and then wrote a poem about this'. She relates his suicide to the depression that his mother was going through at the time, while she herself had become quite a distant figure – partly because she had very problematic issues in relation to her own parents. Sometimes cycles are not resolved but continue.

The conclusion to this section would be that a wide range of different relationships are potentially resolved through grandparenting, though only potentially. But the argument can be taken further. This chapter was introduced via a wider issue around the balance between relationships of obligation and those freely entered into. Grandparenting may also be a model for balance between these two, with balance often proving the key to middle-class sensibilities. As one participant puts it:

I know some friends where they're doing childminding for three days, four days in a row. It can be quite wearing. But I think we're having the best of both worlds. None of our children are asking us. We're stepping in from time to time if they need weekends away. Maybe a couple of hours a week, sometimes they stay here. We're going to stay with them for a weekend, but only once this summer. If they wanted more to be done, we'd be willing to do it. It's more a sense of helping the parents than particularly to have the enjoyment of the grandchildren. I am also quite happy to read a book. But if there's something happening as well, take the book with me. The age range is 13 down to 3 months. It's extremely different from parenting. The terrible twos come and you can get away with it because you're not their parents, you don't have to live with the consequences.

Grandparents may thus also try to limit obligated and regular care, partly because that would deprive them of the freedom to make exceptional efforts if the need arises. Interventions at critical times, such as when a babysitter has let their children down, tend to be much more appreciated, while regular care of grandchildren can soon be taken for granted.

Friendships and loneliness

As is common elsewhere in the Western world, loneliness is a growing problem. One psychotherapist has referred to lonely householders as the hidden population since they do not leave their homes much. In conversation, isolation and loneliness are often associated with elderly male farmers in remote rural areas, particularly with the closure of post offices and harsher drink-driving laws. In a recent study, almost one-third of adults aged 50+ in Ireland experienced emotional loneliness at least some of the time, while 7 per cent often felt lonely.

However, on average, loneliness scores compare well with international standards, and studies have found that loneliness did not increase with age but actually decreased.[18] Among our participants, we found that the majority were embedded in family and wider relations. In general loneliness was much less evident than Danny had found in his recent study in rural England.[19]

The discussion of fraught relations with siblings discussed above is often contrasted with the positive and enduring relationships with friends. Several female participants have spoken of having friends that they made at school, with whom they have been in touch ever since. Mary, Anne and Ellen, for example, attended secondary school together; now in their sixties and retired, they meet a couple of times a month for coffee. These friendships come across as both enduring and supportive, and are occasionally pitched in opposition to family relationships. Most women had cultivated friendship groups throughout their lives, especially if they had children, while we found more problematic issues around a lack of friendship that pertained more to men. As noted in chapter 2, the TILDA study found twice as many older women reporting supportive friendships than men, though our fieldsites might differ from Ireland more generally.

Some men form groups of retirees, meeting with ex-work colleagues once a month or even weekly for a coffee, but the legacy of work varied. A 50-year-old who had spent a lot of time at home with young children before getting a job in the civil service noted that the links he made at the school gate were far deeper than those he has made at work. He assumes that because women do the bulk of childminding in the area, they have access to social support networks that are not available to men. Men may forge new groups through leisure activities such as hiking. Recall

Aidan in chapter 2, who developed a hiking group with previous work colleagues that provides him with a valuable social outlet. Men also often have strong links through sports, which may once have been through playing together in the GAA club or now being involved in supporting the local rugby club.

Several men spoke about the expectation that they would go out for a pint after work as the route to making friendships. Sean formerly worked as a bus conductor. He started on the buses in 1976 and describes how the bus drivers and conductors would automatically go to the local pub for a pint on Fridays and particularly on paydays. They would spend the day there and would sometimes spill out of the pub, where fights might break out. Now if someone is caught drinking on the job they are immediately fired, so no one goes to the pub any longer. Sean himself goes to the pub near his home where he lives alone, but has no other social outlet.

The centrality of alcohol to socialising for men could also be a problem. Mike felt that his unwillingness to drink was the reason he forged few friendships at work during his years in the civil service. Instead he has been involved in traditional music for many years and was an active member of his local trad group. Joe, recently retired from the police force, realises that the friendships that he kept up during work are beginning to slide and that he needs to invest more time in expanding his contacts:

> Because I am kind of quite self-contained, you know. And I know that and I see Ella [his wife] has a raft of friends around and her book clubs and other activities.

Although Joe was in a local history group for 20 years, he does not feel that it helped him to develop any strong friendships and recognises that 'I should have done more'. Currently he is trying to make more friends by taking a postgraduate course. He has identified one man, a migrant, who is also probably lacking a social network, and Joe has decided to invite him to visit some important archaeological sites.

A significant component of friendship is geographical, and traditionally the pub was central for men to meet people (Fig. 4.3). For this age group, however, its role is much diminished. There is just one pub today in Cuan where older men regularly go to watch horse racing after placing their bets and enjoy the banter that ensues. Quite a few men will go intermittently to pubs and it is entirely acceptable for them to go singly, and indeed to sit by themselves. Or they might meet to go as a

Figure 4.3 Evening in the pub. Photo by Daniel Miller.

group to participate in one of the several music 'sessions' and other pub activities noted in chapter 3.

However, pubs are far less important to this age group than the cafés that have become the key site for friendship today. Gender is significant here. By far, the majority of socialising is single-sex. In the main, this would have been composed of women, for example, coming as a group after daily mass, or in one current case to practise silk embroidery. But there are constant, regular and also ad-hoc chats by groups of retired women alongside mother and toddler groups and, in one restaurant/café, a weekly breastfeeding group. Participants said that up to five years ago men were mainly present at weekends. But today they are there in almost equal numbers. Many men have developed weekly meetings, some with former colleagues but also others with men living in the same street. There is also the Men's Shed (chapter 3). The most common mixed groups would be for those taking a break from an activity such as an art or language class. The other major venue for a meeting would be the various sports clubs, such as the sailing club, the rugby club, the cricket club and the GAA. For older men, these are probably now more important as places to drink and meet up than the pubs.

Both cafés and pubs are developing as niche sites relative to age. Retirees in Cuan mainly go to two cafés; a third is a major meeting point for young people and is much noisier as a result. One pub that had been mainly for older people closed down and then re-opened with completely different décor, plus music and events targeted to young people. This was entirely successful and the young completely replaced the previous older clientele. People also meet outside of their locality, especially in Dublin, where Raymond meets with a small number of former colleagues monthly. He comments:

> Amazingly, even after 10 years retired, we still talk a lot of 'shop'; and my wife does something similar. I also meet once a week with a small group of fellow retirees here in Cuan.

People tend to refer to others as lonely, but not themselves.[20] Some are adamant that even though they spend the majority of their time alone, they are not lonely. There are a few exceptions such as Nuala, who talks of the gulf that she experienced when she found that she was bereft of all her previous connections. Another man claims he is happy with life, but did point out that one feature of retirement is the silence of his phone. From being constantly on call as an electrician, he found that suddenly he no longer receives messages. The abrupt transition was difficult to take. This is the other side of the *ping ping ping* that people often complain about – the silence of the phone that may then resound more loudly in his solitary home than when it constantly rang. Josie, who we met in chapter 3, was clear that one motivation for her activities in the local parish hall was to help others alleviate loneliness. She sensitively describes being lonely as something to stave off rather than an all-or-nothing experience. However, because she is so active with the parish, neighbours and friends can over-depend on her. One elderly neighbour asked her to help her 50-year-old daughter get out more, so Josie has constantly to balance her own needs with the demands of others.

Neighbours

As already noted, the institution of neighbours has somewhat declined as people prefer to choose their friends rather than have them imposed by proximity. There is also a historical legacy in which the idealised memory of mutual help disguised an undercurrent of resentment that surrounded the dependency of neighbourly relations during periods of poverty. Perhaps the single most important factor today is simply the pattern of house construction. Since the 1970s Cuan has experienced an almost continuous cycle of estate building that saw the population increase from 2,300 to 10,000. As each new estate was built, it attracted young families who coalesced around the care of children they already had or quickly gave birth to. These connections often developed around the primary school. Today there is something of a shift to still earlier sociality, established through ante-natal and post-natal classes. Having young children was a period when people were in and out of each other's homes. But this is not sustained and it visibly declines as the estate matures.

There is a suggestion that in Cuan neighbourly relations remain closer in the social housing of the Vartry estate than in the middle-class estates, though that is also the place which includes a few 'troublesome neighbours'. The middle-class residents will greet neighbours and chat when they pass either in front of their homes or when walking along the beach, but these tend to be shallower relationships than friendships developed more freely outside of proximity. Rob describes neighbours as:

> Acquaintances rather than friends, I was conscious not to get too close to the neighbours. The guy next door to me, he is 75 and I'm coming 70. He's very keen to talk, which I understand, if he gets me over the garden wall. I'm not interested in different types of grass, but I sense he needs somebody to talk to.

However, as just noted, there are some groups of men from the same street who now meet at the cafés. There are also occasional street parties. All these groups take a while to form and most people who had recently moved into the Brittas View estate did not really know their neighbours.

Relationships were starting to develop mainly through an active Facebook group and the common interests that were developing around certain political protests, such as one related to the water supply, or planning applications that residents wanted to oppose, as well as through the local primary school. Generally, however, friendships seemed to be forming quite slowly.

Feelings about neighbours partly depend upon background. Rob notes:

> I grew up in a small country area and I spoke to everybody because you knew them like your fingers and toes. And we borrowed ladders and machinery and whatever it might be, and we're in each other's houses and all that. And it was a small pool, a way of being in the world, where you talk to people, and all that, I find that true of other country people.

Today there is a kind of unspoken solidarity based not on talking but watching. People check that an older person has been seen out and about, mindful that otherwise one might need to see how they are. They know when neighbours are on holiday and that there should not be sounds coming from that house. Most people agreed that Cuan was the kind of place where no one could die at home without others coming to know of this quite quickly. The demise of one extremely curmudgeonly male, whose death was not noticed, was cited as the exception that proved this rule. Continued high attendance at funerals was also seen as evidence of an underlying sociality.

A surprising finding was that what at first seem quite shallow forms of sociality are actually very important. Greeting people when passing in the street or walking by the sea might look cursory to outsiders, but the degree to which people continue to do this is seen as crucial to the feeling of collective friendliness in public places. In general in Ireland, many people pride themselves on the friendliness that strangers show to each other. In Cuan it was cited as yet more evidence that this was a good town in which to live.

Conclusion

This chapter has considered a wide range of social relations in turn. To bring them all together, consider Gertie and Tom Healy. Tom reached a very senior and responsible position in the civil service and now commands a very decent pension. In the past, this enabled Gertie to follow her dream of becoming an artist. In truth, while she has sold some paintings from time to time, this has remained a largely personal rather than professional pursuit. Today they own a large house on which the mortgage was paid off long ago. Their children are generally as successful as they are and, most importantly, have chosen to settle within Cuan.

Starting from what they would fully acknowledge is quite a privileged position, the Healys have been able to create a comfortable balance between different kinds of sociality and privacy. On the one hand, they are surrounded by a loving family and can indulge the pleasures of grandparenting more or less to the degree to which they choose. At present, this means they have one full day of childcare and two other days when they mind two other grandchildren after school. They are also on hand when one of their children encounters problems and issues, as from time to time they will. The Healys are also deeply involved in community activities, taking on periodic roles as chairpersons, but equally involved in making tea, or whatever else is required. You might bump into them volunteering in the theatre, helping with art exhibitions or giving a talk at the historical society. Tom has weekly meetings with a group of close male friends, mostly other ex-civil servants, at one of the town's cafés. Gertie has her circle of female friends who might enjoy a glass of wine in one of their homes or meet for tea and cake or to discuss art projects. She is also in a book group. They meet other couples for dinner during which they engage in lengthy conversations about art, feminism, religion or the possible consequences of Brexit for Ireland. Apart from planned encounters, there is that constant bumping into people they know when walking by the sea – an activity generally regarded as the glue that binds together the lives of long-term residents in Cuan.

Sometimes they just need a break, and this is where the Healys' cottage in Spain comes in. Situated in quite a remote corner of rural Spain, in winter there is often only one other occupied cottage in their small hamlet. Quite a few of the properties in the area are owned by expats; others are deserted. This is their retreat, where for a couple of months every year they can live without even a television, enjoying the peace and quiet, tending the garden and finding the best local foods and wine. Gertie has taken a serious interest in cooking fine Spanish cuisine. But even this escape can be turned back into sociality. There are two language classes in Cuan, both teaching Spanish, and there is even a group of Cuan residents who meet periodically because they own properties abroad, which gives them a common interest. For the middle class, life is often about balance; this includes striking a balance not only between family and community, but also between privacy and solitude. And at the heart of all this, they have each other.

The case of Gertie and Tom is indicative of people who have the resources and good fortune to craft their social life in much the same way as crafting other aspects of their lives. They can configure a wide range of kinship relationships and friendships to achieve this overall balance between sociality and autonomy. They can be conscientious grandparents and friends within Cuan partly because they can also gain extensive autonomy through their Spanish retreat. Their ethos is egalitarian and socially liberal, and there is no reason to consider them complacent. They are acutely aware that life is very different for those living in the social housing sector of the Vartry estate, which has its own patterns of intensive sociality and autonomy but without these resources. In both sectors, people vary in the degree of sociality they are comfortable with. Some want less. Amanda says:

> I wouldn't be as sociable as my other friends. I like my own company and I'm a bit rigid if I'm really honest about things, that's how I manage my life. I'm doing what I want to do.

What is being crafted is, above all, balance within sociality. This chapter started with a surfeit of obligatory sociality in having to devote oneself almost entirely to looking after one's parent with dementia and dealing with often fraught sibling relationships; towards the end it has considered the conditions of loneliness and isolation that indicate a lack of sociality and friendship. Crafting only works for those fortunate enough to inhabit a relatively clear space between Charybdis, the intense whirlpool of sociality, and the rocky isolation of Scylla. As we have seen, the arena that perhaps lends itself best to crafting is grandparenting when people feel they have quite some freedom to determine how active they will be in that role. The same may be true of friendships. By contrast, they are more likely to be faced with obligations and the dominant agency of others when it comes to their children, their parents and their siblings.

The same set of observations turns out to be one of the single most important insights in understanding how people use smartphones. The smartphone is not simply employed by families, but may also have facilitated significant changes in the Irish family. In a prior study based on the use of social media in an English village,[21] it was suggested that social media are best understood as a kind of 'Goldilocks' solution to the problems of balancing intensive and burdensome sociality against the desire for autonomy and separation. On social media, relationships could be sufficient without becoming intrusive, neither too hot nor too cold. Seen in the context of Ireland (though these findings also applied to Brazil and other fieldsites in the ASSA project), the smartphone seems to have reversed the historical shift from extended to nuclear families. Instead of just seeing the extended family at funerals or Christmas, when conversation is relatively formal, a WhatsApp group can return the twenty-first-century extended family into more frequent and informal conversation closer to that of the historical extended family.

There is an important difference, however. The Goldilocks solution meant that in one sense people could 'afford' to return to the extended family because they were not actually living together; one could reply or converse just when one felt like it. Such a compromise had not existed prior to the smartphone although, as in the example of Niamh, not everyone relishes the result. This is the kind of balance that is also being sought across other social relations. People recognise that they may have escaped their historical economic dependence upon their neighbours, for instance borrowing sugar or anything else that ran short, but they can now join them as part of the wider community through using Facebook or by putting on a play. The separation represented by having children – and now grandchildren – living in another country is at least partly ameliorated by frequent webcam encounters. In short, the smartphone has proved itself ideal as a device for maintaining extensive social relations, but in a manner that does not feel too intrusive or burdensome.

This search for balance is by no means restricted to the impact of the smartphone. The discussion around grandparenting showed how people have crafted quite an extensive balance between personal autonomy and the sharing of kinship responsibilities and experiences of love. This conclusion would also fit with a comparative analysis of how Irish people envisage care for their elderly parents as ideally having residential autonomy but backed by frequent visits from their children.[22] The emphasis at the beginning of this chapter was on a shift from relationships of obligation, such as kinship, to voluntary relationships like friendship. By the end of the chapter we see a more complex picture. People equally value the sense of love and commitment represented by kinship, but are striving for a balance that injects some of the qualities of friendship into these same relationships.

Notes

1. Wills 2001 argues, for example, following Meaney (1994), that in twentieth-century post-colonial Ireland 'a particular construction of sexual and familial roles became the very substance of what it means to be Irish' (190–1). This vision was heavily influenced by Catholic preaching and right-wing politics, but also derives from a wider ideological construction of the familial sphere as intimately bound up with the public image of Ireland as a traditional rural society. See also Canavan 2012 and Seward 2017.
2. See Gibbon and Curtin 1978. For older studies see Arensberg and Kimball 2001 [1940]. Also see DuBois 1941, 460–1, Birdwell-Pheasant 1992, Brody 1973, Harris 1988, Wilson 1997, Byrne and O'Mahony 2012, Peace 1989, Taylor 1996, Wilson and Donnan 2006 and French 2015.
3. For details of this argument see Miller 2017b.
4. See McGarrigle and Kenny 2013, 3 on the profile of the sandwich generation in Ireland.
5. See Statista 2020.
6. See Inglis 2015, 79–80.
7. See Gray et al. 2016, 42–4.
8. For examples see Connolly 2015a. She also acknowledged the continued normativity discussed by Fahey in Connolly 2015a.
9. See Gray et al. 2016, 41–61. They also note that the family was probably more varied in the past than has been previously portrayed.
10. This trend in mid-life is significant because otherwise marital breakdown is decreasing in the general population. In fact there was a decrease of 11,115 separated or divorced persons aged under 50 between 2011 and 2016. By contrast there was a substantial increase of 29,224 persons over the age of 50 between 2011 and 2016. Not only is there an age factor involved, but there are also distinctions in how men and women describe their marital status: more women speak about being 'separated' while men tend to talk of being 'single'. See Hyland 2013. Also see Lunn et al. 2010.

    It should be pointed out that on a national level, death accounts for more single-occupied homes than divorce.
11. Of people aged 50 and over in Ireland, 36 per cent have co-resident children and an additional 38 per cent have at least one child living in the same county. Overall, therefore, 74 per cent of the older adult population of Ireland live in very close or fairly close proximity to at least one of their children. However, there is considerable variation in the proximity to children by age group. There is a notable decline in the proportion with co-resident children from the 50–64 age group (50 per cent) to the 65–74 age group (17 per cent), reflecting the nest-leaving process. Among those aged 75 and over, i.e. the age group most likely to need care and support, 71 per cent either live with their children or have at least one child living in the same county. However, members of the oldest age group are also more likely to have all of their children living abroad than younger age groups, reflecting historical patterns of emigration. See Kamiya and Timonen 2011, 40.
12. Well over half of those people see their parents daily or weekly. Of those with living parents, 53 per cent have face-to-face contact with them daily or several times a week, 24 per cent have face-to-face contact several times per month and 19 per cent have contact several times per year; only 2 per cent have almost no contact with their parent(s). In other words, three-quarters of older adults whose parents are still alive see their parents frequently (daily, weekly or several times per month). See Kamiya and Timonen 2011, 40.
13. The same source reveals that 27 per cent of men and 27 per cent of women aged 50–64 have a surviving mother. This proportion decreases to 3 per cent for both sexes in the 65–74 age group. Social class is associated with the likelihood of having surviving parents. Table 3.2 shows that 25 per cent of 50–64 year olds with tertiary (degree level) education have a surviving mother; for those with just primary education, this percentage is only 15 per cent. Of those 50–64 year olds with tertiary education, 9 per cent have two living parents, compared to only 2 per cent of those with primary education. This is likely to be due to the transmission of the social gradient across generations and its effect on life expectancy. See Kamiya and Timonen 2011, 41.
14. For the context of parenting relations see O'Doherty and Jackson 2015.
15. Gray et al. 2016, 171.

16. Gray et al. 2016, 183. They also note the implications for gender relations more generally as women identify more with work rather than exclusively with their role as carers. See Gray et al. 2016, 184–5.
17. Grandparenting has been foregrounded by a number of studies that arose from the TILDA project, several of which support the arguments made here. See McGarrigle et al. (2018), who also stress this balance between obligation and autonomy and note the basic gender equality in Irish grandparenting, alongside Share and Kerrins 2009 and McNally et al. 2014. The evidence is that obligation is a far more important factor for low-income families, especially where the parent is single. This is also the group where it is more likely that grandparents will be the primary carers.
18. On the University of California, Los Angeles Loneliness Scale figures were low at 2.1 from a maximum of 10; lower scores reflect less loneliness. See Ward et al. 2019.
19. Miller 2017b and Miller 2016, 143–6.
20. There are a number of NGOs dealing with the problem of loneliness in Ireland more generally, for example https://alone.ie/. However, some studies suggest this is less a problem in Ireland than in some other regions, for example Gallagher 2012.
21. A more extensive discussion of this 'Goldilocks' solution to family relationship may be found in Miller 2016, 99–118. For a prior usage see Turkle 2011, 15.
22. See Gray et al. 2016, 190–1.

5
Smartphones and ageing

Smartphone infrastructure

According to a survey conducted by Deloitte in 2019, 96 per cent of Irish people owned a mobile phone, the vast majority of which (91 per cent) were smartphones.[1] By the end of our research, we found nothing surprising in having long conversations with a 95-year-old discussing their Samsung Galaxy. This change could have equally profound implications both for what a smartphone is and what age really means.[2] For example, does the smartphone simply lose its associations with youth or has its incorporation made older people in some sense more youthful? Ireland itself is increasingly dominated by its flourishing IT sector. Dublin is the European headquarters for Google, Facebook, Apple, Twitter, LinkedIn and many tech start-ups, although smartphone use is not particularly cheap here.

Smartphones are now ubiquitous. By June 2018 there were over 6.1 million mobile phone subscriptions, a penetration rate of 126 per cent.[3] In 2019 smartphone ownership in Ireland was dominated by Samsung (33 per cent) and the iPhone (30 per cent), followed by Huawei (14 per cent).[4] Deloitte found that 85 per cent of survey respondents use their smartphones for WhatsApp, 72 per cent to check emails, 60 per cent for daily calls and 33 per cent to monitor their fitness, checking their phones on average 55 times a day. News online was viewed by 84 per cent of respondents. Women make more use of social media, while men use work-related apps such as email and LinkedIn more.[5] Women also make more use of smartphones generally. In addition, the survey reveals

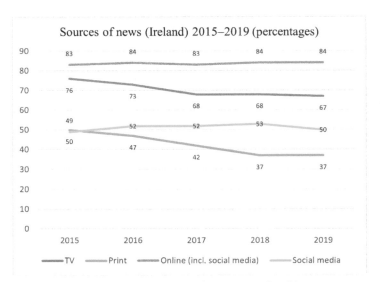

Figure 5.1 Graph showing sources of news in Ireland between 2015 and 2019. Source: Reuters Institute and OII (Oxford Internet Institute). 2019. 'Digital News Report – Ireland'. More data can be accessed at: http://www.digitalnewsreport.org/survey/analysis-by-country/2019/ireland-2019/.

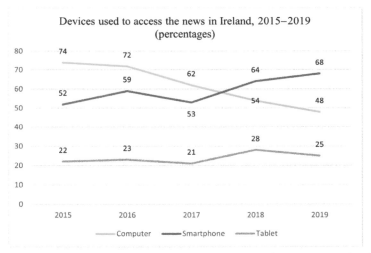

Figure 5.2 Graph showing devices used to access the news in Ireland between 2015 and 2019. Source: Reuters Institute and OII (Oxford Internet Institute). 2019. 'Digital News Report – Ireland'. More data can be accessed at: http://www.digitalnewsreport.org/survey/analysis-by-country/2019/ireland-2019/.

that the older population is now the main growth area in terms of use of digital devices. For example, in 2018 70 per cent of those aged 65 or over had access to tablets, a rise from 57 per cent in 2017.[6] On almost any measure – voice, messaging, email or social media – Irish usage is above both global and UK usage. By comparison, the use of computers and laptops or television for news is in decline (Figs 5.1 and 5.2).[7]

Talking about smartphones

The smartphone is not just a material object. It has also become an iconic presence in the way we talk and think about the world, especially in moral discussions. There is often a marked discrepancy between what people in this age group say about their phones and how they actually use them. For example, many of these participants started by claiming that they just use smartphones for texting and voice calls – that is, purely as phones. Yet as the evidence given below shows, they may typically be using around 25 to 30 different functions or apps. So the way in which they discuss their smartphones seems to be about something other than actual usage.

The problem for many older people is that their conversation around smartphones developed over a period when these were used by young people and not themselves. Opinions about smartphones are therefore dominated by the idea that they are a cause of harm to young people, who become fixated on screens and so lose the ability to communicate properly face to face (Fig. 5.3). Grandchildren who are paying a visit and are supposed to be paying some attention to their relatives take the first opportunity to return to those screens, apparently oblivious to how rude this makes them seem to older generations. Such behaviour confirms accusations of screen addiction or children's short-term attention span.

For themselves, older people worry about privacy; they are concerned that their social media accounts might be hacked or their browser history surveilled.[8] They carefully follow news stories about state surveillance and corporations stealing their data or monitoring their browser history. Although an online survey in 2020 found that 66 per cent of respondents have a Facebook account and over half that number use it daily, the numbers also went down abruptly in 2018 after the Cambridge Analytica scandal and subsequent concerns that their personal data would be harvested for unknown purposes.[9]

Figure 5.3 Photo of a 2018 headline in the *Irish Daily Mail* claiming that social media is making children mentally ill. Photo by Pauline Garvey.

What this means is that there is an increasing discrepency between these negative discourses and people's own, ever-increasing usage. Mostly people live with the ambivalance in surprising comfort, because talking about smartphones occupies a different regime from actually using them. However, there are also examples of more consistent negativity that pervades practices. We see this in the following example involving Olivia.

Olivia is convinced that her continued use of smartphones will cause her actual physical harm. A professional woman in her mid-forties, she has two young children at primary school, where she has been canvassing for the imposition of Wi-Fi-free hours, in line with a similar policy in France. Olivia uses her iPhone 6 mainly for work, otherwise aiming to turn it off and only turning it on again when her childminder is on duty or when she is expecting a call. She admits that this can be difficult, for example when she misses messages or opportunities, particularly from friends who assume having a phone implies having constant access.

Olivia has deep concerns regarding radio-frequency exposure. She notes that the 'Legal' section under 'Settings' in her iPhone claims this remains within safe limits when used against the head or just 5 mm from the body. Why then, she asks, does it also recommend using a hands-free option such as earphones? Initially Olivia also worried whether the smartphone might overheat. Despite her husband's opposition, she kept their landline for her daily calls to her mother. Her worries came to a head when she discovered a lump on her left breast. Thankfully it was not malignant, but she realised that the lump was next to the jacket pocket where she regularly carried her phone. This catalysed Olivia's information gathering on the possible effects of radiation or radiofrequency exposure. She examined leaflets in the doctor's surgery and then perused books. She read the fine print in her smartphone's terms and conditions and she spoke to friends. Finally she asked her GP whether there was anything to worry about, but was not reassured when he said there was not.

Ironically, perhaps, it was online, and through her smartphone as well as her computer, that Olivia discovered the information she sought. A site labelled Environmental Health quotes a release from the World Health Organization in 2011 that tentatively recognises such exposure as a possible carcinogen. Armed with this, she began leafleting her local school and her workplace (Figs 5.4a and 5.4b). Now Olivia scans her environment with a critical eye. She mentally plots where local mobile phone masts stand and wonders if living close represents a threat to her family's wellbeing. She has distributed leaflets to local residents, tackled her employer about her concerns and takes any opportunity to speak out on this topic, whether to hairdressers, nannies or indeed anthropologists, as part of her campaign. She finds that responses tend to cluster around two poles – either in complete agreement or total rebuttal. There seems to be no middle ground.

While Olivia represents one extreme, almost all older people can recite various invectives against smartphones which now form part of a wider moral discourse. They talk about filter bubbles, echo chambers, surveillance, taking personal data and many other issues. They are much more likely than young people to balk at the terms and conditions, noting how they require far more access than the new app could possibly need. Overall, the smartphone has become a key icon within a variety of claims about how the world has deteriorated and become more dangerous. This book does not attempt to assess such claims, though it is worth noting that they have a long history, with analogous claims made about most emerging technologies.[10] The newspaper industry tends to be aligned to these claims, partly because print media is increasingly reliant upon older people for its survival. For these reasons the discourse about the phone has to be regarded as an important phenomenon in its own right. Irrespective of how it may or may not relate to the way that these people use their smartphones, it does reveal another consequence of smartphones. These ubiquitous artefacts now act as a key trope within a much wider moral debate about our contemporary world, its failings and problems.

Figure 5.4a   (caption on next page)

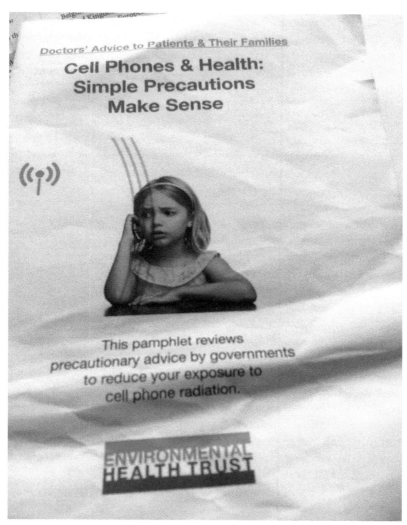

Figures 5.4a and 5.4b   Leaflets about safe technology that Olivia distributes at her local school and elsewhere. Photos by Pauline Garvey.

The wider context

Smartphone use cannot be considered entirely in isolation, but must be considered as part of a wider 'Screen Ecology'. Most people also have a tablet, a desktop/laptop, landline and, increasingly, a smart TV, and they often move seamlessly from one screen to another. Size is increasingly a factor for people whose eyesight and manual dexterity are declining with age, but who also care about weight and convenience. When the iPad became popular, our participants in their eighties and nineties, who had previously resisted using any form of computer, were soon contacting relatives and making photo albums on their tablets. By 2019, however, tablets seemed to be in decline in many countries as smartphones have grown larger and are far easier to carry around. Maria, who used to FaceTime on an iPad, now mainly uses her iPhone, though the iPad is still employed for her creative writing. Many other iPads lay abandoned in drawers. Some have worked out how to cast entertainment directly from their smartphones to their television using compatible Samsung screens or devices such as Chromecast.

Not everyone migrates to the smartphone, however. At the age of 61 Fergal mainly relies on his iPad to read the newspaper, look up history podcasts and, he says, ignore the constant messages from women on his dating app, though he does correspond with some of them through the website. It is the opposite of Tinder, he says, noting that the most recent hook-up involved helping a woman buy a shed. Others, such as Denise, have pointed out that small screens and touchscreen technologies are difficult to manoeuvre with arthritic fingers, which she demonstrates by detailing how she may inadvertently call the wrong person because she is not accurate enough when scrolling down her contact list. Yet others, such as Eamon, have scaled down their entertainment, for example Netflix, from the television to the tablet, to demonstrate their one-size-fits-all commitment to tablets. On a recent pilgrimage to Lourdes, he simply handed over his iPad to the reception desk and, hoping to exploit his age, asked them to 'hook him up' to the internet and to any specialist devices/services for negotiating his way around Lourdes.

Landlines remain important mainly because this age group may have parents in their nineties who will never use anything else. While younger people increasingly watch television on a computer, older people are switching to smart TVs, often with very large screens, which may also be used to watch videos or photos from holidays or weddings. Then there are others for whom their laptop dominates screen usage. They bank online, shop online and generally see online life through laptops as better for manoeuvring, preferring internet-based sites to smartphone apps. One participant, a woman in her forties, finds smartphone apps clunky and inconvenient compared to the equivalent websites and so avoids almost all apps. To conclude, there are different participants for whom the tablet, laptop or television dominated screen usage, though the majority now focus on the smartphone. But none of these are exclusive.

With the rise of cloud storage technology and automatic synchronisation, people happily employ the smartphone when out and about, the tablet when going to bed or for reading the newspapers, the laptop for a sustained piece of writing and the television for an international family Skype session.

Some preferences are simply a reflection of habit. People who state that the smartphone screen is far too small for watching television nevertheless happily watch an hour of YouTube entertainment on their smartphones. Other uses are extending previous practices. For example, one man, whose smartphone was linked to his car through Bluetooth, complained roundly about his friends calling him when they were driving home from work or stopped in traffic. He was very critical of this practice, feeling they were simply calling because they had nothing better to do. Most drivers, however, appreciated the link to Google Maps. There is little sign yet of the 'Internet of Things', which refers to a future replete with direct digital connections between everyday objects, but participants did occasionally control their home security or heating systems through their smartphones. Most people ignore phone assistants such as Bixby and while many of them have Alexa, it is almost invariably relegated in practice to a voice-activated radio.

As well as this Screen Ecology there is a 'Social Ecology', where a smartphone has to be understood in its social rather than individual context. For example Aidan, whom we met in chapter 3, prefers not to use his smartphone and resents his adult children texting or making quick calls as an excuse for not visiting him. As a result it is his wife Jackie who maintains phone contact with friends and relatives, and then relays their news on to him. For his part Aidan does their banking on the home computer, as well as other tasks she is not fond of. If people regard the smartphone as a technical device, and the husband has taken more responsibility for DIY and practical tasks, this makes him the 'natural' dominant user. But if, as in this case, the smartphone is conceptualised as a device for keeping in touch with family and friends, then a traditional married couple see the wife as the 'natural' smartphone user. Obviously if they eschew traditional gender roles, as is the current trend, then neither logic would apply. Couples may see their smartphones as interchangeable, knowing each other's passwords and answering either phone if they happen to be nearest, though this is not typical. More common is to share a single online diary so they know each other's appointments for themselves and their children.

Social Ecology can include many different relationships. Anna, aged 68, describes herself as a 'Liverpool fanatic'; she purchased her Galaxy

Core Prime after seeing how her sister uses hers to check football scores easily. She has synced the smartphone to her laptop, which is where she watches football. She also has fun changing her Google settings, making up random birth dates or refusing to specify her gender. Without a functioning pancreas, Anna must measure her blood count and decide how many carbs to consume every day – a complicated process which she calculates on her smartphone. Her other key connection is through grandparenting; she has a 12-year-old grandson and an 8-year-old granddaughter with diabetes, who downloaded the Minecraft app on her phone. She sometimes exaggerates her inability to download or perform other tasks in order to give the grandchildren minor smartphone tasks, something they clearly relish. They assume Anna knows very little about smartphones and she plays along with this idea. In another example, an older couple may simply not bother learning much about smartphones because they both constantly rely on their 19-year-old daughter. All of these examples reveal the limitations of thinking that research about smartphones is simply a study of individual people with their individual phones. There are generally both other screens and other people that have to be taken into account.

Learning and teaching smartphones

There is another reason for older people's ambivalence. Smartphones are one of the main devices that lead to a devaluation in the skills and knowledge that older people may have developed over the decades. One woman had worked delivering flowers for a flower shop, developing considerable expertise in finding her way around the countryside as a result. She is quite upset at the capacity of Google Maps to make her knowledge redundant. Who cares what older people know if you can simply look things up on Google? In turn, this resentment may be expressed in what seemed an absolute refusal among most research participants ever to download an app that they would have to pay for. Since these typically cost less than a cup of coffee, their reasons are unlikely to be due to thrift.

Despite these resentments, older people recognise that they may have to progress their skills simply to be able to perform everyday tasks or deal with online bureaucracy. Melissa, a former nurse in her mid-fifties, was now unemployed. She had two adult daughters, both of whom refuse to help her with her smartphone. She suspects she was sold a phone that the shop assistant wanted to get off his hands. Melissa is unsure if her Pixi

One Touch even is a smartphone. What she really wanted was WhatsApp to stay in touch with her local book club group. Her name had 'dropped off' the WhatsApp group, so the book club convenor had to send her separate text messages. Melissa is afraid to press anything on her phone, feeling especially fearful that she will be then charged for something.

After her daughters refused to have anything to do with it, Melissa went to a neighbour for help in setting up WhatsApp. But when WhatsApp then disappeared, she was too embarrassed to return and ask for further help in reinstalling it. She would rather 'admit' her lack of ability to a stranger than to friends or neighbours. She is familiar with the language of downloading, storage and megabytes, but cannot translate or apply such jargon to the actual smartphone in her hand. Along with many participants, she has no idea about the difference between Wi-Fi and data. Many participants assume downloading a film at home through Wi-Fi would be expensive. As just noted, they balk at the demands a new app makes for unnecessary access, but young people scorn their refusal to agree to terms and conditions.

For people like Melissa, their inability to manipulate the smartphone leads to the feeling that they are 'dumb', with the associated sense of deficiency and embarrassment. She had bought the smartphone because the shop assistant said it was the easiest to use, but actually it was unfamiliar to others, leaving her not only digitally isolated but also lacking the confidence to do something about it. For Melissa, seeking help really just means humiliation. Such stories became more familiar when we started teaching smartphone use to older people, first as volunteers with the charity Age Action in a Dublin library and then offering something similar at a local community centre. The key problem is that young people imply that smartphones are easy to use because they are 'intuitive'. The older 'pupils' are then told to download an app. They look at their phone and press an icon called downloads, which gets them nowhere at all. What is intuitive about the relevant icon for downloading their banking app being called Google Play? How should they know the new meanings of 'packages', 'the cloud' or 'crashed', which are all the more misleading since they are apparently intelligible? Then they are told to 'go on the internet'. Looking at their smartphone screens, they see one icon called Internet and another called Samsung Internet, but young people have mentioned other icons such as Safari or Chrome or just Google. Which is the wretched internet? What is the difference between a pre-installed icon called 'the Gallery' and another called 'Photos'?

One of the primary causes of anxiety among older people is the fear of being charged. As already noted, most are confused both by data and by phone plans. Since they regard smartphones as machines, they assume that when the smartphone does not work it must be broken. What do young people mean when they tell them they cannot 'break' a smartphone and that they just need to go back some steps and take a different path? Older people constantly fear that they will thereby do something irreversible, such as deleting their precious photographs. They also have problems in that phones are not designed for fingers that are starting to become arthritic. Young people tend to learn as a peer community and seem completely oblivious to just how un-intuitive a smartphone actually is.

Sometimes help comes from other sources. Sarah and Aoife are best friends who take long walks together a couple of times a week and text each other most days. Aoife works as a nurse while Sarah, now in her fifties, stopped working full-time 30 years ago when she had children; she then took up childminding part-time once her own children had grown up. Her Huawei smartphone was lent to her by her daughter's boyfriend because she simply could not work out how to recharge the 'big fancy Samsung' her family had bought her for Christmas. Aoife introduced Sarah to messaging and WhatsApp, but her children tend not to text since she seldom answers. Aoife keeps an eye out for club activities or messages which Sarah might miss. When some local cousins invited her onto Facebook, Sarah suggested coffee instead.

Sarah has become aware that family members and friends are modifying their behaviour to accommodate her. She now has to rely on her husband to book travel or communicate with family. This was especially hard when her teenage daughter phoned them from Paris to say she might have meningitis. Her husband immediately sprang into action, informing the family and checking about doctors. Their daughter turned out to be fine, but Sarah had felt excluded and incapacitated. She had once worked with computers, but had fallen behind when she became a stay-at-home mother and now feels as though she is stranded in a different time zone with an ever-growing gulf. Her only hope is that friends such as Aoife, who has offered to come with her on a computer course, will help her to rejoin the digital world around her.

The problem we found is that even most routine jobs today seem to require proficiency with smartphones. Travel does not just involve the specialist apps; there is also the basic proficiency that is required to be included in the background chat and organisation. Stranded like beached whales without smartphone skills, older people may feel even older and out of touch. Yet if they do then master the smartphone, this goes into complete reverse. They have now incorporated skills that have become seen as youthful, and they, in turn, may see themselves as having become more youthful as a result. We have met plenty of people in their eighties and nineties who bristle when sales assistants suggest they ask their son or daughter for help – one woman, aged 81, remarked loudly that she had a home computer before the sales assistant was born.

Smartphone apps

For all the negative discourse about smartphones in general, older people become much more enthusiastic when talking about particular apps. They praise the Dublin Bus app, for example, whose real-time information means they do not have to wait in the rain for the next bus. As coastal communities, people in Cuan and Thornhill have tidal apps and sailing apps; they explain why the Norwegian app YR is best for the weather. Apps form part of general conversation, especially for those at the younger end of our population. People ask each other what they think about Spotify or have they seen this on Instagram, if they are younger, or that on Facebook if they are older. If they come to a smartphone course, it is often in order to be able to use a particular app such as WhatsApp or the news.

As part of our research, we conducted 57 interviews in which we asked people to open up their smartphones and systematically go through every single icon, discussing which they used and how they used them. If the intention was to obtain clear quantitative results, then this exercise failed. There are simply too many factors that intervene. Firstly, while one person may have the Tripadvisor app, another may access Tripadvisor through Chrome or Safari. Our figures relate to apps they actually use rather than being simply present on their screens, but sometimes they would claim to have only used an app once, which led us initially to discount it; only later did subsequent conversations reveal more extensive usage. Other people may use the app on their smartphone, or they may access the app through another device. For all these reasons, we see any figures we use as essentially visualisations of qualitative findings.

Apart from apps, there are also inbuilt features to most smartphones which almost everyone will use, including the camera, the clock/alarm feature, the torch, the voice phone and text messaging. Next come apps that at least 80 per cent of users would employ, including WhatsApp, an email app such as Gmail, a calendar app and an internet browser app such as Google or Safari.

The apps that the majority of people (albeit less than 80 per cent) would use include transport apps such as Dublin Bus and Irish Rail, news apps such as RTÉ news, Journal.ie, the BBC, *Irish Times*, the *Independent* or the *Guardian*, weather apps such as Met Eireann or YR, photo apps such as Gallery or Google Photos, radio apps such as RTÉ radio, airline apps such as Ryanair or Aer Lingus, video telephone apps such as Skype or FaceTime, music streaming apps such as Spotify or iTunes, maps such as Google Maps, Facebook, Facebook Messenger and YouTube.

Then there were apps that around one-quarter of older people might have used, which would include games such as Candy Crush, social media platforms such as Instagram or Twitter, a television-related app such as Netflix, a sports-related app such as apps for streaming football or rugby, a language translation app such as Duolingo, a shopping app such as Amazon or SuperValu, Dropbox, a Notebook app, a step-counting app, a banking app, a taxi app and Airbnb.

Finally there were some apps that would be represented by something like 10 per cent of users. Examples include a religious app, a book reading app, a dating app, a parking app, Pinterest, sailing apps, Sky Entertainment, podcast apps, a home speaker system, local tides, Alexa, Tripadvisor, Viber, Wallet, health insurance, fast food apps, hotel booking apps, guitar or other instrument tuning apps, phone finding apps, eBay, a savings app such as Groupon or DoneDeal, an ancestry app, relaxation app and a more specialist health app such as one that aims to treat sleep apnoea.

You can see a visualisation of these apps on the following page (Fig. 5.5), although the illustration is not comprehensive.

Typically an older user might use between 25 and 30 functions and apps on their smartphone; for users at the younger end the number of actively used apps can reach as high as 100. There are some differences between the two fieldsites. Those in Thornhill used Facebook, Maps and YouTube less, which may be related to the degree that they tended to be a little younger than those in Cuan. As noted above, the most common phones were the Samsung Galaxy, followed by the iPhone. Generally people take up a new model when their phone plan has expired, i.e. every two years, so that new smartphones tend just to come through the structure of payment plans rather than from a sense of need.

In effect, there seem to be three main components to smartphone usage. Functions that give capacity, those that are sources of information and those used for social communication. These may overlap and contain sub-categories, for example, 'social communication' conveys information. To start with capacity, a few see the smartphone as their primary watch and far more use it as their alarm clock. Bluetooth is mainly used to enable people to make phone calls or listen to music in their car. The smartphone

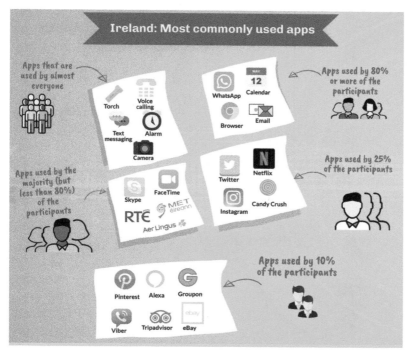

Figure 5.5 Visualisation of the most commonly used apps in the Irish fieldsites. Created by Georgiana Murariu.

is usually where they have a calculator. The calendar/diary has become essential for organising their day-to-day lives, reminding them not only of appointments that day, but also of special occasions or annual events such as birthdays. People constantly consult calendars to check whether a time slot remains free. Other frequently used functions will include settings, contacts and often cloud storage such as Dropbox. By contrast, it is very rare for them to use apps preloaded by corporations, such as Samsung or Microsoft apps.

The camera provides a good example of how the smartphone changes their lives. At first adoption is conservative, being used for holiday or wedding pictures, just as previously cameras would have been used. Gradually, however, the smartphone has come to transform the nature of photography itself. New genres appear, such as functional photography, where people take pictures of notices about forthcoming meetings or a page in a book to retain this information. Rather than a way of remembering the past, the orientation is shifted to the extreme transience of photographs shared immediately on WhatsApp and other social media. Photography becomes part of a more general shift towards what our ASSA project calls 'Perpetual Opportunism',[11] which pertains to many other uses of the smartphone.

A common functional usage connects people with transport, and not just the Dublin bus. Apps are used for parking or to summon taxis. MyTaxi, or FreeNow, is used more than Uber in Ireland, but Uber is used on holiday. Chapter 2 listed a swathe of other apps employed for going on holiday. The very occasional use of phones to control home devices such as central heating and security has already been noted. Step counters are quite common, but older people rarely use any bespoke health apps other than the quite sophisticated one used to expedite claims to their medical insurance company.

A major part of the function of the smartphone now includes entertainment. Most smartphones include games which, as the film about Deirdre demonstrated (see Fig. 3.1), may well be relevant to this age group. Much more extensive is the use of YouTube for videos and, increasingly, music through Spotify, though most older people still listen to music mainly through the radio, which may itself now be an app. Smartphones may contain links to television, usually the Irish RTÉ or the UK's BBC, as well as a television guide app. This is also an age group much given to reading books. They rarely read books directly on smartphones, but Kindles are increasingly popular, as are apps linked to the library or other ways of obtaining books.

The second major segment of smartphone use is obtaining information. The smartphone is now the main route into the internet. The hub of this activity is usually just called 'googling', and Dr Google is discussed in the next chapter. The smartphone is where people find out what is going on, but it is also a massive encyclopaedia of knowledge. It has become hard to watch a television series without simultaneously searching on the smartphone to check where you previously saw that actress, but information may range from comparison shopping to looking up a philosopher.

Seeking information is, equally, part of the previous review of functions. The smartphone is used one minute as an airline boarding ticket and the next to check up on times of departure. It is used to make a payment and to find out how much money is in the account. The latter is a genre of use where older people remain anxious, and as yet many prefer to bank using computers rather than directly through the smartphone. They also tend to be conservative about shopping apps, though shopping online saves them a journey into Dublin city centre and with Covid-19 may have seemed more of a lifeline. In addition, many participants are tempted by the savings and bonus point schemes that may be available through shopping apps.

The sense that older people are in the midst of a transformation in everyday practice is especially clear in the usage of Google Maps. Some will only consult the app before setting off, using it as an analogue map. Others follow their route on screen, but are reluctant to listen to a voice that instructs them where to drive. Yet others will use voice-based driving support – but relatively few as yet would employ Google Maps while walking, except when in a foreign country.

During this period participants tended to follow the news avidly, although Irish politics did not generally carry the same fascination as either the US politics surrounding President Trump or the UK politics regarding Brexit. Anne, for example, spends two to three hours daily on 'Trump' News, shifting between Google and newspaper apps, including the *Washington Post*, Al-Jazeera, the *Guardian* and the local Irish papers. She listened to radio apps and followed US television stations such as Fox News. This was complemented by using YouTube for various satirical programmes or tweets from *The Onion*, as well as Facebook coverage. In the morning Anne listens with headphones on, so as not to wake her husband. It is possible that the majority of older people now look at the news on their smartphones before they get out of bed and before they turn off the light to go to sleep.

It is hard to exaggerate the importance of sport for some men in their sixties and seventies. It is their main source of entertainment and the content of their communication; for some, betting is also an important pastime. For them, Twitter is the primary means of keeping up with a specific celebrity sportsperson. Facebook is used for following sport, but also for discussing it with friends, while YouTube is for watching key moments in the game. Specialist sports apps include the GAA app to follow Irish sports such as hurling and Gaelic football, plus a rugby app or Premier League football app. As a group, older men may share news about an Irishman cycling the globe or the fortunes of the Irish rugby team abroad, with some using the smartphone to organise a trip to watch them. If Rob's smartphone is mainly devoted to golf, it is because Rob is mainly devoted to golf. For those with teenagers, Teamer was a popular app to arrange football, rugby or GAA matches, invariably accompanied by WhatsApp groups as the site for banter.

The third major component of smartphone use is communication. Voice calling, the original function of a phone, has mostly declined, although landlines are retained for long calls to one's mother. Texting is generally preferred as less intrusive and time-consuming. Video-based communication through Skype and FaceTime was already common even before the rise of Zoom during Covid-19, especially because most Irish families have relatives living abroad. For the same reason WhatsApp is now also a major medium for free webcam-based communication, and indeed voice calls.

Older people are less drawn to the social media dominated by the young such as TikTok. A few post on Instagram, but they often use it mainly to follow their children. Some follow Twitter, but the key transformation has been with Facebook. A few years ago older people were telling young people to leave Facebook as a trivialising of life. Now they are asking young people to stay on Facebook as a means of remaining in touch. Danny was rather amused when a lady in her seventies complained that young people kept pressing her to take up WhatsApp. She believed instead that they should leave older people to their own preferred and better-suited media, namely Facebook. Ethnography is often the study of short memories.

Older people often use Facebook firstly to keep in touch with family and friends. One participant explains:

> I am more one of these older people that just keeps an eye on it (Facebook) and what's happening is I am seeing my sister's gorgeous daughter who has three beautiful babies and they are in England, so I will always check Facebook mainly four times a day.

Facebook is now also the main means of finding information about community projects such as Tidy Towns, various sports and other societies and activities around the town. One participant noted that they go on Facebook several times a day to look at sites concerned with swimming. They also followed two closed groups, one called Community Talk and the other buy/sell/swap as well as a kayaking group. In Cuan the Facebook site for the local news magazine proved particularly popular. As a result Facebook, once viewed as an icon of narcissistic individualism, has morphed into being the main site for maintaining community involvement.

WhatsApp

For most people, the single most important function of the smartphone is WhatsApp. It is the app that marks the fundamental difference in capacity from older phones. As well as communicating with individuals, most people have several WhatsApp groups on their phone as shown in the infographic below (Fig. 5.6).

Typically such groups consist of those caring for elderly parents, those interested in seeing new pictures of a grandchild or simply everyone within a household. Some groups are further afield, such as cousins in California. Next in frequency might be groups of friends, the ladies who meet periodically around the town or people who reciprocally celebrate their respective birthdays. Also common are sports groups, especially golf but also football, GAA or triathlon. Several have WhatsApp walking groups. Then there also are committee groups, such as the Men's Shed or the Town Twinning group, or groups for those taking a course in

Figure 5.6 Infographic showing responses to the question 'How many WhatsApp groups do you have on your smartphone?' Created by Georgiana Murariu.

common. There was even one puppy with its own WhatsApp group – but at least there was only one.

When your mother is in considerable pain at a nursing home at some distance, your brother is in Scotland and your sister in Northern Ireland, then WhatsApp is an unalloyed blessing, as Bernadette describes:

> When my father was dying in the nursing home and then he was moved to the hospital, the constant WhatsApp to each other and also to our friends as well – it's hard to imagine life without that. It's all free which is unbelievable.

Responsibilities are often intergenerational. WhatsApp is used to organise babysitting a grandchild because something has come up at work for the parent. In one instance, a 35-year-old adult child was experiencing depression and threatening suicide; the participant explained that you would never forgive yourself if you were not there when they needed you. This is why, as one person put it, 'you answer immediately, even if it means spilling things on the floor, and you go back home to get it [the smartphone] if you find you have left it behind'.

People often complain about the sheer number of WhatsApp messages that flow into their smartphone every day. Some of this reflects the intense sociality of this vibrant community. But if every time someone texts that their child or grandchild has scored a goal in a football match, others then feel obliged to make an appreciative comment; eventually the aggregate number of notifications can become extremely tiresome. A group set up as part of a town committee similarly complains that certain members effectively hijack the WhatsApp group because they feel everyone should hear about their latest holidays.

There was a marked absence of discussions of Irish politics on WhatsApp groups, though Brexit and Trump are present. This is because opinions regarding the latter topics are generally consensual. WhatsApp groups are mostly sites to build consensus rather than bicker and debate, so more divisive political issues tend to be avoided. A woman in her mid-fifties who worked as a GP removed herself from a group because she had a strong objection to an unfolding conversation about health. The group was established for parents to collect children and simply did not seem to her the right environment for arguing these points. Another woman of similar age left her women's volleyball group because she found the pressure to be constantly funny and upbeat on their WhatsApp group exhausting.

Personalisation

The previous sections imagine the smartphone as a collection of apps used in combination to accomplish certain tasks. But it is equally important to cut this cake a different way, to forget apps and tasks and instead acknowledge the resultant intimate and expressive relationship that exists between a person and their smartphone.

Eleanor's iPhone is a marvel: aged 69, she has turned her phone into a kind of life manual of several hundred pages. There are no individual app icons. All her apps were organised into a nested hierarchy, grouped in fields such as finance, sports, news, utilities or arranged around work-related functions. This vertical order was complemented by a horizontal order where she made full use of the capacity of different apps to be linked. For example, her calendar would have a task, such as paying a particular utility bill. That event was linked to her notepad, where you would find a step-by-step description of the process involved in paying that utility bill, including the password and relevant website address. She then described how on her smartphone an app related to a job function might be linked to a collection of all the PowerPoint slides from the presentation she had attended about how to carry out that particular work most effectively.

Eleanor has also provided herself with visual aids to help her to organise relevant information, including a whole series of emoticons. So a pin indicates that this is medical information, a car stands for transport and a flash sign represents any payment that has to be made that day. As a result, at any time, faced with any particular task, within three or four taps of her fingers she could locate the instructions as to how that task might be accomplished. Another example would be her use of the app provided by Laya, her health insurance company. She immediately photographs any receipts from her doctor and sends these in through the app; she is then guaranteed to be paid back within ten days.

All Eleanor's photographs are date-stamped so that she can more easily order and share them. Her camera has also become central to her organisational work because she sees it as the main device for collecting and storing evidence, which might relate to a car repair or to her timetable for water aerobics. Her phone alarm is not just for getting up in the morning – she will also set it to tell her when she needs an injection or when she is supposed to be leaving the house for some task. Eleanor has a whole section of the phone devoted to money management: she does not have much, but she likes to move her funds around frequently to keep them active. She also has a food section, which includes a link to a site called rhubarb-central.com, which features 250 recipes for rhubarb.

Eleanor talks about her phone in terms of cleaning, clearing and housekeeping. The mass of PowerPoint slides and other photographs can threaten to overflow and needs constant editing, deletion and re-ordering to remain useful and close to hand, which is what she requires from her phone. She is constantly updating her calendar. Everything was securely backed up so that, when her smartphone was stolen in Spain, she was able to neutralise its functions immediately. Using back-up provisions, she was able to repopulate a new smartphone with its entire contents very quickly.

The one thing that Eleanor has not taken to is Siri. She has tried both male and female voices but is not comfortable with either. Indeed, she resents not just the interference from Siri, but the whole trend of using artificial intelligence to pre-empt her with suggestions. Nor does she like the way that Netflix tries to give her ideas of what she might like to watch based on previous viewing experience. She dismisses such things with the comment, 'it's trying to be helpful, but it's clumsy'.

This seems to fit a pattern. Taking her life as a whole, Eleanor has less control over her work or her health than she would like – which may help to explain why she wants to maintain this degree of control over her iPhone and resents the competition represented by suggestions from the smartphone itself. The smartphone expresses not just Eleanor's skill and creativity, but thereby also her personality. She sees herself as a consummate professional, with the organisational aptitude that comes with it. She has spent her whole life trying to achieve a work position that would reflect this and fully utilise these abilities. Her work situation has not always recognised this in her, but it is the person she wants to be and who she believes she really is. Currently the best expression of herself, the only place where Eleanor can see the real person that she feels she actually is lies within her own smartphone.

At the other extreme is a man who says his family have been fishermen for 150 years. He comes across as the icon of a particular kind of masculinity, characterised by a rugged and practical self-sufficiency. He did not need other people or television because he was never bored and always active, whether with sporting activities or practical tasks. Every single usage of his smartphone had to be legitimated under the strict criteria of necessity. He was entitled to use Skype for the two years that his daughter was in Australia, but he was very firm that he has never used it either before or since. Social connectivity is mostly reduced to his ideas of necessity. One advantage of mobile phone development is that he no longer needs to use voice communication, which he dislikes, but can replace that with terse text messages about when, for example, his train will arrive at the station.

The point is that the masculine minimalism of his smartphone is just as expressive of who he believes himself to be as is Eleanor's highly organised smartphone. These two characters thereby make clear something that less extreme examples might not, namely the capacity of a smartphone to extend and reflect back an individual. The smartphone is a mirror: a person can gaze at it and see reflected back the kind of person they believe themselves to be, more rounded and more profoundly than in any actual mirror. This becomes still clearer when the person is regarded as more eccentric.

Gertrude, for example, had three phones because she was obsessed with the idea that she would see some image or aesthetic composition that she needed to capture with her phone and then send out on Instagram, or sometimes also Facebook and Twitter. It might be a landscape, a selfie of herself in a particular situation or just the constellation of colours. She was terrified that she would not have the means to capture this at the precise moment she encounters it, so she constantly has on her person two iPhones, a dongle, in case there is no wireless, and a spare battery charger. However, Gertrude understands this process as precisely the opposite of anxiety. This aesthetic disposition is viewed as something she has created for herself. Rather than focus upon the body as prescribed by mindfulness, she sees her relationship to the aesthetics of the external world as contemplative, even transcendent. As with mindfulness, it is her way of being with that moment, seeing the aesthetic possibilities as creating a deeper relationship with the world.

However, Gertrude carries merely three phones at all times. When Melvin emptied out the pockets of his jacket, he revealed no less than four Nokia mobiles plus a cheap Alcatel smartphone (Fig. 5.7). In his case, the primary concern is music rather than photography. Melvin is constantly recording 'sessions', that is live performances, usually in pubs, of traditional Irish music; when one phone runs out of storage, he turns to the next. He also travels a good deal to places such as the UK or Corsica, employing different phones to communicate with people in each place using local phone plans. He also duplicates information since he worries that a phone might be lost or stolen, and he may also carry a spare battery. Melvin is used to people seeing him as eccentric in various ways. He was perhaps the least surprising person in Cuan to be found carrying five phones in his pockets.

One of the reasons why the smartphone has achieved this unprecedented intimacy and resonance with individual personality is that it is designed to be reconfigured by the user. While very few people make much use of the pre-installed apps on a smartphone, the survey of

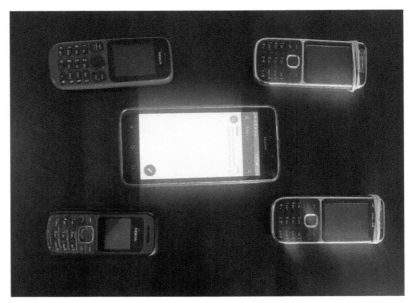

Figure 5.7 The five phones from Melvin's jacket pockets. Photo by Daniel Miller.

apps they did use demonstrates the diversity of downloading. While we are often told about the smartphone's use of algorithms and AI (artificial intelligence) to learn from the user, this process seems as yet to play a minor role, compared to this reconfiguration of the smartphone by users.

Inspecting the smartphone may not always reflect personality – it can often reflect simply the dominant life interests of that individual.[12] Jacinta, aged 56, had worked in the tech sector for 26 of those years, but had retired early due to the stress of her job. Early retirement for Jacinta is an opportunity to do all the things she did not have time for when she was working, a collection that turns out to be quite formidable. It started when she created in her smartphone a list of 55 things to do at 55 – a kind of bucket list that she is working through (Fig. 5.8).

Jacinta started with an art class, which included sharing the results with friends and family through her smartphone. Since she spends half the year in Tenerife with her husband, she uses the app Daft.ie to rent out her house in Ireland for that period. She also keeps a close eye on weather apps to check whether golf is an option for the next day. Jacinta plans cycling holidays with friends and, in a quiet moment, will look up routes following major European rivers (because rivers flow downhill) that are not too demanding. Jacinta invested in a Fitbit that works in the

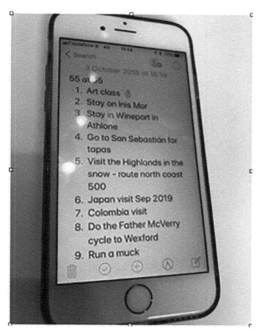

Figure 5.8 The smartphone owned by Jacinta, one of the research participants. It shows her Notes app which has been populated with '55 things to do at 55', a bucket list that she is working through. Photo by Pauline Garvey.

water and which she can sync to her phone; this has suited her retirement ambition first to learn how to swim and then to take part in a triathlon (Fig. 5.9). Each accomplished goal gets ticked off her smartphone list. Another case of a smartphone almost entirely dedicated to activities is that of Stephanie, but in her case it is the single activity of looking after her bedridden father, for details of which see chapter 6.

The main caveat to all these discussions is that the emphasis has been on the way the smartphone comes to mirror the individual user. The evidence therefore, has to be tempered by the earlier sections on Social Ecology, which showed that a smartphone is just as capable of expressing the personality of a relationship as that of an individual.[13]

The Irish smartphone

Smartphones can characterise more than either the individual or a relationship. After all, these are not just individuals and couples; they are

Figure 5.9 A second photo of Jacinta's smartphone, showing her swimming data based on her Fitbit app, which works in the water. The Fitbit is synced to her phone and uploads new swims each time she completes them, specifying the total distance swum and other information. Jacinta is preparing for a triathlon. Photo by Pauline Garvey.

people who were born and brought up in Ireland with particular cultural expectations and values. The extensive discussion of what happens to a couple on retirement is, equally, an insight into how gender relations have changed in Ireland. The masculine minimalism of the smartphone of a man from a family of fishermen reflects an older conception of gender. We noted during fieldwork a tweet from a young woman who had just been included in a WhatsApp group called 'funerals' and suggested that this was the most Irish thing that had ever happened to her.[14]

Whatever is common and characteristic in Irish life is likely to be equally so on Irish people's smartphones. Chapter 4 noted how people only relaxed in each other's company when they had established which other Irish people they know in common. Smartphones tend to reflect this form of networking to strangers through first establishing familiars. Smartphones can also facilitate change as well as continuity. Most people in Cuan were born elsewhere in Ireland, making this an example of a new kind of community. The smartphone is important in helping to create the new bonding based on their active participation in Cuan life.

Another contemporary characteristic has emerged from Ireland having a vastly larger diaspora population than its in-country population. There is now huge interest in ancestry.com and similar online platforms, which have allowed people to find and re-connect with extended family. In the film shown in chapter 3 (Fig. 3.1, p.51) Deirdre talks about staying up until 3 a.m. chasing down ancestors. Many people are now submitting DNA samples to make this link to specific relatives. They use the not so recently dead to create new living connections.

Sports and cultural events may also express Irish nationalism or, as in content about hurling, the GAA and traditional music, they may express Irish particularism. A factor that might help Irish people see the digital as something local rather than a foreign intrusion is also the centrality of the technology sector to the contemporary Irish economy. The same point follows for this volume more generally. The smartphone is facilitating and reflecting not ageing in general, but ageing in middle-class Ireland.

Conclusion

There is considerable overlap between this chapter and our contribution to *The Global Smartphone*, the comparative ASSA team book. The final chapter of the latter, however, provides much more detail of the general, analytical and theoretical conclusions that follow from a comparative study of smartphones. Some of those concepts have made an appearance within this chapter. Reference has been made to Screen Ecology, which situated the smartphone alongside other devices in simultaneous use. Social Ecology, on the other hand, indicates that an individual's smartphone needs to be understood in the context of other relevant individuals, for example, both partners in a long-term marriage. Reference has also been made to Perpetual Opportunism, a concept that reflects the way in which the smartphone is always available and the impact that it has had on people's use of photography, the recording of information or the sense of security for the older person, knowing that if they have a fall they can quickly contact someone.

The Global Smartphone introduces the idea of the smartphone as reaching 'Beyond Anthropomorphism'. In so doing, it indicates the extraordinarily intimate relationship we have with these devices. Smartphones may not resemble people in the way a robot might, but they do possess an extraordinary capacity to take on the traits and values of users such as Eleanor, thus becoming perhaps more human than any robot. In turn, users in Ireland often manifest Irish culture, which makes their smartphones also somewhat Irish.

Finally, *The Global Smartphone* develops the concept of the 'Transportal Home': a sense that the smartphone is not so much a device we use as a place within which we now live. This feature may be of particular importance to older people in Ireland, since ageing may result in decreasing mobility and the threat of relative loneliness and isolation. At the very stage of life when people may lose some capacities, the smartphone bequeaths them new ones. This Transportal Home is a far more sociable place to live than their bricks-and-mortar home. At any moment they can portal direct to their relatives in Australia or to children living in London, and can feel, via webcam, almost in the presence of their grandchildren. Covid-19 may have exposed all the deficiencies of online communication compared with face-to-face contact – but it also felt as if the entire world were contemplating in horror what this experience might have been like without apps such as Zoom and WhatsApp.

There are thus good reasons for thinking that it is this older population who are gaining most from smartphone usage, not least through accruing the connotations of youth itself when they start dating and downloading their favourite rock music onto those smartphones. Yet in conversation they are far more negative about smartphones. If older people gain more, they also have more to lose. The same capacities of the smartphone mean that knowledge and skills developed over decades become worthless almost overnight. A fundamental shift has occurred in the power relationships between the young and the old, which to date young people have shown little sensitivity to, exploiting the new dependence older people have on them. The claim by many young people that the smartphone is intuitive would be laughable if it were not also humiliating. Stories often refer to the impatience of the young though, of course, there are others that tell of kindness and solicitude. To be fair, older people are now also being hoisted on their own petard, following a decade of denigration of young people's reliance on these same devices.

These conclusions, considered alongside those of other chapters, enable us to rethink the experience of ageing. The spread of smartphones from young to old was so rapid that it was as if the smartphone still carried the angst and the acne of its teenage associations. As such, for older people, it was instrumental in the wider shift towards becoming modern and even youthful that is being documented across this volume – associations that are helping older people somehow to reclaim a place in the contemporary in their own right. Unlike most discussions of smartphones, this chapter has generally avoided passing judgement as to whether smartphones are good or bad. Our evidence is that most of its effects are simultaneously contradictory. It both joins you to people and separates you from them; it provides a focus but also a distraction. There are gains and losses in capacity. These contradictions are what make the smartphone so powerful – and so much like ourselves.

Notes

1. See Deloitte 2019.
2. For a much more detailed discussion of this see Miller et al. 2021.
3. See Commission for Communications Regulation (ComReg) 2018a.
4. No other phone brand in Ireland has a market share greater than 3 per cent. See Deloitte 2019.
5. Women use their mobile phones for online games more than men, with 38 per cent of female participants saying that they play online games daily as opposed to 22 per cent of males. The reverse was found for online gambling, with 27 per cent of males saying they gamble online as against 16 per cent of females. In their responses 12 per cent of males and 13 per cent of females say they have used online dating apps. Despite these differences, there is only a small difference in the amount of times male and female respondents look at their phones per day and usage for men and women is generally consistent. See Deloitte 2019, 5.
6. See Deloitte 2019. Also, according to the ComReg report Q4 2018, the average person in Ireland sends 70 texts, talks for 213 minutes and uses 6.4 GB of data per month. According to their 2016 report, Average Revenue Per User (ARPU) was approximately €24.51 per month compared to approximately €24.75 in the same period in 2015 and €24.98 per month in June 2014. See Commission for Communications Regulation (ComReg) 2018b.
7. Source: Reuters Institute and OII 2019. More data is available online: http://www.digitalnewsreport.org/survey/analysis-by-country/2019/ireland-2019/. See also Statista 2019.
8. According to a recent report, a government department sought tenders for media monitoring, including the monitoring of social media platforms and broadcast media for 'keywords'. This was seen as gaining access to the expression of people's opinions as an important news source. But in the face of global controversies such as the Cambridge Analytica scandal research participants in Dublin voiced suspicions over the disclosure of personal data, particularly if they suspected it would be harvested for state surveillance or political interference. See Edwards 2018.
9. In a radio interview David Cochrane, online editor for *The Irish Times*, noted that 66 per cent of the Irish population have a Facebook account and over half that number use it daily. Facebook represents one of the primary sources for election candidates to reach voters, he said. Facebook numbers reduced in 2018, amid privacy concerns, but were soon on the rise again. See RTÉ News at One, 15 January 2020. We discuss these issues in much more detail in Miller et al. 2021.
10. See McCullagh and Campling 2012. For example, there are several studies that document the suspicion that surrounded the introduction of the telephone in Ireland. The first Irish president, Éamon de Valera, compared television to the atomic bomb in its threat to social order and moral standards.
11. See Miller et al. 2021.
12. For a clear example of this, see the discussion of Matis in chapter 6 of Miller et al. 2021 that has not been repeated here.
13. Several examples of how the smartphone reflects relationships are provided in Miller et al. 2021.
14. Thanks to Dr Gillian Kenny for allowing us to cite her tweet from 6 December 2018. See Kenny 2018.

6
Health and care

This chapter begins with an outline of the Irish health system and its mix of private insurance and state health. However, visiting doctors and observing biomedical health practices is only one part of people's self-care activities. There is an increased interest in wellness as a more holistic approach, ranging from diet and fitness to the use of complementary health treatments. This chapter suggests an affinity between older people and complementary health systems because older people tend to experience multiple health issues alongside more general concerns such as stress or contextual factors; a holistic approach is thus closer to their own experience of feeling unwell. Evidence of an ambivalent attitude to health services, in which patients may be less than honest both to doctors and themselves, is also presented. The chapter then focuses on menopause as a clear example of an age-related physical change. It also discusses how researching health information via Google exacerbates class distinctions and ends with a discussion around dementia, cancer and death.

Health services, insurance and complementary health

Unusually for a relatively affluent European country, Ireland does not offer free universal primary health care. Currently 60 per cent of the population pays about €52 on average to see a GP while two-thirds of the population pay up to €144 per month for drugs; they will also be charged for other primary care services.[1] Medical cards are available for around one-third of the population who qualify as low-income, which provide them with primary and hospital care without charge.[2] In addition, those aged over 70 and under 6 are eligible for free GP visits only.[3]

The health system in Ireland is often described as 'two-tier': those who can afford to pay privately and have health insurance can get faster access to diagnosis and treatment, even in the public hospital system. This is reflected in the relatively high level of private health insurance in Ireland, which stands at about 46 per cent of the population.[4] However, the long waiting lists for treatments have been a high-profile source of public anger, and the 'crisis' within the health system was pivotal in the 2016 and 2020 general elections. In May 2017 a cross-party Parliamentary Committee published a report known as 'Sláintecare', based on a consensus across the political spectrum to establish universal, single-tier health.[5] In the meantime, the majority of our participants in middle-class populations such as Cuan and Thornhill have private health insurance. It is quite common for people to have an app for one of the main insurance companies on their smartphone, making claims quicker and more straightforward.[6] The Irish government also created a 'Fair Deal' policy by which older people would receive support for the costs of nursing homes and other facilities, but would have to put a proportion of their assets towards the costs. With an ageing population, this scheme faces severe challenges.[7]

Our research participants are generally conscientious in visiting friends and relatives in care homes. In Thornhill several participants volunteer to help out in the large local nursing home that is run by a religious order. However, a major issue for people in Cuan is that there are no local care homes. Visiting care homes features prominently among many people's activities; having none local meant that organising transport, often involving smartphones, had become an important issue. This, alongside transport to the local hospital, was the subject of the main Age-Friendly committee initiative during the period of fieldwork.

Among the many challenges that the health system faces are a growing population and longer life expectancy. The Irish population is expected to reach 5.19 million in 2031; average life expectancy for men is currently 80 and for women 84. In the years between 2000 and 2010 life expectancy rose by 4.5 years for men and 4 years for women, but these gains have slowed considerably in more recent years.[8] A further challenge is the significant undersupply of GPs in Ireland. There are around 2,954 full-time equivalent GPs working in Ireland; this provides 64 per 100,000 people, well below the OECD average. More than 2,800 doctors withdrew from the medical register between 2015 and 2017, including a larger number of Irish doctors emigrating annually. According to Dr Doyle, President of the Medical Council, 'the culture surrounding the practice of medicine in Ireland' – by which he meant long working hours and a poor work-life balance – was to blame.[9] Similarly, a 2017 study found that more than three-quarters of hospital doctors reported significant work stress. A doctor is now twice as likely to take his or her own life as a member of the general population.[10] The average patient visit lasts 14 minutes,[11] and state funding for each visit has dropped from €41 in 2008 to €29.4 in 2013.[12]

Finally, there is one more element crucial to understanding the complexities of health services available to older people: the pharmacy.[13] The pharmacy's role has become much more important precisely *because* health services come at a cost. As a pharmacist comments:

> In the UK, nobody goes to a pharmacist for that because why would you?[14] You get your doctor for free. So you automatically go to the doctor and hence there's a huge weight on doctors now… Here they would go to a pharmacist first and see, should they go to the doctor? Is it worth spending that money going to the doctor? Like what other professional person do you go to and don't pay a consultation charge? Nobody.

At the same time pharmacies are relatively expensive, and people do not always appreciate that they will be charged a dispensing fee each time they buy prescription drugs. Some, therefore, look for cheaper alternatives such as trying to get their medicine in Northern Ireland or other countries.

Responding through wellness

In 2018 broadsheet media reported that people in Ireland typically visit their GP three times a year. They spent an average of €171 on each visit, including the cost of the visit and prescribed medication. The research found that those forced to take time off work end up spending six hours on average to visit their doctor.[15] The survey also found that four out of ten adults agree that the average waiting time to see a GP is too long. Given this context, in which healthcare is already seen as closely related to costs in time and money, it is perhaps not surprising that people are drawn to the idea that there might be less expensive alternatives.[16] Of equal importance is the sense that formal medicine, including GP visits, feels relatively abstract and distant. The traditional concept of the family

GP who knew their patients and might make a home visit if required has been replaced by the image of someone hunched over a computer and watching the clock during the 10 minutes allowed for the consultation. There are also now a host of other practitioners who make their living by offering alternatives, based on various claims for holistic treatments and wellness.

The changing relationship between biomedical and complementary health is reflected in the plans of the major health insurers in Ireland. A recent newspaper article noted that at least some of the plans from the three biggest providers, VHI, Laya and Irish Life Health (ILH), refund around half the cost of up to 12 visits to a homoeopath or a reflexologist. They also refund costs for tests for allergies and, in the case of one company, ILH, they will also pay for a visit to a medical herbalist.[17] One effect of these payments is likely to be greater medical legitimation for complementary health. The payments are doubtless a result of insurance companies seeking competitive advantage by offering to cover such treatments.

The same element of competition is true of Irish pharmacies. One pharmacy in Cuan does much of the prescribing of complementary medicine since they have a very well-known shop assistant, seen as the local expert on dispensing 'natural' medicines. She works much as the private herbalists do, taking people through a sequence of possible remedies on the shelves for problems such as insomnia. She knows which complementary practitioners she likes and she has a very enthusiastic personality, so her recommendations are valued. She might say of a complementary medicine, for example, '60 per cent of those who come here find this works and don't need anything else'. This particular pharmacy is part of a chain, however, and the treatments are often extremely expensive.

Meanwhile, there is also evidence of movement in the opposite direction. A health food shop is now partly modelled on the trappings of a pharmacy. The manner in which the owner dispenses various herbal remedies, following extensive discussions, tends to follow the language and style of the pharmacy, with the experience presented to the customer as a kind of free consultation.

The range of services is evident in the Social Prescribing research described in chapter 3. In both fieldsites the GP surgeries may themselves include a chiropodist or a psychotherapist. In Cuan several other psychotherapists share one premises and a range of complementary therapists share another. There is a pain clinic and a health food shop that doubles up as a herbalist, as well as an individual practitioner who specialises in both acupuncture and Chinese herbal medicine. Because of the emphasis upon sport, many services are orientated towards sports injuries. An international mindfulness business also operates from the town. There are pop-up healers, too – for example, a woman who claims to have inherited her powers from her grandmother and operates by placing her hands in proximity to the patient's body. This woman holds the occasional whole day 'open office' at one of the pubs, where she accepts voluntary donations for her healing and may see up to 40 patients on the day. There are various forms of Pilates, with pop-up Pilates sessions on the beach as well as a regular class. These services may align with the age spectrum. In general, it is t'ai chi that tends to attract an older age group since it involves more standing and is less strenuous than the alternatives. By far the most extensive service is yoga. Some of those who teach yoga offer merely one session a week, but one young woman was at one stage teaching up to 40 classes a week.

One of the complications in understanding the position of complementary health is that on the one hand some individuals understand their role as the antithesis of biomedical health and are extremely negative about formal health services, while others provide an almost seamless bridge that shades between biomedical and complementary health. The former tend to include those offering a range of complementary therapies such as cranial sacral therapy or reflexology. Their practitioners may criticise GP visits on the basis that a 10-minute consultation is focused upon a single health issue which is then treated in isolation. By contrast, they present themselves as having enough time and a listening ear, enabling a patient to describe in full why they feel unwell, and to explore the wider context of any symptoms.

It may help to see health provision as a kind of triangle. The doctors are viewed as essentially a resource dealing with physical problems and lacking the time to talk. They are complemented by the various psychotherapists and psychologists, seen as the appropriate response to non-physical problems such as mental wellbeing or stress. They will discuss matters with a patient, but may not deal directly with physical issues. Many of the complementary health practitioners have colonised the obvious niche left by these two positions (Fig. 6.1). The concept of holistic medicine sees physical problems and non-physical problems as two sides of the same coin and argues that these need to be treated together. Typically, an older patient going to a reflexologist will present with muscular pains, for instance in the shoulder or ankle, migraines and stomach problems, which the patient feels are somehow related to each other. In turn they describe a general feeling of stress, tiredness,

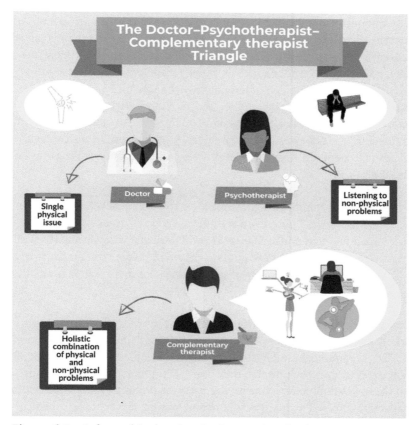

Figure 6.1   Infographic showing the Doctor–Psychotherapist–Complementary therapist triangle in Ireland. Created by Georgiana Murariu.

depression or sleeplessness, which may then be related to wider issues in their life, such as problems with relatives.

Whatever an outsider's views of the direct efficacy of a focus upon, for example, the heel or the head, the appeal of a complementary therapist is more subtle. It is likely to lie more in the fact that while the patient's foot is being massaged, they are using the time to discuss problems relating to the family and other factors that are seen as the cause of stress. In turn, stress is assumed to be a major underlying factor in the physical problems that have been described. These observations correspond to the experience of many older people, for whom ill-health has become an integral part of life rather than an aberration.

Practitioners of complementary medicine provide holistic narratives that assume the interconnectedness of their problems. This corresponds more closely to the way in which older people understand, and in turn narrate, their experiences of ill-health. The range of practitioners then shade off in different directions, including not only the world of yoga and Pilates but also those who advise on diet and nutrition or physiotherapy and exercise. All of these link to the general maintenance of a healthy body, a concept that may have a particular appeal here because of the centrality of sport to people's lives in Ireland. One patient summed things up as follows:

> I've often said myself, you would go to your local GP and if you're lucky to get 15 minutes, 8 minutes usually, whereas if you go to an acupuncturist or a herbalist they will sit down with you and the first visit is normally 2 hours, when they will take a complete history, talk to you and engage with you; each subsequent visit is normally an hour.

Many of these older people would prefer not to go to a psychotherapist, whom they may associate with mental illness. The fact that they are seeking treatment for a physical condition gives them licence to talk at length about the problems that they face at this point in their lives. In turn all these developments intensify the pressure on, and create unrealistic expectations of, GPs – many of whom now want to leave the Irish medical profession because of the high levels of stress associated with their work.

This same attention to the wider context of ill-health may also be found in services that perceive themselves as fully within the nexus of biomedical health and science. An example would be the pain clinic. The young man who runs this usually starts by making a video of the patient's mobility routines, how they get up from a chair. He refuses to see things as right or wrong, but rather as alternative forms of mobility that cause more or less pain. For him the visualisation is key since he also feels much of this is a psychological issue, the way patients think about and visualise their mobility. Since he feels the key to his success is understanding his patients' motivation and working with that, his session may last up to an hour and a half, with lots of discussion. He talks about the lack of awareness about how mild depression can manifest itself as pain. He also notes that he might deal with specific pain, but that there remains a residual fear in the patient about lifting children or playing with them that needs to be addressed. He further argues that a common problem with healthcare is that we focus on telling people what they cannot do, rather than showing them pathways to continue doing the things they want to do and which mean so much to them. Overall, in running his pain clinic he sees his interventions as extensions rather than repudiations of biomedical treatments. A similar attitude was found with some physiotherapists. There are some who clearly situate themselves in juxtaposition with biomedical treatment and may be located within a GP's practice, while others lean further towards complementary health.

Complementary medicine also has an ambiguous relationship to financial considerations. On the one hand, its practitioners tend to espouse an anti-materialistic ethos, seeing mass consumption and salary pressures as closely related to stress. On the other hand, they are at least equal in cost to the biomedical profession, without the government concessions for young, impoverished or more vulnerable members of society. Complementary therapies tend to be associated with the middle classes, and quite a number of their practitioners supplement their incomes with 'alternative' brands of products such as dietary supplements or substances that claim to cure a wide range of ailments. In promoting these, their pitch is often not far removed from the salesmanship they claim to condemn.

There are also constant contradictions between ideology and practice. Mary was a relatively extreme example. She worked within a medical institution, though not herself medically trained, but also devoted much of her life to seeing herself as the personal incarnation of an ancient time, infused by New Age reformulations of Irish mythology. She says she has had amazing results from flower essence homeopathy. The contradiction became most acute from her awareness that the people she mainly mixed with would follow and support the anti-vaccination movement, while her experience within the medical profession set her in the opposite camp. She was desperately trying to get the medical authorities to take a more empathetic stance to anti-vaccination supporters and not dismiss them as crazy. Mary aimed thereby to develop a more open and accessible dialogue that might persuade these people to change their minds and accept vaccines. She saw the current condemnations of the anti-vaccination movement as just fuelling its popularity.

At the same time there was a very widespread view about the institutional arrogance within the medical profession – an issue seen as a major contribution to the dilemmas that these professionals were now facing. Medical consultants were the subject of particular criticism. This was again brought to public attention early in our research by a current affairs programme on Irish television that investigated how some consultants were treating large numbers of private patients while leaving public patients on the waiting list.[18] When it comes to GPs there is, not surprisingly, a spectrum, ranging from those seen as empathetic and good listeners to those deemed autocratic and dismissive of patients' views. Several mentioned that although they googled symptoms, they hid this fact from their GPs in order not to antagonise them.

This idea of an arrogant health service was as much directed at the overall state service as against any individual medical practitioner. In 2018 an example came up around the issue of women's health. Irish laws regarding contraception and pregnancy termination were among the most restrictive in Europe until 2018 when, as previously noted, two-thirds of the population voted to *legalise* abortion, in contrast to the two-thirds of people who had voted to *restrict* abortion in 1983. The optimism in terms of women's bodily autonomy was short-lived, however; that same year a national scandal dominated the media, when it came to light that approximately 221 women had been given incorrect information regarding their cervical cancer tests. This issue became public when one of the women affected, Vicky Phelan, settled a High Court case against a US laboratory subcontracted by CervicalCheck to assess the test. The 2011 audit showed that the test Ms Phelan took the same year was a false negative, yet she was not informed about it until 2017.[19]

The controversy surrounding this issue was a constant feature in the press and hotly discussed among our research participants. Protests took place in several cities, including Dublin, with anger fuelled not only by the non-disclosure of errors in the cervical smear programme, but also the reluctance of the Health Service Executive to admit full liability. Participants noted the silence, secrecy and obfuscation that characterised the Health Service's reaction when the problems within the screening programme came to light. The debacle led to a formal apology by Leo Varadkar, formerly a GP but serving as Prime Minister in October 2019, for the 'litany of failures' of the screening processes and procedures. In this he promised that paternalism would have no place in Irish healthcare.[20]

In this context there was an accompanying scepticism around many other aspects of health policy. For example, people might suggest that the promotion of the Healthy Ireland Programme has more to do with the Health Service trying to save money by making people responsible for their own health than an actual concern with wellbeing.[21] In a way, both doctors and the state seem to be occupying the invidious position of a kind of parental-like authority, with the consequence that patients view unhealthy behaviour as a kind of freedom from authority. Such a perspective becomes very evident in the next section.

Age, attitudes and behaviour

The ethnography was confronted with a vast range of opinions about both biomedical and complementary health. Many participants believe that mainstream biomedicine has lost some vital ingredient that can be found in Chinese or herbal medicine, acupuncture, reflexology and similar approaches, whereas others view all forms of complementary health as utter nonsense. Some have maintained the more traditional link with their GP, sometimes over generations, and feel the GP maintains a kindly and personal relationship with them. Overall, though, the evidence suggested that, in practice, it tends to be younger and female GPs who are viewed as attentive and friendly. Older male GPs are characterised as more financially-driven; they are accused of time-watching during consultations and being prepared to discuss only one issue on each visit. The result is that while a minority work exclusively with biomedical services, for the majority within the middle class the biomedical has become not the only – sometimes not even the primary – place to which they turn. Indeed, some participants only visit GPs as a last-ditch exercise that lies outside the frame of their efforts to live good lives.

For example, some of the older male participants in Thornhill made a point of detailing their self-sufficiency when it came to management of their health. Many have no routines for visiting GPs, only doing so when it was strictly necessary. Joe, for example, aged 61, declared:

> I don't go to the doctor. I have desperate blood pressure and anytime I see the doc he asks about it and I say 'yeah, it's grand, I had it checked at work', and the same with getting my heart checked. If he asks, I'll say 'it was checked at work'. So I lie to him.

Further discussion revealed other men in their fifties and sixties who either lie to their doctors or go out of their way to misinform them. Joe explains that he gives up alcohol and fatty foods for a month before his annual check-up. He says he gets a 'clean bill of health' and comes out of the surgery announcing 'I'm in great form' before returning to 'drinking like a fish' for the rest of the year. When he confessed this behaviour to another male friend, his mate admitted that he does exactly the same. Intrigued, Joe mentioned it at work and discovered that out of about a hundred colleagues, at least three other men have said they do the same thing. When we discuss why his friends do this, he emphatically announces 'self-delusion is where it's at, gobshites, how to fool yourself into thinking you're healthy'. Laughing, he adds:

> I don't lie to the doc. I'm economical with the truth because I have an intimate knowledge of medicine from Google. I know the doc would nag me to go for more tests. You've exposed the lie – thank you!

So Joe goes every six months to get his prescription for blood pressure renewed, even though he has a blood pressure monitor at home which he bought from Argos and he knows what the normal and abnormal range is. He is on medication for cholesterol and knows himself what to do to alleviate symptoms. The point for him is not that he does not look after his health; he clearly does by walking about 16 km along the local beach at least four times a week. A social element is present here too, as he jokes that sometimes his solitary walks are 'disturbed' by the presence of friends who accompany him. Breaking his jovial demeanour for a moment and speaking seriously, he says the walking is to clear his head and to 'be there' for his adult daughters and he frequently leaves work early to get out and take long walks, using up his generous annual leave on sunny evenings.

Joe is thus very serious about his health, but very flippant about his relationship with his doctor. The concept of holistic is not just about complementary health – for Joe, his walking works also as a social outlet, to combat stress from work and to fulfil obligations to his daughters. He links walking to his volunteering to pick litter once a month, another way of keeping in touch with people he likes. Out on the beach is also where he consults his dating app, away from the prying eyes of teenage daughters. In all these ways he reflects the experience of most older people for whom ill-health has become integrated within what they regard as ordinary life.

Frank, a retired civil servant aged 66, has a similar attitude. He walks between 10 and 15 km most days, starting with dropping his adult son at the train station on weekday mornings and continuing for an hour. He avoided going to the doctor for 15 months, but then realised his cholesterol was a bit high. He thought he could deal with it himself through exercise and diet, but a recent blood test failed to show any improvement. More worryingly, his failure to get a blood test meant that a rise in PSA levels (a possible indicator of prostate cancer) had not been detected. Frank acknowledged that he should follow recommendations to see his doctor twice a year but, even after mentioning his elevated PSA levels, he is still unsure as to when or even whether he will next visit the doctor. 'They say you should go every six months, but who can remember when six months has passed?' he explains.

For others, such as Brian, a bank manager in his sixties, the avoidance of doctors has more to do with the cost of visiting the GP and subsequent medication. He has high cholesterol, but complains that the medication costs €45 for six months in Ireland but only between €5 and €6 in Spain. So he researched the generic medicine he requires and buys in bulk while abroad.

> Now I buy for six months and then forget about going to the doctor. I was buying abroad, so for two years I wasn't going to the doctor. Generally speaking, I was supposed to in six months to fill the prescription. But I am not going.

For Brian, managing his health involves a rigid routine of eating salads a couple of times a week alongside regular exercise. He used to play football a lot and, although he is now less active in that regard, he does watch his alcohol and meat intake. When we speak about health worries, he is less concerned about his present high cholesterol, but more worried about the prospect of cancer; his wife had cancer some years ago and its spectre lingers. His local GP is tangential to his health efforts rather than central to them. Nor is Brian particularly unusual: women in Thornhill on long-term medication for chronic illness also reported how they share the names and addresses of particular pharmacists in Northern Ireland and post their prescriptions there.

Lastly, older women in Pauline's craft and coffee group speak of feeling guilty if they are unproductive. Trish, aged 59, joked that the only reason she goes to the gym twice a week after work is to assuage a sense of guilt that she would otherwise feel for being inactive. She jokes that resistance training for her means trying to resist chocolate. Others referred to activities in more positive ways, as working towards something life-enhancing. Vincent, for example, walks every day because he wants to keep his weight down, whereas others emphasise the future benefits in mind and body that will come with 'keeping active'. As we saw in previous chapters, both men and women who take daily walks are eloquent on the benefits of getting out of the house and getting some exercise and developing a routine. The retired and elderly men and women that we have met talk of health and nature, and sometimes transcendent values such as spirituality, in a way that is not easily disentangled.

Menopause

Menopause is of particular significance to our study because it is a transformative process directly associated with age, though an earlier age than other conditions for this demographic; it is also an inevitable event for half of the population. In addition, menopause is a condition that reprises many of the issues discussed above with respect to biomedical treatment as against complementary therapies. In this case the debate is not simply because of complementary treatments but, more fundamentally, because of what menopause is.

In Cuan, several women were concerned with radically shifting the meaning of menopause from being seen as a medical problem to a positive progression in the natural life of women (Fig. 6.2). These included trying to develop various forms of celebration that they thought might link to earlier Celtic ideas about the moon or other symbolic systems. The historical context of such aims is significant. In an era without contraception, some women speculated that their mothers passed through a period consisting of a constant cycle of pregnancy and

Figure 6.2   Menopause meme shared in the Irish fieldsite.

birth. Without plentiful resources, large families represented a financial and physical burden, and some participants noted that the large size of families had been more than their parents could cope with. The finality that came with menopause may therefore have presented itself as an almost unalloyed blessing. It may also have shifted women's roles in society, allowing them both the freedoms and respect that they may not have previously enjoyed.[22] By the late twentieth century, this situation had gone into almost complete reverse. As women have been increasingly able to control their fertility, menopause has shifted from being seen as a liberation to becoming a series of disruptive changes that many women we met felt unprepared for. The women mentioned above are trying to swing the pendulum back to the historical viewpoint of celebration.

Not surprisingly, women who use complementary therapies and natural childbirth methods tend to criticise what they view as the overmedicalisation of menopause. Some regard hormone replacement therapy (HRT) as a route to breast cancer and make considerable efforts to avoid it, something confirmed by the pharmacists. They object to treating menopause, which they regard as a natural process, as though it was simply another illness with a litany of symptoms. Others take more or less the opposite attitude, believing that menopause is something they really do not want to bother with or think about; they simply want a prescription that will make any unwelcome effects disappear, whether it is for HRT or some other treatment. One woman referred to the experience as 'a slow puncture', an inexorable loss of energy and *joie-de-vivre* that was more profoundly debilitating than any single symptom.

The average age for a woman in Ireland to reach the menopause, defined by the absence of periods for 12 months, is 52. Menopause is often associated with a series of physical and emotional symptoms, but most women do not seek medical treatment for these. For those who do, several problems have beset its treatment, the first being the reluctance to discuss them and the second the sheer diversity of experience. As with all such topics, there is a variety of reportage; some women came from families with open discussion and easy access to information. However, it was far more common to hear that the previous generation made no mention whatsoever of menopause and for our participants to have had no particular advice from mothers or older sisters. Melanie, a 51-year-old from Thornhill, wryly observes that 'my mother says I invented hormones'. Alongside the other topics previously discussed as taboo, this was something that had to be dealt with in private.

The older women in our demographic had gone through these changes some time ago; for others it was still current. The majority of women described two main symptoms as clear indicators of menopause: hot flushes and night sweats. Although they were sceptical, some felt it was not entirely implausible that some of their mothers could claim to have hardly noticed menopause. Against these claims are a significant minority who passed through one or more additional significant symptoms – in some cases finding their lives turned upside down by severe changes which they may or may not associate with menopause. Furthermore, even regarding the universally recognised symptoms of hot flushes and night sweats, the experience varies from one that is unwelcome but not especially problematic to those who feel as though they are broadcasting flames to the rest of the office or are woken up time after time in soaking sheets. As one woman noted:

> God, I know, it's awful, yeah, but I didn't go to a doctor. You might say to your colleague – could you just take over for a moment? – and then not explain why you would disappear because you had a flush and you needed to remove yourself. I remember my colleague saying – when does this ever end?

Most also report ignoring or trying to ignore menopause since they had family work and other responsibilities. For many, however, the experience simply cannot be ignored. For example, Linda, aged 45, works part-time in a city community centre. She suffers from depression and anxiety and is currently taking antidepressants. She reported having recently gone to her GP, where she asked about hot flushes and other problems, which she said she indicated by waving her arm in a circular motion over her groin area. Because she was still having periods and taking precautions regarding pregnancy, she had not considered menopause. Now she talks to her sister, who normally never talks about bodily issues but who rings her up occasionally to tell her that she is 'feeling brutal', and that she has problems with sweats and bad relations with her husband and another friend – who once phoned her husband and said she was going to jump off the extension of their house, which she blamed on hormonal surges of PMT (premenstrual tension). Linda teases her, in part because the home extension is not at all high, but also because her reaction sounds extreme; they wonder what she will be like when menopause really hits. To Linda's disappointment, the GP told her that her problems were due to the 'peri', something that Linda had never heard of before. To her dismay, she was also told that there was nothing to be done. She could not go on HRT because her mother died of breast cancer at the age of 36, when Linda was only six years old. Linda thus finds herself with another medical problem to add to her existing anxiety and depression. She felt that the GP was no help, but she was thinking of downloading an app called Calm, which someone had recommended to her and which helps through mindfulness and meditation. She has not done this yet, however. At the moment she deals with things by smoking, after which she feels guilty.

There were quite different opinions about the degree to which menopause is now discussed. Many women reported that previous generations did not talk much about the menopause, though a Thornhill GP dismissed this as 'nonsense … women have always spoken to each other about the menopause',[23] insisting that because it is transient and easily treated it is not the live topic that some people think. By contrast, Collette argued that menopause is not spoken about because it becomes an easy shorthand for a panoply of behaviours and experiences that might have nothing to do with hormone fluctuations – or, worse, become a reason to exclude or denigrate the sufferer. 'It's like the whole hysteria thing,' she said. Several noted that the topic might be raised, but often through flippant remarks such as 'she's having one of her turns' – a dismissive reference that minimise what women are actually going through.

The sheer variety of experiences added to the problems. One woman commented on the strength of her feelings:

> I could be quite murderous. I could just go right through you. I would have no compunction or feel guilty. I often felt I could just drive the car right into that wall – never did.

Physical symptoms could have emotional consequences. Another woman tended to flood and was hugely embarrassed at dinner when she stained the white chairs of her host. Evelyn saw the effects of menopause as less physical than an alteration in her sense of herself in ways that she did not anticipate or understand.

> There's definitely a slump going through it and I don't know that you're prepared for that … I would have been 'peri' for a lot of my forties. The way my mind works – if I understand what is wrong with me, I can deal with it – but it's when I don't when I think I'm just a lunatic and there have been times that I've wondered about that. You have to know what you're looking for and know what is wrong with you and looking back you realise what it was.

Feeling confused, Evelyn went to the GP and consulted library books. She tried drinking soya milk, taking evening primrose oil and ginseng, using pharmacy-sourced medication and even wearing magnets in her underwear. Others talked about avoiding spicy food, looking for 'no-nonsense' books and the standard remedies such as HRT. For many, it was hard to separate menopause from the wider context of growing older. Veronica, aged 61, felt when she was not sleeping she found it difficult to concentrate on both her relationships and her teenagers. Instead she was left wondering:

> Is this me or is this outside of me? Do I just keep going mad? Before people did not know who to turn to, and if you go to the GP he might say you're not post-menopausal because you're still having your periods. They don't treat what is happening inside.

Another source of evidence was interviews with women working in pharmacies, psychotherapists and those working in complementary medicine. Overall these suggest knowledge about menopause is quite limited and is derived mainly from television or newspapers. They report that most women find the topic embarrassing to talk about even with other women and usually only do so under the cover of jokes. They also noted the degree to which women may not associate symptoms, such as dramatic mood swings or long-term insomnia, with menopause.

Women varied greatly in whether they associated menopause with issues of bone density. Some have had DEXA scans for bone density but many had not. One of the common problems discussed with complementary health practitioners was vaginal dryness, which could have significant impacts upon sexual intercourse. As a result, most women are unaware of treatments such as local HRT ointments. A similar issue was that of urinary incontinence, which one physiotherapist, who specialised in women's health, claimed was the single most common reason women came to consult with her. Once again the pharmacies may be seen as the initial resource; some stock a wide range of expensive herbal remedies such as sage for hot flushes and treatments made from red clover or soya. As the pharmacist noted, 'the first thing they say is "I don't want to go on HRT", but they are much less certain regarding any alternatives'.

Of particular relevance to our study was the association with ageing. This is a time when women may be concerned about putting on weight and focus on this as the core issue. For others it was the memory that 'old' people sit around and talk about their hip replacement operations and now it is *them* who are becoming concerned with osteoporosis and taking measures to prevent loss of bone density. For others, again, problems of vaginal dryness or lack of libido coupled with increased grey hairs or wrinkles were indicators of ageing as a kind of steady decline. Lastly, some commented on the positives of this recognition too: one woman who stopped dying her hair commented on how delightful it is to be unnoticed by young men. Caitriona, now aged in her fifties, found that she could walk past a group of young men and be completely invisible to them.

Taken in the context of ageing, it is not surprising that men also occasionally made similar remarks. One recently retired man described feeling like he had lost his 'drive' when he turned 50: 'Life just seemed to have lost something; if it was a colour it would be grey'. He complained that, among friends, the company would sit and talk about how menopause affected their spouses, but no one discussed how it affected them. The difficulty that Martin saw was that what he was experiencing did not seem to have a name: the grind of care many people this age are involved in, looking after elderly parents and sometimes simultaneously troublesome teenagers, the myriad relationship problems, the loss of the bloom of youth, but also the positives such as self-confidence and new freedoms. Middle age is not a single thing; as one participant said:

> It comes down less to age than to where your career is or where your family is – are they young or have they moved out – contributes to a very different way of seeing oneself.

Taken in the larger context of the 2018 referendum and the scandal regarding cervical cancer tests, menopause is related to a path of societal progression being mapped onto women's bodies. Silences around menopause that seemed to be a hallmark of previous generations were, therefore, becoming reversed, which partly explains the diversity of women's comments on the extent of discussion. The media had suggested that a singular feature that swung the referendum was women telling their personal stories in such a way that 'stories expanded the public sphere's capacity for distributing empathy among all citizens, a political prerequisite to allowing women fuller participation in civil life'.[24] The year 2018 also saw the arrival of the 'Menopause – The Musical' and the opening of Ireland's first Menopause Clinic. The latter's founder created the 'Menopause – No taboo' event in association with Irish Nurses and Midwives Association in 2019.

To conclude, most women saw menopause as perhaps the clearest example of the sensibility that they also associate with complementary rather than biomedical perspectives – that is, something whose symptoms cannot be separated out and seen in medical terms alone. Rather they see these changes in the context of everything else going in their lives at that time,[25] much of which comes back to the basic association with ageing and the gradual increase in the experience of issues around health and wellbeing.

Googling for health information

Many of these issues around menopause concern information, whether regarding HRT or the range of symptoms that might actually be associated with menopause. An associated problem had been the lack of intergenerational discussion; most women discussed menopause, if at all, with long-standing friends. Sharing stories with friends help them 'normalise it' (this phrase emerged a couple of times), but when they wanted to learn about actual symptoms they either went to the library or, increasingly, to Google – often referred to as 'Dr Google'. This practice was facilitated by the ever-present smartphone. [26]

Mary, aged 71, commented that Google was not around when she had cancer in the 1980s, a condition that triggered early menopause. At first she was on HRT, but as soon as she came off it she was plunged into full menopausal symptoms. She described these as 'dreadful' with 'sheets wet in the middle of the night'; her worries were compounded by being unsure if that was 'supposed' to happen: 'Was I the only person to have menopause after chemotherapy or does it happen to everybody?' She did not talk much about how she was feeling because no one wanted to hear.

> The girl I worked with would say 'you're radiating'. I didn't talk about it to people, no one wanted to hear. You looked after yourself and they said to take soya milk and ginseng and all that, remedies.

Mary now recognises that her daughter is currently going through menopause but still notes 'there isn't much talk about it, never was', even though she is in constant contact with her daughter. They text daily while they are watching television (they watch 'Love Island' at the same time and exchange views on the characters: 'he's a wally' and similar comments). Mary appreciates that her daughter suffers from mood swings.

Oh she is menopausal, really bad mood swings, but you can't say it, it is as if that word is enough as if you don't need anything further, but this is a condition.

Even though she has a good relationship with her daughter, she does not feel she can offer advice in person.

If the person is touchy you don't want to say it is menopause or they'll go wild … might be easier to point to an app which explains how to remove the tension and treat the symptoms.

Another woman suffered from tingly feet at night, which she described as an itch under the skin. She googled the symptom to see if it was 'a thing', feeling this was less embarrassing than asking her friends. The problem was that when googling she accepted the first piece of information that she found. 'I didn't care where the science came from,' she asserted, 'or who wrote it.' Despite that, armed with this information, she went on to tell her friends that tingly feet are a symptom of menopause.

Menopause is merely one example of health issues that seemed to lead inexorably to the practice of googling for health information. Brian, who featured early on in this chapter, told us how he replaces his visit to the doctor with numerous health-directed initiatives. These have included googling – although as with Joe, also mentioned above, he comments that he also stopped googling because 'it would scare the crap out of you'. So whether it is because of potential embarrassment or the desire to avoid having to visit the doctor, or simply because as a parent you are worried about anything and everything that your child is experiencing, googling provides a route to apparent expertise that is difficult to access otherwise. However, there are a whole series of problems that surround the information available on Google.

We intend to write more extensively about the impact of googling health information in a further publication, which will also provide more detailed evidence. The primary conclusion of our study is to suggest that googling for health information has become a highly significant factor in exacerbating class differences. The problem is that Google appears to be a simply neutral facility: an additional source of information equally available to all. But listening to the details of how different individuals access and interpret this information suggests something entirely different. At one end of the spectrum are the substantial proportion of our participants, who were university educated. Most of them tend to look for government or university-backed authorities, or other reputable websites such as the Mayo Clinic. They may even follow through to the original science papers that the medical professionals rely on. They may do this directly or through a member of the family, since it is quite common in contemporary Ireland for people to have at least one distant relative who works within the Health Service. They would trust these people to help them interpret the information available through Google, and to help adjudicate authoritative as against untrustworthy sources.

At the other end of the spectrum are people with more limited education, less used to undertaking research. Many of them tend to look at whatever comes at the top of the Google results page, accepting these at face value. Almost invariably they are drawn to websites that increase anxiety, link almost any symptom to incipient cancer and then link in turn to commercially-driven sites that give the appearance of objectivity but are designed to sell expensive, often unsuitable, treatments often including scary claims or promises of instant relief. The main effect of googling, therefore, is that those who were already quite well-informed and comfortable with the idea of research become better informed, while those who were not well-informed become far more misinformed. This extension of class inequalities, in turn, impacts upon their relationship with GPs and other medical professionals.

Dementia and dying parents

In chapter 8 we will discuss not only the importance of funerals, but also the tradition around avoiding discussion of death. This is now changing; both death and cancer are starting to surface as issues of public discussion, facilitated by the gradual rise of hospice provision. Such an acknowledgement is hugely important to our demographic, simply because so many of them are dealing with the death of parents typically in their nineties. Overall, people generally accept mortality but fear the manner of dying. As one of our participants puts it:

> If I died suddenly don't cry, just say wasn't mummy a lucky bitch, she got her way. I've no fear of dying, it's inevitable, but I don't want to be suffering.

To be more specific, something that participants said again and again was that what people feared was not so much death but dementia. As life expectancy has grown, so has the incidence of dementia, which means that many of them had either direct experience of looking after someone with dementia or knew others who had. Although there is a growing public education campaign to try and lower the fears and anxieties around dementia, our evidence is that the trend is in the opposite direction. Fear and anxiety are growing with the incidence of dementia. People talk of their elderly parents who had always been quite stoical, trying to keep medical interventions to the minimum, and who are now refusing to accept they have this condition and its consequences. The problem of older people finding the promise of retirement thwarted by the need to look after elderly parents was discussed in chapter 4.

In 2019 Danny accompanied Aisling, aged 53, on a visit to her mother in a home for people with dementia. The care home was in a nearby town and is one of the main two homes in which those with dementia from Cuan tend to end up; there are no facilities within Cuan itself. This home is private – the public dementia home is in a different town. In general, the treatment of dementia patients is exemplary. All forms of force are now prohibited by law; everything is achieved by persuasion and by trying to create a very calm, placid environment so that the patients do not get disturbed, the usual cause of difficult confrontations. Aisling goes to visit her mother six out of seven days a week and has done so for around a year. For what can be quite extended periods when a parent is developing dementia but there is still the possibility of their living at home, this care becomes a more or less full-time occupation; it may indeed be the immediate cause of retirement, as it was in Aisling's case. She therefore appreciates the quality of care in the care home, but still has to deal with the concomitants of dementia, for instance when her mother is convinced someone there wants to murder her or connects a current event back to the brutality of the nuns she experienced when at school – or simply forgets who is visiting her.

Caring for parents with dementia was one of those circumstances where smartphones, and most especially WhatsApp, have become extraordinarily prominent. In Ireland the most pressing health concern for the generation that was the focus of research was often caring for their elderly parents. Scrolling through Frances's phone history, it is evident that around 80 per cent of all voice calls and text messages were connected to organising the care for her frail father. Since a recent fall he is more or less bedbound and needs to be changed, washed and cared for in his bed. The state provides Frances with 10 hours of care a week, but for the rest of the time this has become her full-time work – so much for her dreams of retirement.

In the last month Frances sent 270 texts concerned with her father's care on her smartphone. For example, she has a specialist voice recorder that records all her phone calls because she can then use these recordings as evidence of her conversations with the care authorities when they dispute her claims about promised care. She carries a power bank everywhere to ensure her phone never runs out of battery. Of her four WhatsApp groups, two are family groups concerned with organising her father's care and two concern sailing. Her father has a *Doro* phone, specifically devised for use by the elderly, so that he can talk with his sister. Given that the sister in question is in the early stages of Alzheimer's, these may be long conversations that can drift in many directions.

Stephanie purchased the same phone for her 89-year-old mother-in-law. The use of WhatsApp groups to organise care for elderly parents has become astonishingly common in a remarkably short time. This practice of sharing out the care for parents does not always work smoothly, of course. A woman reported the problems her mother was having with dementia in full, only to have her brother reply angrily that she was just trying to spoil his holiday because she was jealous of him. He followed this accusation with all the reasons why he could not – and would not – help with their mother's care.

Dementia is not so much seen as becoming elderly but as dying slowly, on a par with other physical conditions that lead to death or disability. In chapter 2 we argued that it was frailty and dependency that finally lead to people being categorised as elderly. But this category, in turn, is being fractured by the entry of smartphones and other changes. Digital devices have a considerable capacity to ameliorate the problems of immobility and certain forms of frailty. But while physical decline associated with immobility may be diminishing as a factor in making people feel old, there is commensurate stress on cognitive loss as an irredeemable sign of a transformation in who one fundamentally is. This may be why dementia and cognitive loss become framed more in terms of dying, rather than simply ageing.[27]

Conclusion

One participant recalled that when young she kept finding herself sitting among old people, having endless conversations about their hip replacements or their cataracts. The trouble is that she now sees herself as reproducing that trend. More than anything else, it is this that makes her feel that she is becoming old. Naturally experiences vary; some people are fortunate enough to remain unscathed until well into their nineties. We found women are still far more likely to form groups having long conversations about health than are men. Our fieldwork, however, seemed to coincide with a kind of coming out for men, inasmuch as topics such as prostate cancer seemed a much more prominent issue of public debate by the time fieldwork was complete. The topic of health in relation to ageing is vast and this chapter does not try to take a comprehensive view; we have barely mentioned hip replacements, for example. Instead the chapter focused on just a few elements which resonate with wider themes in this book, such as the role of the smartphone and the extent to which people craft their responses to issues of health.

The chapter started with an examination of the wider context in Ireland. Older people today may have more assets, proportional to younger people, than was the case in the past. Health insurance is a dominant topic for more affluent participants, while being eligible for a medical card is a primary concern for those with lower incomes. Chapter 7 will discuss the development of new strategies towards assisted and supported living as alternatives to people moving directly into a care home. And, as we have seen, there has been a huge increase in the use of complementary therapies.

Into these trajectories has come the smartphone, which has made itself almost instantly a hub. It would now be quite unusual in conversations about health for no one at some point to suggest that they follow up that conversation by googling a symptom or treatment. Our evidence is that googling information is not neutral. It changes the relationship between patients and doctors as well as exacerbating differences of social class and education. WhatsApp is becoming equally important as the hub for organising care for elderly parents, especially ones with conditions such as dementia. Apart from the specialist apps such as Fitbit or step-counters and health insurance apps, most employ general apps such as maps for visiting a specific clinic or health site, YouTube to look up the exercises suggested by a physiotherapist or apps for practising yoga or mindfulness at home.

Two of the main topics of this chapter have been complementary therapies and menopause. These turn out to be important indicators of more general changes in the relationship of older people to health. It might have been expected that complementary medicine is a younger person's more faddish interest, while older people would have more trust in established medicine. In some cases this is true, but there are structural links here. As people age they tend to experience co-morbidity, that is a set of simultaneous and related problems rather than a single illness or condition. On retirement they may be more contemplative about the way in which illness relates to wider issues in their lives. As illness becomes more central to their lives and conversations, it may become a kind of hub around which many other topics are discussed. These range from stress and depression through to family relations, pensions, holidays and everything else that is going on in their lives at that time. The suggestion in this chapter is that older people are becoming drawn to complementary therapies partly because health itself has become a more holistic experience. As a result, they may feel less attuned to the doctor-patient relationship, based on a tradition of trying to focus on a single health problem for each visit. Instead older people may prefer practitioners who have more time to talk about their problems in general and are not subject to the structural pressures and safeguards that doctors are. Complementary medicine has also moved to fill the niche between the 'talking cures' of psychotherapy and doctors' attention to physical symptoms by transcending such distinctions.

Antipathy to the authority inherent in orthodox medicine was also evident in the discrepancy between what some older men in Thornhill knew they were supposed to do and their actual behaviour. For women menopause seems to be a catalyst for this change in perspective. More than just a key sign of ageing, it is also among the most holistic of all health experiences, a prime example of a constellation of emotional as well as physical effects. The condition may impact sleep, mood swings, memory, sexual relations, bone density or urinary incontinence. While menopause starts among the younger end of our age spectrum, symptoms such as insomnia may continue for decades. All of the above may account for the high incidence of middle-class, middle-aged and older people who are involved in regular yoga, mindfulness classes and conversations about diet and wellbeing more generally. Significantly, they are also prepared to spend considerable sums of money on complementary therapies.

The other impact of these complementary resources is that they correspond to attempts to incorporate health within the wider field of crafting, a theme explored throughout this volume. People in retirement with financial resources and time on their hands can simply give more attention to their bodies – for which purpose they mix and match a wide variety of health-related facilities. People configure not only biomedical and complementary health, googling and discussion of hip replacements, but also keeping fit, a range of possible diets and an overall concern with wellness into a tapestry of daily life. Here wellbeing takes its place in relation to activities, to sociality and in ensuring that they do not take for granted life itself. This emphasis upon the body has become such an important part of their lives that the theme continues into chapter 8, where wellbeing is now found to be a central component of their overall sense of life purpose.

Notes

1. Burke et al. 2018.
2. See Central Statistics Office 2016c.
3. In 2019 Prime Minister Leo Varadkar announced that free GP care for the under-12s would be rolled out over the coming three years. See Wall 2019a.
4. Market statistics for number of people with private health insurance inpatient cover. Health Insurance Authority Ireland (HIA) 2016. See also Health Insurance Authority Ireland 2020.
5. Burke et al. 2018.
6. The average annual cost of health insurance in 2016 was €1,177 with VHI as the largest provider with 50 per cent; other major players are Irish Life and Laya. See the Health Insurance Authority's 2016 report for more data.
7. See Wall and Horgan-Jones 2019.
8. Malone 2019.
9. See Wall 2019b.
10. Hayes et al. 2017.
11. Pierse et al. 2019.
12. See Collins and O'Riordan 2015.
13. For information on pharmacies see van Egeraat and Barry 2009; see also Gorecki 2011 and Gallagher 2016.
14. People in the UK may now in fact use a pharmacist, largely because of the time it takes to get a doctor's appointment.
15. See the research conducted by Amárach for online consultants VideoDoc in Weston 2018.
16. People had mixed feelings about the possibilities of webcam 'visits', with older people more resistant and younger people more positive about not having to take time off for a visit. What no one anticipated was the rapid shift from face-to-face visits resulting from the pandemic.
17. See McBride 2018.
18. 'RTÉ Investigates – *Public v private: the battle for care*'. Thursday, 1 February 2018. See Raidió Teilifís Éireann 2018.
19. Vicky Phelan's case was not in fact exceptional – more than 200 women were affected. See Drążkiewicz 2019.
20. See O'Halloran 2019. Traditionally, also, religious orders were heavily involved in Irish healthcare, a role that many people currently object to. To this day, a number of the largest Irish hospitals are owned by religious orders (The Sisters of Mercy own the Mater Hospital while the Sisters of Charity own St Vincent's University Hospital, among others).
21. See Healthy Ireland Framework 2013–2025 in Ireland Department of Health 2013.
22. See Carolan 2000.
23. We had access to the doctors in Thornhill, but not to those in Cuan.
24. Barr 2019.
25. In the United States anthropologist Michelle Ramirez writes about expert representations of menopausal symptomatology that frames menopause and the ageing female body as 'the site of dysfunction' and consequently the root cause for a variety of other problems that women experience at this time of life. Ramirez 2006.
26. Accessing information for health was one of the main reasons people in this area first connected with the internet. See Ward 2003.
27. The traditional stereotypical image of an elderly person sitting on a rocking chair, staring off into space, is outdated. However, it endures as an image associated with cognitive loss and dementia.

7
Downsizing

Introduction

Both authors of this volume were trained in the tradition of material culture studies. These aim to integrate the study of artefacts within anthropological approaches to social relations by examining the way in which objects both express and create people and relationships. In our previous research, the attention has been as much to home interiors and furnishing as to the house itself.[1] This chapter begins with a brief description of housing in Ireland in terms of state policy and the conventional expectations regarding the changes that come with ageing, summarised as downsizing. However, against both policy developments and public expectations will be set our ethnographic observations. These show that the phenomenon of moving or not moving to a new house for older people is remarkably different to anything we might have expected. In accordance with the findings of previous chapters, downsizing will be seen to be more about how people in this age group become younger, rather than how they become older. The focus will start with the house, but will also consider how people divest from possessions more generally. Relinquishing possessions turns out to be another way in which older people re-align their values with those of younger people.

Housing is perhaps the single most overt material symbol of how Ireland has grown from poverty to relative wealth as, unsurprisingly, the family-occupied household remains the standard of a good quality of life. Most Irish people are familiar with the claim that Ireland has a high proportion of homeowners compared to other European countries (Figs 7.1a and 7.1b).

Figures 7.1a and 7.1b   Two typical Irish streetscapes. Photos by
Pauline Garvey.

There is no single reason for this. One significant factor is the state's prioritisation of housing as a form of distributive welfare for much of the twentieth century.[2] Instead of emphasising health, or even education, to the same degree as neighbouring countries, the Irish state prioritised helping people to buy houses. Home ownership rose steadily, peaking in 1991. However, the last census shows that the number of owner-occupied households fell following the economic crash of 2008, with the overall homeownership rate dropping to 67.6 per cent,[3] a level last seen in 1971. The 'housing crisis' was one of the most prominent issues in the general elections of 2016 and 2020; here, as elsewhere, it concerns the unaffordability of housing for young people, for many of whom property ownership is far out of reach.[4]

One result has been a perhaps inevitable clash of perceptions about the consequences of ageing. Government initiatives may seek to encourage older people to downsize in order to release housing to the young, but older people regard their homes as an achievement signifying their struggle out of poverty and now their futureproofing, a tangible pension in bricks and mortar. Our starting point was a recognition that many of our research participants treated with scorn the government blandishments aimed at persuading them that releasing their properties contributed to the common good. As one respondent observed, no 40-year-old would expect to have diminished rights to a large house just because others also need one.

Alternatives to residential care

One way in which the state has tried to tackle institutional care for older people is by first acknowledging the general antipathy that exists towards care homes. Research participants confirmed that for many the greatest fear is not downsizing but being moved into a 'home' – meaning residential care, which they associate with a complete lack of autonomy. When respondents spoke about death, they invariably said they hoped to die at home and never have to enter a care home. One woman called them 'prisons'. A Thornhill GP confirmed this widespread fear:

> You'd have to drag them kicking and screaming out of their home. They won't tell you they are sick almost. They won't go to hospital and the idea of a nursing home is anathema to almost 100 per cent of the population. Something must be done about it.

Several housing initiatives have been suggested in recent years. During the period of our fieldwork Eoghan Murphy, Minister for Housing, suggested working with the Department of Health to encourage homeowners in care homes to lease out their vacant houses. The measure was met with concerns from organisations such as Alone and Age Action Ireland on the basis that older people should not feel obligated into leaving or selling their home. Other government-led initiatives included setting up a website to identify vacant houses, taxing second homes, subdividing houses in what is popularly called the 'granny flat grant'[5] and remodelling houses to allow people to live on different levels. Notably, at the end of February 2019, a report was launched that advocated the building of specific types of housing to house Ireland's ageing population. This report, *Housing Options for our Ageing Population: Policy statement*, points out that ageing represents a significant demographic problem. By 2030 those aged 65 and over will number one in six of the population, while the number of people aged over 85 will have doubled. It points out that 85 per cent of people say they wish to stay living in their home. The majority also wished to remain within their own communities and maintain existing important relationships, indicating that staying in a familiar location is just as important as staying in the family home.

Central to current thinking, the report notes, is the creation of a spectrum of specialist accommodation. This would start with building ordinary homes in which people remain autonomous, but which have additional medical and security features. Other housing schemes could then incorporate additional medical and security features, but only as required by a deterioration in the condition of residents.

All of this seems sensible with respect to future planning. However, despite the upbeat tone of this report and the argument that people are willing and interested in downsizing given the right conditions, it contrasts with the reality, according to estate agents in Thornhill. One agent suggested that the current emphasis on downsizing, retirement villages, sheltered accommodation and dividing homes into upper- and ground-floor apartments to rent unused space is completely unrealisable. This is particularly true as at present developers are given carte blanche to build the type of units they prefer, with no active intervention from planning authorities that might have designated some land for low-rise small houses more suited to an ageing population. In conclusion, although initiatives for 'smart ageing housing' recommend a gradual transition[6] allowing maximum autonomy for as long as possible,[7] the feasibility of implementing this seems remote. Finding empty sites for building these specialist accommodations is difficult and expensive, and siting them far from present communities sunders people from friends and amenities.

A further problem is the under-provision of social housing in Ireland, especially since the economic downturn. This is particularly the case in Cuan and Thornhill, both primarily middle-class residential locations. Most people living there would be ineligible for such housing, little as there is. In response, and in typical Cuan style, a self-generated movement called the Cuan Sheltered Housing Committee published a 48-page survey in 1999 to make the case for a private sheltered housing project. In 2018 Danny observed a public meeting held because the committee felt it did not have the requisite expertise in law and finance. The meeting successfully recruited both legal advisors and two individuals who had previously been chief financial officers, one for a housing project. Yet none of this resolves the problem of the lack of suitable sites for such a scheme around Cuan.

Meanwhile, the local Age-Friendly committee encourages soft-infrastructural solutions which help people stay in their own homes. These may include a toilet and bedroom on the ground floor, non-slip floor surfaces, outside lights, alarms, storage for mobility aids, chairlifts, intercom, bathroom aids and adaptations and ramps. The Age-Friendly committee has been particularly successful in altering pavements to make them suitable for electric mobility scooters and to offer step-free access. It is very common to see these mobility scooters on the streets of Cuan. Government policy supports an aim to help individuals futureproof housing in Ireland so that both residents of private and social housing have more options (including home-sharing or house-splitting) as they age.[8]

Not downsizing

A common thread running through initiatives for step-down housing for older people is the expectation that this implies downsizing. The term downsizing refers to the assumption that when people are older and their children have left home they will move to a smaller residence which will be more appropriate to their needs. In Ireland downsizing is a common and colloquial term. The far less familiar term 'rightsizing' was recently coined to challenge this assumption – a perspective supported by a recent report from the UK which suggests that most moves in the UK by the over-55s are to four-bedroom properties.[9] One-third of respondents had 'upsized' to larger properties and around half had put more money into this move, rather than releasing equity. These observations are all far removed from the general assumption that people would downsize at this stage in life.

In Dublin too we found that people often consider downsizing but rarely act on it.[10] Hunters, a Dublin estate agency, produced a booklet in 2017 called *A First Time Sellers' Guide,* recognising that most people had never actually sold a house and were daunted by the task. Hunters found that many older couples or singletons found themselves stuck after the economic crash. Only in recent years have they been able to realise the equity in their properties, thus making a move more financially viable now than at any time in the previous decade.

For all these reasons, our evidence suggests that the travails of young people in struggling to purchase properties are not, as yet, having a noticeable impact upon the actions of older people. According to solicitors we interviewed, there was no evidence for younger people trying to promote downsizing in order to release their parents' equity, probably because they would have got short shrift from those parents. One Thornhill resident described her resentment at being pressurised when 'there are plenty of 40-year-olds in four-bedroom houses and nobody has said a word to them'. She continued:

> I inherited this house and paid for its upkeep from my wages since I started working fifty years ago. Now the boys [meaning government ministers] are talking of taking my first floor?

In an echo of the complaint above, another resident pointed out that 'no one expects a singleton in her thirties living in a three-bedroom house to downsize, so why should I?'

So, although it is very common for participants at least to consider downsizing to help adult children secure family homes, we did not generally find these impulses were acted upon. A research participant called Claire, now settled in Thornhill, considered selling to release equity for their children, but her solicitor advised against it. Age is often accompanied by higher medical or care costs; holding on to a valuable asset, such as the family home, would give her and her husband greater financial security. On reflection, the couple agreed. In another example Kate, a participant in her mid-seventies, noted that she considered downsizing because her son and his family moved away from the area last year to live more cheaply in the west of Ireland. He now travels to Dublin on Sunday evenings and stays with her until Friday, when he returns to his family. Kate is worried about him and feels the loss of her grandchildren's company. She joined an Active Retirement group and talked with her husband about how they could help their son financially. Downsizing was their initial consideration, but that posed its own problems: 'What would we do? Gerry lives with us, and what would we do with all our stuff? He is lonely and we have our own routine…'.

Meanwhile Joanne and Arthur, in their late seventies and eighties respectively, say that they think about downsizing 'constantly'. Living in a large detached house in the centre of Thornhill, a home they share with their 48-year-old unmarried son, they realise that they do not need so much space, but cannot think of an alternative suitable arrangement.

So although we found that many participants considered downsizing in order to help offspring, in general they had not acted upon their concerns. There is further evidence from Cuan. At one end of the town is the Brittas estate, which is typical of new housing estates. The houses cost around €350,000 for a three-bedroom property and €450,000 for a four-bedroom one. Although officially mortgages are supposed to be restricted to 80 per cent, there are various ways to secure a 90 per cent mortgage. An interview with the individual who does much of the property conveyancing for this estate indicated that young families are struggling to pay deposits of around €30–40,000. This suggests that they are not getting sufficient financial support from parents – even supposing the latter are in a position to help. During fieldwork, Prime Minister Leo Varadkar came under fire in the media for suggesting that first-time buyers should get their house deposits from their parents, as well as through more conventional routes such as working or staying at home until they have raised sufficient funds.[11] Families were larger until relatively recently; financial help for multiple adult children trying to buy houses would be prohibitively expensive, even if the desire is there. According to a TILDA survey,[12] several participants mentioned that they would like to help adult children financially while they are alive, but this support may be limited in practice; our participants are also quite keen to keep their money for themselves and their future. They envisage not only future holidays, or even buying property abroad, but also, importantly, keeping a reserve for medical expenses and general strategies of 'futureproofing'.

In conversations, participants sometimes speak of state taxation as another reason for not being able to assist their children, i.e. that they [the parents] should spend their money while they can, since otherwise the state will take it in tax.[13] People also cite the tax implications of the Irish state's 'fair-deal' system, in which a proportion of assets is taken by the state to pay for residential care for the elderly – although sometimes people talk about it as if the state was going to take it all. Given that these conversations somewhat exaggerate the effects of policies such as fair-deal, this may be in part a legitimation for their retaining their assets. Finally, many of their children are now in a vastly better financial position than their parents would have been at that age.

Other factors also mitigate against downsizing. Many (though by no means all) people retain a strong sentimental bond with homes that they have owned for a long time, often where their children were brought up. Gertie reminisced that, even though her memory of her own parents' house was that living there was horrendous, she still felt a great sense of loss when it was sold. Older people also see large houses as still required because children and grandchildren come to stay. Their families may now live abroad; when they come to visit, they expect to stay in the family home. So even if it is only occasionally that the house is full, at Christmas or St Patrick's Day or similar holidays (and people acknowledge that it is only two or three times a year), they would not want their families to have to stay in a hotel. Furthermore, in Cuan, unlike Thornhill, there are no real hotels; even with the rise of Airbnb, it is a very difficult place to find accommodation when visiting. Some older people still have elderly parents to look after and may convert their children's bedrooms into granny flats for their parents. Many families also report 'boomerang children' who they thought had left home for good but who, owing to changes in life circumstance, choose to return to the parental home. For example, a couple in their seventies are currently preparing their home, since a married daughter with a husband and two children is about to move back in. The agreement is that they will stay for two years in order to have saved enough to buy their own property locally. This event has occurred 12 years after the parents thought the last child had left home.

The Cuan estate agents note the pent-up demand for two-bedroom homes (less for one-bedroom), but this is predominantly from outsiders wishing to retire to this seaside location. Concerning local people, the estate agents note that, at best, downsizing means moving from a four-bedroom to a three-bedroom property, in places such as Brittas estate. Quite a few of the properties there have been purchased for retirement by people such as Ciara, who notes that three other retirees from Cuan live within a few houses from her own. People talk about bungalows, but on the new estates these are very expensive and poor value. From the builder's perspective, they take up an unprofitable amount of land compared to a three-storey house. If anything would tempt people to move from Cuan, it would be the prospect of a very large garden, but it would need to be a similar seaside resort such as Dungarvan in the south or Kerry in the west. As we can see, the discussion of downsizing refers almost entirely to privately-owned housing, which dominates our fieldsites. There is a cluster of social housing in Cuan, but these houses are quite homogenous, conforming to the two-up, two-down standard common in Irish towns. There is consequently little prospect for people to downsize within social housing if they are to stay within Cuan.

Downsizing

Notwithstanding all the factors just mentioned, there is certainly some downsizing that would accord with traditional ideas of this trajectory and its causes. This film introduces this topic from the perspective of both the estate agents and one specific individual (Fig. 7.2).

Not surprisingly, in times of illness, frailty or bereavement, the prospect of downsizing becomes more urgent and several people spoke of downsizing when they found themselves living alone. Mary, in her seventies, for example, downsized after her divorce. She suffers from bowel problems as a result of previous cancer and is very aware of the worries that beset her adult son and daughter if they cannot contact her. She owned a large three-storey house some miles away which she sold to order to purchase a two-bedroom/two-bathroom apartment close to her adult daughter.

> Definitely, I went through everything: sickness, falling, arthritis. The arthritis is stalled, but they are not going to fix me and my house didn't have a downstairs toilet and I have bowel problems, so I couldn't wait to run upstairs.

Figure 7.2 Film: *Downsizing*. Available at http://bit.ly/_downsizing.

There is a further striking dimension to this movement. Many female research participants pointed to their mothers, who had little opportunity to venture out. As with Mary, steps to downsize are coloured by the experience of a deceased mother who aged prematurely due to her inability to move beyond the confines of house and family. As an alternative to the gradual decline that she observed with her mother, she regards the sale of her large house in favour of a new apartment as 'taking control' of her health and preparing for the future. She now lives close to her daughter and can enjoy the benefits of her proximity to the city and Thornhill's amenities. For others, it is often a dramatic change in their circumstances that precipitates their move. For example, some participants consider downsizing when partners become ill or die, with the subsequent experience of living alone becoming a catalyst for action. One woman, aged 63, said she would love to live in Thornhill forever, but that given the cost of housing it is just not worth it.

> Well, not when Mark is alive, I mean not any time soon. I wouldn't move out and let them have my house. But I'm thinking later in life I'd love to move into a small cosy house…

Another example, Cora, in her late seventies, downsized some time after her husband died.

> Jim died in 2006, and I stayed for five years on my own, coping with travelling and big gardens and was perfectly capable, but after five years I was 70 years old and I decided I'll be out of here by 71 and took steps. My eldest girls helped me get it ready and I sold that house in 2011. As my second daughter had married and lived (locally) I looked for a place around here and I got a three-bedroom house in a new building complex. There are 16 townhouses there as well as apartments. It was a dream home for me to buy that and still have money to enjoy myself and not be left alone. I'm near daughters but it was perfect not being too close – you can see too much of people too, although I can help out a bit with the children. I have very good friends around here from the Irish Countrywomen's Association and you know people from all over the country. I know people around here and I love the sea and golf. I walk my daughter's dog every day and it suits me perfectly.

The concept of downsizing is generally linked to the need for smaller properties as a response to frailty or, as just noted, the death of a partner.

However, the ethnographic findings suggested that when people in this age bracket moved house it was mostly for rather different reasons. A functional reason might be matched with the sense of the move as expressing a shift in values. According to the estate agents we spoke to, the primary motivation for moving is that a typical four-bedroom home occupied for several decades now requires all sorts of modernisation, has poor insulation and is expensive to upkeep. As a result, people in this age bracket seek out new-builds, which are compact and cheap to run. These are still pretty large, three-bedroom houses designed for families. A wealthy couple built a gorgeous two-storey property overlooking the sea as their ideal retirement project, then self-published a book showing the design and building of their house.

Moving to a more modern house may start as a functional imperative, but then comes to express new sensibilities. Maria, aged 80, was brought up on a working farm and laughs when she listens to radio programmes today discussing a return to self-sufficiency: that had been pretty much all she had. It was a time before electricity was normal in such farmsteads. She married an accountant and they had four children (and now ten grandchildren). The family came to Cuan in 1975, where they bought a lovely, five-bedroom house next to the sea with an extensive garden. They were among the first newcomers, referred to as 'blow-ins', to a town of only 2,800.

Even after her husband died, Maria would have liked to have kept her house or had her children live there, but she realised that she could not in this way be fair to all four children. She thus looked within Cuan for nearly a year, but simply could not find anywhere suitable. 'I didn't think for a heartbeat that I would leave Cuan,' Maria admits. She then bought a house further into the town for €500,000, having obtained a good deal more for her previous house. The additional assets were given to her children, reflecting her belief that 'It is better to give with a warm hand than with a cold hand' (i.e. while one is still alive).

The house that Maria purchased is now occupied by one of her sons with his family, while she built herself a bungalow in the garden to a carefully worked design in which she was very involved. Her daughter-in-law managed the building project. Maria's kitchen overlooks the remaining garden.[14] Her design carefully allocated places for things that spoke to her memories from the farm and her previous house, such as a large grandfather clock and a cabinet for china. But these are set within what is otherwise an extremely modern and bright bungalow, decorated with paintings by herself, as well as about 50 pictures of her family. There is also a nineteenth-century painting of Cuan. She has a spare room with its own bathroom that she knows will be useful 'if I need somebody to look after me'. Maria is aware of her fortunate position: 'I know I'm lucky because not everyone could do that (i.e. afford it)'. Her bathroom has a walk-in shower and other disability aids, none of which she currently needs but she is explicit about futureproofing.

This is an extremely modern house. All the furnishing Maria actually uses is brand new, in white or bright colours, influenced by her son's minimalism. None of it is from her old house although, as noted above, retained objects and mementoes such as china, crystal or silverware have been turned into a form of symbolic decoration.[15] This turn to the modern still represents a kind of family craftsmanship; carefully designing things so that both the past and the future have been slotted in as a feature of the present. Maria's children took very little of her mass of big, heavy, dark furniture from the old house. Instead it was sold or given away as she philosophically explains:

> It wasn't that hard to part with it, because my life had changed. You fit into another sort of life.

Maria considers this to be an entirely successful downsizing, which also worked out cheaper to build than it would have been to buy. In short, this move is not about continuity; it is about finding a new modern shell for a new modern crab.

Another example appears in the film about Macrina (see Fig. 7.2, p.164). Living alone, downsizing represented an enhancement of her life rather than a curtailment of it. She also emphasised the modernity of her new apartment (Figs 7.3 and 7.4). Although Macrina has brought furniture from her childhood with her, all the pieces have been upholstered to look stylish and 'modern'.

Expanding the home to accommodate family rather than downsizing is also common in Thornhill, where a high proportion of households have adult children living with their older parents. For several research participants, this distributes the care requirements not only to partners and perhaps elderly parents but to grown-up children as well. Marion, aged 63, complained that the exorbitant prices of small houses are preventing them from downsizing; she is consequently wondering about expanding their homes by building a granny flat.

There has recently been quite a lot of discussion about cabins called *Seomra* (Irish Gaelic for 'room') or log cabins after Dublin County Council passed a motion to allow log cabins to be built in back gardens in November 2018. This was universally reported on as helping young

Figure 7.3 Macrina showing us her apartment on the day of filming. Photo by Pauline Garvey.

people save for a house deposit during a housing crisis, but some older participants were commenting on it too. They saw such structures as a way of 'futureproofing' their homes and creating a space that would be small and comfortable for them, while keeping family members close by.

Fred provides a slightly different perspective. He retired at 65 from his role as a sales manager for a car parts store. In 1981 he had bought a four-bedroom house in Cuan, where he had three children; he has now also one grandchild. Fred then purchased a two-bedroom flat for his mother-in-law so she could be near them in Cuan, with everything on the ground floor, but unfortunately she died before she could move in. An estate agent then suggested that instead of selling it, they consider moving into it themselves. Even though it is probably smaller than Fred and his wife would have chosen, the flat is entirely modern; there is no vestige of their prior furnishings or even possessions, his children having got rid of the previous stuff. The only exception was that Fred kept his motorbike, which is in their yard. No one was sentimental enough even to keep the paintings of their grandfather, who had been an artist. So once again this move signified a shift to the modern – but, unlike Mary, there is no retention or incorporation of pasts and futures.

Figure 7.4 Macrina's apartment. Photo by Pauline Garvey.

As long as people have their own houses, there are usually tasks that need doing and these may be critical to the issues of our next chapter regarding retaining a sense of life purpose. Brendan, aged 84, was a perfect example of this point. When he said that they were planning to move out of their four-bedroom house, it seemed obvious that this would be to downsize. Yet it turned out the plan was to move to another four-bedroom house further along the same road – a house that was not at all modern. It gradually transpired that the main reason for moving was that Brendan was a pretty good handyman; a member of the Men's Shed, he really liked doing up his house. Indeed, much of the interview was spent walking around his current house with him pointing out all the work he had done to modify the rooms, adding this or that facility. Meanwhile his wife had created a lovely garden. But the tasks were all finished: there was just nothing left to do. Brendan was moving house primarily to provide a new subject for his house improvement projects; aged 84, he was actively looking for new challenges rather than relinquishing them. Similarly, we assumed that older people would want to move into town, so they were closer to other people and facilities. But one of the couples had retired out to the peripheral Brittas estate, because actually what they wanted late in life was more privacy. As one of them observes:

> People don't mean any harm, but it was very hard to keep your own business. My husband hated that, he didn't like people being intrusive. Pretty much we knew everybody on that road and he likes to be separate.

Looking across these various case studies, it is clear that again and again the motivations were not as we anticipated.

In addition to expanding, there are various ways in which homes are being repurposed or adapted. Examples were found of people adapting their homes to make them wheelchair-compatible, or to have a downstairs toilet and bedroom so that they can remain there as long as possible. As noted above, various organisations such as the Age-Friendly committee provide advice about such adaptations. The great advantage of a granny flat is that owners can initially secure an income from them, but later on can move into them themselves, renting out the house that they presently occupy. Such forward thinking is in recognition that the burden of costs as older people age is more likely to fall upon them.

> Who is going to pay for all these old people in future? Not the state, it can't afford to pay all those pensions, and when I go into the local supermarket I often think everyone here has hair my colour (grey).

Ellen, aged 67, likes to travel extensively. However, she recognises that to fund this she would need to dip into her pension or else rent out her house on Airbnb, emulating her neighbour.

Not everyone is so sanguine about the prospect of change. For example, Emma, now in her late fifties, says it is 'just wonderful' that her adult daughter and grandchild are living with them and that they all get on really well. They circulate pictures at Christmas of Ellen, her husband and grandchild all in the same pyjamas and sitting in front of the Christmas tree. But occasionally, she wonders about the long-term viability of this situation and speculates on when she and her husband might move into some comfortable cabin in the garden if they become too frail to climb stairs. Yet at other times Ellen jokes that she cannot really imagine being in a 'shed in the garden', looking up at her children occupying her home.

To conclude, the very term 'downsizing' turns out to be something of a presumption. It is now clear why the alternative term 'rightsizing' is currently gaining traction. The state is largely concerned with an entirely different set of issues, those suffering from ill-health or frailty or those in social housing. The state is responding to the need for sheltered accommodation rather than nursing homes or helping people stay in their own homes. Yet such a focus leaves out most older people, who are either not at all frail or are middle class and ineligible for state support. Consistent with the other findings of this book, people from their fifties to their nineties are bracketing off frailty as that which necessitates such changes in accommodation. Until that happens, if they are moving house, they want to see this as something other than simply a trajectory towards ageing. Instead, they are more concerned to use it as an opportunity to become more modern and to find an appropriate setting for the life they hope to continue to enjoy while in reasonably good health.

Divestment and decluttering

The previous section suggested that the key imperative for downsizing is to find not a smaller home, but one that is modern and easier to manage. This preference is not just about the building, but also reflects a change in attitude to possessions. The development of a family home has usually meant a massive accumulation of things. Homeowners may be reluctant to remove the possessions of their children if they think there is some chance the children will return, or they may be able to reuse books and toys for grandchildren. Also, until recently, possession of a large, full house may have been something of a status symbol. By contrast, today they are more likely to hear their friends talking about downsizing in terms of relief at having got rid of all that stuff from the past. They appreciate that an alternative to downsizing is simply to stay where they are and instead take on the project of decluttering. It is partly the same logic, but avoids actually moving home.[16]

Women in particular talk of clearing out, tidying up and removing detritus in order not to leave clutter to their descendants. Denise complains that she can barely get into her garage because 'my brother has things there too, lots of my parents' and grandparents' things, papers and whatnot, still in boxes in the garage'. In response, she has drawn up a schedule with her niece to clear it out. It is not a job she wants to tackle alone and so together the women 'will have a go'. As she explains:

> I bring my niece swimming on Tuesday so she has promised … an hour a week to go through the garage and clear the attic.

Denise still has her retirement gifts, which she keeps in a cupboard because she does not know what to do with them (Fig. 7.5). She continues to make ambitious plans to:

> go through the garage and work up to the attic. The bureau there is all that I kept of furniture … I have some dishes that belonged to my mother. I don't know why I bother with crystal glass as the next generation of nieces and nephews will inherit all this, but they don't want crystal.

Figure 7.5 Gifts given to Denise on her retirement that sit untouched in her cupboard. Photo by Pauline Garvey.

When Denise's neighbour died, she recounted how his wife cleared out his clothes on her own. This had saddened her when she found out, appreciating that it must have been 'really hard to do tackle his clothes, she should have got someone to do it with her'. Later the neighbour realised she should have asked her nephews and nieces whether they wanted anything. At the time it had not occurred to her to ask, but then she realised she could have given them his silk ties.

According to professional declutterer Lorraine, who works with estate agents in the Dublin region, more and more Irish people are decluttering their homes in their advanced years. To explain this, she drew similarities with a Swedish practice called 'death cleaning', which describes cleaning out one's home and putting things in order in anticipation of death. For example, she had worked with an engineer who decided to move into a care home after his wife died because he was lonely. Having saved wires and cables over a lifetime of work, his house was full of electrical items that he had thought might come in handy sometime and he needed help to remove them all. Another of Lorraine's clients was the woman who called her in to help clear the bags of possessions that were clogging up her living rooms and living spaces, so that she was too ashamed to invite people in for coffee. After spending a week clearing out the older woman was delighted; she hosted a book club, the first one in years, because the burdensome weight of insignificant possessions had been lifted. Yet as Lorraine talked through her examples, it seemed clear that what was being described was not death cleansing for the benefit of family members after they have died. Instead, it was a case of people taking action to enhance their daily lives for the present.

Two more of our participants, Ciara and Brian, say they would like to turn the house upside down and throw away everything that falls. Another woman from Thornhill said she had bought a book on decluttering, only to realise that she had lost it in the clutter.

The sociologist Anthony Giddens has written about the way people, from time to time, reconstruct the primary narrative they tell other people and themselves about their lives.[17] Certain events tend to drop out of these narratives after a while to make way for more recent ones. The anthropologist Jean-Sebastian Marcoux showed how this also applies to moving house through his ethnography of house-moving in Montreal, which examined how people make choices about what to take with them and what to leave behind.[18] It is another way of bringing their biography up to date, keeping objects that relate to more recent memories and discarding those connected to events and people that had faded in significance. When older people downsize or declutter they may also unravel certain aspects of themselves – distributing some items to certain family members, but also reconfiguring the material foundations of their lives so that they can be freer to develop new interests and ambitions.

Several participants had parallel ambitions with regard to their social connections. They had realised that there were long-term friends and more extended family with whom they had felt obliged to meet at intervals and talk about nothing much, because they long ago had ceased to have much in common or to be interested in each other. At this point in their lives they felt free to divest themselves also of such social 'clutter' and concentrate only on the relationships they really cared about.

Decluttering from things and people is also seen as a way of putting things in order. As James, aged 62, noted:

> It's the tidying up, getting your affairs in order, knowing where things are, not having to rummage for papers, basically creating order where there wasn't order before. If I dropped dead in the morning, they would have to unravel a few balls of twine to figure things out.

For many of these people, hoarding practices are also now being challenged by new environmentalist ethics in which frugality is a virtue rather than a necessity. James talked with pride about how he just had one good working pair of shoes, rather than 20. Older people are well aware that they are living through a radical change in the way people relate to possessions that reflects the growth of ecological concerns. They may be involved in movements such as Tidy Towns, where the emphasis is now shifting from simply making the town look pretty to being in the vanguard of new environmental initiatives. Many of those involved in such movements are retirees.

As they increasingly identify with the general rise in green values, older people feel a growing antipathy to their accumulation of possessions. Where once possessions might have represented status and a cause of envy, they look down on neighbours who seem to need a new kitchen every few years as vulgar materialists. Now status and indeed personal pride often lies in abstention and buying organic or fair-trade goods, and in voting Green.[19] Older people may feel a responsibility to the young to demonstrate their concern with climate change and the future of the planet. As a result, a process such as the divestment of possessions, which might seem inevitably orientated to the reduction and selection of stuff in order to manage continuities, is actually being hijacked by another trend towards a modernity best expressed by new environmental goals. As James noted:

> I am not materialistic, but then I would recycle and I don't like people who abuse resources and I don't like that. I am learning to throw things out, the house is not cluttered but I have attics with things in them, stuff that I got, and slowly and surely I am getting rid of stuff.

For other older people there was a direct link between these new environmental ideals and an ethic of frugality that they were brought up with as children. The same goals accord well with the movement to homes that are easier to maintain, since the householder can equally well claim that they are more energy-efficient. Decluttering here is part of a much wider context in which older people may be in the foreground of environmental initiatives ranging from allotments to keeping bees, protecting trees or complaining about waste.

Environmentalism is an area of ideology in which older people can even claim they are surpassing the younger generation in their adherence to this new modern outlook on life. As already noted, for many householders the problem is not so much getting rid of their things, but the fact that their children insist on using their parental home for continued storage of the things they used as children. Such objects are regarded as treasured, but not sufficiently to take them into their own crowded homes. Younger families may vote Green and have the same commitments, but they are almost inevitably accumulating possessions at this stage in their lives rather than relinquishing them, especially if they have children. It is therefore the older generation who can claim to be living more in accordance with this new ethic and expressive virtue.

Conclusion

For a book titled 'Ageing with Smartphones', there is a noticeable absence from this chapter: a discussion of the smartphone itself. But having a chapter about a different set of material objects helps to put the basic relationship between ageing and smartphones in perspective. The smartphone looms extremely large in the lives of older people today despite its small size: it has become a genuine complement to the house. In our comparative book *The Global Smartphone*, one of our primary theories for what the smartphone has become is called the 'Transportal Home' (chapter 9). Instead of viewing the smartphone as something external to the person, it is understood more as a place in which we live. Even when sitting with other people, we zone out from the proximate world and return to this other home, without having to move physically. Similarly, the smartphone acts as a kind of portal allowing us to visit other people or places from our Transportal Home. People talk about tidying and decluttering their smartphones as though they signify domestic space. Often they organise them into a series of 'rooms' or areas where they can play games, read the papers, do their homework or watch television.

From the perspective of this volume, however, the key distinction is that the house was already there, while the smartphone is new. The smartphone acts as a catalyst in helping older people to embrace a new modern life previously associated only with the young. But that does not make it the cause of this aspiration. The evidence from this chapter shows how older people can equally foist their new values upon one of their most established possessions – their house.

Previously, the primary image of downsizing was one of descent. Once they have reached the high point of life in the size and scale of the family home, there then came an acknowledgement that the rest of life's trajectory was to be a relinquishing downwards that marked a road to final oblivion. The main issue was often caused by having accumulated possessions signifying all those experiences and relationships accrued over a long life. Now many of them would have to be let go, as they no longer fitted the spaces of this reduced world as one moved to a more appropriate small dwelling. In those days this process of divestment might more likely have been seen as a sad and difficult parting from one's own history, a process that reduces the person. As people age, it is expected that their material footprint will shrink alongside their ambitions and, eventually, their physique.

It is these prior expectations that make the findings of this chapter so significant. While this traditional form of downsizing exists, mostly these research participants have moved 180 degrees to make a change in housing expressive of quite the opposite sentiment. It has become a sign, parallel to that of the smartphone, which enables them to transform their external environment, modifying their situation to catch up with the person they are now becoming. It is the house that got old, not them.

With their renewed self-confidence and ability to exploit their retirement, much assisted by the smartphone, older people willingly dispense with the memorabilia, or create a special kind of museum space or mantlepiece to mark the symbolic space of the old. In all other respects they move to homes whose primary feature is that they are modern, efficient and easier to manage. Even the facilities they add in case of future frailty are bright, white, modern accoutrements that will help to sustain them in these homes.

Similarly, by linking divestment to the most contemporary of ideals, the Green ideology of anti-materialism, they can leapfrog the young, whose needs require continued accumulation and who are less able to manifest this commitment symbolically through getting rid of stuff. The same may apply to rethinking social relationships, both those of obligation (such as kinship) and those of choice (such as friendship). This transformation may not appear positive to their children, since those more traditional obligations may have included a greater willingness to sacrifice their own interests on behalf of their children and grandchildren. Today our participants are thinking more about their own future and potential medical costs, holidays they are planning and the prospect of giving things directly to their grandchildren. As a result of their continued aspirations, often combined with a decision not to downsize, the generation below them are struggling. The alignment with Green ideals may also correspond to the distinctions of social class, giving status to those who can afford to divest themselves of possessions and thereby denigrating those still in need of accumulating possessions.

From the perspective of older, middle-class people, the divestment they make is from what is now seen as the oppressive burden of stuff and people that tie them down towards a material world. Such a trajectory is better aligned with the freedoms that they now enjoy. Of course, there are many variations, many exceptions to all these conclusions, which inevitably overgeneralise. Yet it is still worth noting that in the main, downsizing has shifted from being a major component of growing old to a useful instrument in becoming young. Along with seizing upon the youth connections of the smartphone as their Transportal Home, the traditional home has been repurposed from an expression of ageing to the opposite. There will be a further twist to this story, which will be explored in the next two chapters: the way in which the term 'sustainability' manages simultaneously to convey this new sense of obligation, both to themselves and to the world at large.

Notes

1. Garvey 2018a, Miller 2001, Miller 2008.
2. A point supported by UCD professor of social policy Michelle Norris. Large-scale housing programmes also provided local authority homes to low earners, who were encouraged to buy long before the idea caught on in other countries. See Norris 2020 and Norris 2017, 37–59.
3. Total public funding for new council housing fell by 94 per cent between 2008 and 2013. See Norris and Hayden 2018.
4. The second half of the 2010s saw growing numbers of new homes built, year on year, from a low of fewer than 5,000 completions in 2013 to more than 20,000 homes in 2019. However, the vast majority of those homes – almost 90 per cent – were either estate housing for sale or one-off housing. Some commentators argue that what is needed is replacing the standard expectation of semi-detached homes with back gardens with more European-type high-density apartment living, which would particularly suit smaller households and downsizers. See Lyons 2020 and Lyons 2017.
5. The 'granny-flat grant' was among the proposals for the Irish budget in 2018. Shane Ross, Minister for Transport, Tourism and Sport, introduced it in order to encourage older people to transform the upper floors of their houses and rent them to lodgers. See Collins 2018.
6. For example, one government proposal in late 2017 proposed to help alleviate the current housing crisis by incentivising older people in care homes to rent out their properties.
7. A useful summary of this aspiration is found in the report 'Housing for Older People: Thinking ahead'. See Amárach Research et al. 2016.
8. See Ireland Department of Health 2019.
9. This is a publication by the Housing Research and Guidance NHBC in the UK called 'Moving insights from the over-55s: What homes do they buy?' It is based on a survey of almost 1,500 homeowners who had moved between 2010 and 2015. See NHBC Foundation 2017.
10. This impression was backed up by Derek Allen from the Retirement Planning Council of Ireland (hereafter RPCI), personal communication.
11. See O'Halloran 2018 in *The Irish Times*.
12. For more information see McGarrigle et al. 2017.
13. The current rate of inheritance tax in Ireland in 2020 is 33 per cent. It has been this rate since December 2012. Capital Acquisitions Tax (or CAT) is a tax that is charged on money or property that is gifted to or inherited by someone. See Money Guide Ireland 2020.
14. This arrangement of having a parent live within the grounds of the children's home accords with remarks in chapter 4 about the idea of residential autonomy backed by family support. See also Gray et al. 2016, 190–1.
15. The basic principle is metonymic. A single item carefully placed within the new home stands for perhaps a whole room or period of life.
16. See Garvey 2018a, Daniels 2010.
17. Giddens 1991.
18. Marcoux 2001.
19. See, for example, Isenhour 2012 and Norgaard 2011.

8
Life purpose

An advantage of the wider Anthropology of Smartphones and Smart Ageing (ASSA) project is our comparative perspective. Asking about the meaning of life in Japan might result in a conversation around *Ikigai*, an established term that roughly translates into life purpose. Asking a question about the meaning of life in Ireland would be more likely to result in references to Monty Python. This makes it difficult both to research and discuss the issue. Simply asking people directly about the meaning or purpose of life provides little useful insight. More helpful responses can be gained by extrapolating from what people may be observed to be doing with their lives, and then situating that in the context of wider changes in Irish society.

This chapter will not then try to deal comprehensively with these issues; instead it will focus mainly on one theme. In recent decades Ireland has undergone an astonishing transformation from a country dominated by a powerful and controlling Catholic church to a largely secular society. We clearly need to understand both the legacy of Catholicism and the nature of contemporary secularism, including people's current sense of spirituality. Equally important is the rise of new commitments, suggested by what people actually spend this period of their lives doing. As documented in previous chapters, a significant element of retirement activity involves crafting their wellbeing through keeping fit, remaining healthy and taking responsibility for ensuring, as far as is possible, that they remain in good shape and independent of other people. This may superficially appear to be a shift towards individualism and materialism. On further investigation, however, such activity may also contain and continue prior religious and spiritual concerns.

The age group that we have concentrated upon has become atypical of Irish society over the last two decades, to the degree that they hold on to the religious faith and practice that most younger people have abandoned. This may, of course, be deceptive: retained practice does not necessarily indicate retained belief. The continued involvement of older people is not surprising, as Ireland held on to a strong Catholic tradition long after other countries in Western Europe became secular, with religion being a major component of the education system. At the time when our participants were born, it was very common for at least one sibling to become a nun or priest, especially in large families. The nation's continued adherence to religious faith is also a legacy of the Independence movement and the bloody civil war that followed. Éamon de Valera, the victor in these conflicts, embarked upon a programme to build an authentic Irish identity free of British colonialism, which he felt was best achieved through the reinvigoration of an Irish Catholicism largely subjugated during the colonial period.[1] The relationship to religion and its associated social conservatism then became closely entwined with Irish identity and politics.

In the most recent census, the population within the administrative area in which Cuan is situated was 77 per cent Roman Catholic. The religion with the next largest following, that of 3.7 per cent, was Orthodox Christianity, reflecting immigration from Eastern Europe; 2.8 per cent were Muslim and 2.3 per cent belonged to the Protestant Church of Ireland. Over one person in 10 (12.1 per cent) said they had no religion. In Thornhill the population was 70 per cent Roman Catholic, with 18.1 per cent professing not to adhere to any religion. Both areas are more secular than would be the case in rural regions far from Dublin.[2] Actual religious practice is another matter. Young people may be actively associated with the church until they take communion, but otherwise it is mainly the elderly who attend mass today.

If Ireland was unusual among European countries in its wide adherence to religious faith, it was also unusual in the rapidity of subsequent secularisation. An important factor was the trauma of sex scandals and clerical abuse, which emerged chiefly during the 1990s.[3] Scandals involving the neglect of women and children given over to church-run orphanages and industrial schools caused irreparable damage to the authority of religious orders. Even those with faith observe the subsequent lack of religiosity among the young and see themselves as perhaps the last generation to practise their beliefs regularly. The overwhelmingly liberal ethos today is evident from the numbers of people who voted for the repeal of legislation that had restricted abortion in 1983 – 74 per cent for the Thornhill region and 72 per cent for the Cuan region respectively.[4] Sociologist Tom Inglis, among others, has written extensively on these changes and considers what they imply for more profound shifts in Irish society.[5]

Yet the religious infrastructure remains in various, less obvious ways. In Thornhill this includes the architecture – not only the church itself and the community centres, but also the large local nursing home run by religious orders. These form a kind of scaffold upon which many community activities are built. The Catholic and Protestant churches run the local primary and secondary schools; up until the period of this fieldwork, their policies privileged children of their respective religion. Since these religious schools are well regarded academically and parents are anxious to get their children into them, the parish boundary has proved an important factor in choosing where to live, with estate agents tracking a continual rise in house prices. One woman claimed she had her 4-year-old christened in the Church of Ireland 'at the last minute' when she was refused a place at the local Catholic school. These admission policies caused a good deal of anger from disappointed parents, and in 2018 Richard Bruton, the Minister for Education, signed an order to outlaw the use of religion as a criterion for primary school admissions in all but some minority religions.

The churches in Thornhill also have active parish centres. One of these runs a Meals on Wheels scheme, a large Active Retirement group catering to about 70 people (mostly women), a crèche, an art class, a dance class for seniors and ballet for children, language lessons for children and band practice for folk music on Saturday evenings. It is the venue for Christmas parties for the parents of these children and has a large notice board, making it the 'go-to' place to find out what is happening. Visitors to the centre also spill out into the café across the road, and occasionally the large Catholic church, making the three buildings something of a nodal point to meet friends and get involved in local activities, not necessarily with any religious aspect. There are few other public spaces to meet, in fact, except for cafés, eateries or the park. The equivalent activities in Cuan are not associated with the church.

For all its continued institutional involvement, attitudes to Catholicism have markedly changed. One male participant, aged 72, sums the mood up well.

They're the questions which people are struggling with all the time. Certainly now, with the fall of the Catholic church in Ireland, people are wondering how we do it – it bound us together for so long. We always had that commonality, but now we don't have it. We still like to do the rituals, the weddings, the funerals and all the rest of it, but it's only the gathering together which makes sense. We like to do that and it's a need to do that on those occasions. But umm… the Catholic church – Christ, they've done so much damage no one will have anything to do with them now.

On various occasions, individuals in Cuan made statements that were variants upon the theme that they were born Catholic but, as a result of the church's self-destruction through scandal and abuse, they felt themselves now free to become Christian. The implication seemed to be that Christianity stood for a core ethical commitment that had been released from the constraints of a religion more concerned with obedience and authority. The same sentiment is echoed within the Catholic church itself, with services now placing far less emphasis upon sin, guilt or church authority. Instead, the focus is on ethical benevolence and concern for others. Some retain strong feelings regarding the perceived authoritarianism of their upbringing; one Thornhill man described the Ireland of his youth as 'Taliban without the sunshine'. He and his wife brought up their own children as atheists, but found that even non-practising neighbours and friends were 'quite disapproving' of this decision.

Of course, there is a spectrum. Around 27 per cent of those in our two fieldsites voted against introducing abortion legislation in Ireland, many of whom are likely to be in our research participants' age group. In Cuan there are a group of fervent Catholic Charismatics who hold weekly services, while another equally fervent group have joined a Pentecostal church that meets in a school. For these groups life purpose is almost entirely the task of carrying out God's will to the letter, as they understand it.

More typical of older people would be Lilian, aged 78. She still goes to mass about five times a week and describes religion as being 'fairly important' to her. She goes on to explain:

I wouldn't be as religious as some people, but I'd be lost without it, to be honest. While I wouldn't say, I spend a lot of time thinking about it. I think I believe in the afterlife, but I don't know.

Maeve is an example of someone who might claim they no longer follow or believe in the faith of their youth, but for whom it is very much present in practice. For Maeve, religion is invested in everyday life:

> It's knowing that something else exists. I know about angels, I'm aware, 'cos they've answered my prayers so many times. And I do say the rosary ... every time I said the rosary, it worked... I gotta say the rosary to find my bloody bank card.

While others might not focus so much on institutional religion, they might still pray to St Anthony for help in finding lost property or St Jude for lost causes. Yet others ask for advice on WhatsApp in a tongue-in-cheek way, for example about where it would be best to situate the Child of Prague religious statue in their garden for maximum spiritual efficacy. Several participants describe themselves as practising Catholics but are noncommital about how close their beliefs lie to church teaching. Fiona goes to mass every week, for example, but says this has little to do with institutional religion; others echo this sentiment. While most people talk about going to mass in their youth as something basic and compulsory, some were brought up in a secular way even then; they recount how, as children, they went only rarely to mass and got away with that. Most of our participants not only went to mass regularly, however, but saw that education as well as social and moral values as strongly imbued with religion.

There are some research participants for whom this claim to have finally become a Christian is of great importance. Bernice, for example, was born into poverty in a very deprived part of Dublin. Her father was well-read and his negative experience of Christian Brothers schooling had led him to atheism and seeing religion as superstition. Unfortunately he was also a gambler, while her mother was an alcoholic. Even without being religious herself, Bernice recalls a pervasive sense of religion as fear, as sin and as hell. She used to have nightmares about Christ being crucified, believing that she could really feel the suffering. This sense of guilt and sin became particularly strong when, aged 22, she had a child with a Protestant man out of wedlock. Bernice needed counselling, an experience that had a considerable impact upon her. Eventually she was herself able to become a counsellor, which led in turn to an interest in spirituality. She spent some time learning about left, feminist and alternative ideas; the reading of Indian gurus was particularly influential and meditation became a major part of her practice. Bernice's experience was not necessarily exceptional: by the twenty-first century many Catholics, including nuns, were also seeking a more liberal route to spirituality. At one point she went on a pilgrimage within Ireland where, as she explains:

> I put my feet in … feeling the mud and [my] toes. I got this sudden sense that we're all forgiven for all the awful things. The Jews and Indians and all the races we had persecuted. I really knew that all is well.

It was mainly through a month spent in India at spiritual retreats that Bernice finally became convinced that there was no such thing as heaven and hell. She has now escaped the fear of her youth and can instead see other possibilities around joy and peace. She recently had a meeting with 20 nuns at which they discussed the idea of a cosmic Christ. Her current beliefs mix liberation theology with Hindu ideas on cosmology with an emphasis on miracles and mindfulness. What all this has enabled is a shift from the focus upon guilt and suffering that dominated her early life to a sense of peace and reconciliation that makes her quite a joyful person today. While she was never previously a believer in traditional Catholic notions of the afterlife, such as heaven and hell, Bernice does now believe in a kind of humanist version of the afterlife.

Another example is Ava, who, over the years, has been very involved in the Church of Ireland. As was surprisingly common for people in these fieldsites, in her twenties she was into Eastern religions such as Zen Buddhism, but today she no longer sees these as necessary or helpful. She wants to help others strip away concerns with doctrine and death. In her own way Ava sees herself as reformulating the foundational tenets of Protestantism as she seeks an unmediated relationship to what really matters. She remains inspired by something that happened as a child, when she had a vision of:

> the whole world as a cosmos, a plateau full of light and peace … that underpinned everything for me in life afterwards, a light over my life that is still with me. I can only call it a deep joy that I find in things. I find it in poetry, sometimes in reading scriptures, it would come upon me.

Ava hopes that she is thereby releasing the dove of spirituality that has become buried in the detritus of institutionalised religion. She knows, from several failed attempts, how difficult it is to get people to discuss topics such as faith and spirituality directly. Relevant discussions may take place within the context of creative writing groups or walking groups, rather than necessarily within the church. For Ava, this is best done through the direct discussion of doubt. It is also evident to her that many elderly people feel under siege because of the trenchant criticism of the established churches. She suggests that many respond simply by keeping terribly busy, constantly doing small tasks within the church and engaging in wider philanthropic activities.

These examples represent different ways in which Christianity continues to have a powerful presence among many people within this age bracket. More common today, especially for younger people, would be those who now have very little connection with established religion but would claim to believe in some form of spirituality outside of Christianity. They might suggest that there has to be more to life than merely our existence as the current outcome of evolution. They appear to have retained some interest in their readings about Eastern religion that was common in the 1960s, sometimes linking this with an interest in Celtic mythology from the 1970s or 1980s. Anne believes more in spirituality than in formal religion and this is not uncommon; another of our participants talks about how she finds spirituality more in nature, or her garden, even though she calls herself a Catholic. Almost inevitably, however, any attempt to make such discussion more concrete failed. People could not give any substance or specificity to this claim to spirituality, and often feelings of spirituality seemed to emerge when participants were involved in other activities, particularly those involving nature.

The conclusion seemed to be that most people at this age no longer have a belief in any specific spiritual dimension. Rather they thought that they *ought* to have such a belief and that there *ought* to be such a dimension. Probably of more significance in practice was the point made in the last chapter about an affinity towards Green ethics and the sustainability of the planet. This is often a deep commitment for older people. One reason may be that environmental concern is something that can be turned into everyday practical activities, such as curbing materialism or recycling, as well as re-aligning older people with contemporary mores. Being founded on a powerful ethical commitment to the sustainability of the planet, such beliefs are perhaps the most successful current candidate for taking up the mantle of religious ideals, the cause where it seems most natural to see people as 'devoted'.

Among the older population, there is also another trajectory that is at least as powerful, leading towards the complete repudiation of religion. It is summarised by Terry:

On the matter of religion, like many people, I am definitely against 'organised religion' and, despite its good points, its unwitting capacity for engendering conflict and evil. Logically, it is hard to believe in a 'benevolent God'. I think that the human race should remain agnostic and devote its energies (freed up by becoming secular) to humanitarian issues. In my opinion it is highly unlikely that the human species will ever solve the huge question of how this universe arose and developed. However, I am all for continuing our efforts to try. Although I'm only guessing, I feel that very few people in this country actually believe in an 'afterlife'. I think they go along with whatever form of 'organised religion' they were brought up in, as it is convenient and comfortable to do so. The rituals around the baptising of babies, marrying ceremonies, burial rites, etc., are social occasions and life would be poorer without them. Accordingly most people, I think, are content to participate in these charades. Doubtless many people find consolation in religion. Even though they don't believe the claims that most religions make, they've almost 'conned' themselves into taking comfort from what all their friends and families seem to believe.

As Terry suggests at present, irrespective of beliefs, the Catholic church remains important in terms of life ceremonies. Several entirely secular families explained why they have agreed for their child to take Holy Communion. The pressure comes from the fact that the whole class do this together. Indeed, journalists have observed how the Irish population can overwhelmingly vote for abortion in 2018 and yet at the same time happily attend Catholic rituals such as Holy Communion for their children.[6] The Catholic church in Cuan has now brought in a secular blessing to enable non-Christians in the schools also to take part, though this may be unusual. However, the ceremony that most fully expresses the continuity in the church's social role is the funeral.

Death and funerals

There are two very evident and connected observations that pertain to our research participants – the degree to which people do go to funerals and the degree to which they do not discuss death. At the height of the Covid-19 pandemic, one frequent complaint in the national media related to the prohibition of having more than ten people attend the funerals of family members. In Ireland funerals are generally recognised to be important ritual events,[7] and many older people avidly follow death notices online. One website, RIP.ie, lists every funeral taking place on any particular day, with details of how to get there and times of associated events. People expect to go to funerals of friends, neighbours and relatives, even quite distant ones.

For example, Edward referred to the many people who 'take three days over their funerals, but don't talk about death. It is like they are dealing with it in another way'. Olive, aged 72, recalled how 'growing up in the country you had to go to all the funerals, in the same way as you had to go to mass'. Funerals tend to last a couple of days; they are preceded by a wake, often in the home, where the body is laid out for people to visit. This is followed by the 'removal', when the body is brought to the church, and finally the burial, often followed by a meal or reception in a local hotel or café. Funerals are widely seen as important moments to come together and show support for the family. The etiquette is contested; one woman in Thornhill was accused of being a 'corpse chaser' – meaning that she went to a few more funerals than her peers felt was appropriate, funerals also being associated with free meals.

It would be common for people of this age to go to at least six funerals a year. One participant finds she goes to some by default:

> Sometimes, it happens by chance – I go along with realising there's going to be a funeral at that time. It's only during the week, never on Sunday. Some are quite nice actually. Some are just awful, they go on for so long and you get so many eulogies. It's not necessary.

The same speaker also touched on the experience of her husband Paul's funeral, where she was touched by

> the number of people that came to the house. And some were lovely. One man Paul had given advice to when he was leaving college and it was a time when there were hardly any jobs. He came and just was saying so much about Paul and how that had made his life and all the things that happened because of it. People are very good that way. And I even got letters from people Paul worked with. People take their time to bother, which was incredible. I thought it would

be a very tiny funeral, but we had, I would say, a very respectable turnout. In the days beforehand, the undertaker advised to give them a set time on a set day beforehand. So we did, we had three hours on a Wednesday and he was buried on Thursday. A lot of people came. As my girls grew up here, of course, a lot of their school pals came in. They brought two lemon drizzle cakes, apple pies and things like that. I was amazed at how kind people were. The other thing I think, all that ceremony and stuff, it helps you accept the person's gone. When my mother died, I was in England and she was in India. She was dead and buried before I knew it, because communication was so bad in those days and they have to be buried straight away. I don't think I ever accepted it, not for a long, long time. And it was only when I managed to get to see her grave I sort of did. I think people here like a good funeral. Most people would turn up to a funeral even if they were second cousins. All these second cousins they'd lost touch with, the only time they meet is the funeral.

Attendance at funerals thus seems entirely compatible with avoidance of death as a topic, an issue that was introduced in chapter 6. Our participant Aideen noted that:

When I was young, we were taught that we could be certain of many things. We were certain about God and religion, certain about getting married and having children, being housewives. But one by one all our certainties have fallen like dominoes. Now all the dominoes are collapsing and all you're left with is yourself … We have tackled everything else in Ireland, we have tacked institutional religion, we have tackled sexuality, but death! Death is the last taboo. No one will talk about it, no one in the seniors' club talks about death.

Aideen had a very good friend who was a nun. They would talk about whether there is life after death and, when the nun was dying, Aideen asked her to promise that she would come back after death if it was at all possible. 'But she hasn't come back,' Aideen said with a smile. Asking one 78-year-old retiree if members of the Active Retirement group talk of death, she chuckled and said:

They think they are going to live forever, most of them. I've always been conscious I might be gone tomorrow, and I've always been conscious that death is somewhere down the line. But most of them make plans that don't involve any change of plans... I've lived a lot longer than the dearest and nearest to me. No one close to me lived as long as 78: my father died at 68 of cancer and my mother at 63 from a heart attack and my grandmother of a heart attack at 69 and my aunt of a stroke, so when I was in my sixties, all through my sixties, I felt something might happen to me: at any minute I might have a stroke or a heart attack... In my seventies they're all gone, and here I am going strong, and I don't feel old at all, well sometimes.

It is hard to gauge the impact of secularisation on our participants. Does anything need to replace religion's role in giving consolation for the inevitability of death, through promulgating a belief in the afterlife? Some imply that there could be a kind of inner being that does not die, or some form of essence that lingers. This suggests a legacy of the prior belief in the soul. By contrast, an entirely secular male notes that:

One of the advantages of getting older, I find, is that one no longer fears the prospect, for example, of death. A type of fatalism sets in, as in: 'Well, I'll probably become ill and die in my seventies – so what, I've had a good life' but, like most people, I imagine, I would be concerned about the process of dying and would hope that I would not be a burden to others. If it happens, it happens, there's nothing much I can do about it, but hopefully none of these will occur and I'll slip away peacefully in my sleep! ... Our grandchildren will probably remember us, our great-grandchildren probably won't remember us (and probably never meet us); at most they will see old photographs of us. Our great-great-grandchildren probably won't even get to see our photographs or have any interest in them. In the light of the above, I have no great interest in a legacy or being remembered – other than, hopefully, earning the regard of my family and friends.

It does not necessarily follow that modern secular people will face death in the way they claim. A woman who was an equally clear rationalist for most of her life simply could not come to terms with her descent into advanced cancer. All her conversation was about what she will do when she recovers; right until she died, she could not bring herself to acknowledge publicly that she was dying. A taxi driver noted the number of occasions when seriously ill people seem to have returned to a concern for religion. As he put it, 'there are no atheists down the foxholes' (i.e. the trenches of the First World War). He talked of a person in hospital who took communion for the first time in decades.

Most of the evidence, however, pointed in the other direction. It seemed that it was rather people in their forties and fifties who are concerned with, and afraid of, death. Those in their seventies and eighties had, speaking more generally, come to terms with the finality of a secular death. A recent development has been that the Green ideology to which participants now commonly subscribe is associated with a spiritual dimension. People who are increasingly concerned with climate change and preserving nature may also see death as the dispersion of their individual life, a process of returning more generally to a more universal life. They may investigate new forms of burial that reflect this return to nature and refer to the immortality of the atoms of which they are composed.

Generally, however, this was only a topic of conversation because of our enquiry. It was more natural for people to turn from the discussion of the meaning of death to their more pressing fears, which concerned the manner of their death and also the fear of dementia. For example, someone might say:

> The thing I would fear most is getting a stroke, being laid up in a hospital for a bad time. I would fear the way of my death. It's just that a brother-in-law of mine had a stroke and he's been lying there for two and a half years. That terrorises me.

People are very conscious of the need for living wills, in which they can state that they do not want to be resuscitated under certain conditions. They may also be concerned with their own funeral:

> I'd like to think when I'm dying, hopefully, I get the chance to have my family around. I'd like to die at home. I wouldn't like to die left in one of those funeral parlours. Probably cremated. I would like a humanist burial. My friends and family would get together, I like that idea.

The role of ethics

As religion declines as the medium for expressing life purpose, other forms of moral and ethical concern may take on that role. In this section we consider various candidates, focusing mainly on examples of ethical practice but also touching on individual activities and commitments. The spiritual dimension of environmentalism has been discussed, but this is equally often a practical commitment. During the local elections that took place during fieldwork, the Green Party did particularly well in both fieldsites. By far the largest political protest during fieldwork in Cuan was directed against cutting down trees on pavements, although an alternative voice argued that this was required in order to make pavements easier to negotiate for disability scooters. However, the latter argument was muted compared to the vociferous demand to protect the trees themselves. By far the largest civil action group is the Tidy Towns competition, which has gradually shifted from simply removing rubbish to the implementation of environmental concerns. Aspects of the Green agenda often come up in conversation, ranging from general discussions about climate change to local issues such as the availability of organic food or beekeeping. Many of the new activities have this orientation, such as a movement to try and repair household objects rather than buy new ones.

By far the most high-profile collective action in Thornhill was the mobilisation to challenge the grant of planning permission for high-density residential development on land formerly owned by a religious order and currently used as a school sports ground. The land in question was originally part of a much larger park and was surrounded by the park on three sides. After planning permission was granted for this development, the residents' association swiftly orchestrated a campaign to oppose the proposed action. Thousands of residents and local organisations such as children's sports groups met for speeches in the local hotel and marched in the park. The residents' association set up a dedicated website, as well as Facebook and Twitter accounts, and individuals volunteered their time to collect donations for the significant legal challenge that they co-ordinated. One of the main arguments put forward to justify the opposition to the housing development was the knock-on effect on flora and fauna, the loss of tranquillity and the possibility that yet more development might further encroach on the parkland, jeopardising an amenity that should be available for future generations. Children featured strongly in the marches and pictures, as if to underscore the point that green space must be conserved for their future.

Not everyone agreed with this stance. Dublin is in the midst of a severe housing crisis. In discussions with participants about the controversy, the multi-million sum made by the religious order and the original landowner was often cited as an example of the corrupting influence of greed; another concern was that the resulting houses would cater for the luxury end of the housing market, rather than providing affordable homes. The campaign created a website that focused on the history of the controversy; it followed media attention to key players and posted similar controversies current in other parts of Dublin. By focusing less on the housing crisis and more on wholesome green space versus the profits, the campaign sought to align a specific cause with the more general rise of Green ideology and politics.

A 2018 report from the TILDA study suggested that older adults in Ireland have the second-highest volunteering rate within the EU; 18 per cent of adults volunteer at least once per week and 56 per cent volunteer at least occasionally. Volunteering was highest among those aged between 65 and 74.[8] There were several routes to becoming involved in charitable activities. Some research participants regularly travel to places such as India in order to help directly as volunteers. Others assist local charities devoted to autism or youth depression or serve in a local St Vincent de Paul charity shop that helps to alleviate poverty.

In these fieldsites, it was hard to discern any clear pattern to volunteering. While some were deeply involved, others who were retired, with plenty of time and seeming to possess similarly empathic personalities, had no active involvement in volunteering. Danny had discerned a pattern in his prior UK study which showed that English people prefer to volunteer for organisations where they will not meet people whom they know.[9] In this research in Ireland it tended to be the other way around; people gave more time and attention to neighbours, their local community or Meals on Wheels in preference to a more distant institutional charity. Some older people were deeply involved in activities related to their key interests, which combine mentoring others with enjoying the social outlet that the activity represents.

Keeping active

This degree of involvement in charitable and social activities was often understood as equally beneficial to the volunteer under the more general rubric of 'keeping active'. The phrase 'keeping active' applied obviously to the task of remaining physically active and healthy, but it was more than just a physical concept. There is an equally strong concern that wellbeing depends upon keeping socially or cognitively active. Life is meaningful if life is used. This ethos incorporates the findings of chapter 3, which documented the sheer number and range of activities that contribute to the inhabitants' pride in their locality.

It was common to discuss a variety of strategies for keeping active. These are most explicitly linked to the idea of life purpose when presented through the idea of a 'bucket list', in which people explicitly enunciate the things they aim to have done before they die. Take Jacinta, for example, whom we met in chapter 5. She took early retirement from a stressful job in an IT business where she was managing a difficult, aggressive person. Her first task on retirement was to list all the things she still wants to do, which she called '55 things to do at 55' – the list that we noted on p.125 (see Fig. 5.8).

> I want to take an art class, stay in Inishmore, I want to go to San Sebastian, go to Japan in 2019, go to India – I've done that. I want to swim with dolphins – I haven't done that. Make a will – done that. Buy a bikini – for God's sake, obviously a mid-life crisis there as well, and I did buy it but never wore it; in the end I gave it to my sister. The art classes are just great. Runamuck is a cross-country obstacle course over either 7–10 km, so I haven't done it yet 'cause it's hard to get people to do it with you.

After this exhausting list, she continues to describe her activities. She explains that on retiring she immediately took up swimming lessons in a city centre swimming pool; earlier that day she had completed 64 lengths. So first she had to learn how to swim and then she set herself the task of swimming 1 km, then a mile. Her current plan is to complete a triathlon. 'So now I swim Mondays and Thursdays and I have a friend from work who is now a manager in a post office; I meet her for coffee afterwards and we shoot the breeze,' she reveals.[10]

The problem posed by making activities and staying active into a kind of life mission, or perhaps even a substitute for religious goals, is that they may develop into this kind of frenetic trajectory conveyed by Jacinta – a situation that, some participants suggested, derives from the fear of what might erupt during any inactivity. Not surprisingly, a parallel movement has developed that balances this with a focus on cultivating inactivity and allowing the body to rest; here the goal is instead the achievement of calm.

During the period of our fieldwork the dominant example was the proliferation of 'mindfulness', which took centre stage in debates over how to promote calm as an aspect of health. Mindfulness had become ubiquitous. During 2018 both the Department of Education and questions within the Irish Parliament focused on the place of mindfulness in schooling.[11] This followed the recommendation of a Joint Committee on Education & Skills that mindfulness be included in the national curriculum, a proposal that, in turn, reflected a more general shift to holistic wellbeing.[12] The state was kicking against an open door. Several teachers mentioned that they now use mindfulness at school to 'calm' their classes, and parents reported teenagers arriving from school having studied mindfulness within their class on religion. Similarly meetings of older people, sponsored by local councils, commonly included a mindfulness exercise as part of the proceedings. In one case mindfulness was sandwiched between a performance by the local ukulele group and the one act monologue comedy about the way older people are treated, delivered by Peig, whose film featured in chapter 3 (Fig. 3.2).

Increasingly these private and social activities are becoming orientated around a life purpose that comes under the umbrella term of 'wellbeing' or 'wellness'. Nowadays they are matched by an increasingly explicit concern at the level of the state and NGOs that now commonly promote this ideal of wellbeing. For example, there was the launch of the 'Healthy Ireland Framework (2013–2025)', a government-led initiative which aims to enhance the population's health.[13] In this initiative, health is presented as a public good. The tone is quite moralistic, as it suggests that the maintenance of individual health affects the quality of everybody's life experience. There is a focus on the possibilities and responsibilities for the individual in doing what they can to stay well.[14] This is why it was noted in the introduction that the shift from church authority to a focus on health and wellbeing is not necessarily a movement towards individualism. It has rather been appropriated as a social, national and moral agenda. In the 1960s spiritual wellbeing may have started as a rejection of organised religious authority, but this has gradually morphed into the concerns of the state with wellbeing more generally. Wellbeing is now also an instrument of pedagogy increasingly applied to all age groups.[15] For example, the national curriculum of primary and secondary schooling dedicates classes to social, personal and health education (SPHE). Increasing emphasis is currently placed on the health and wellbeing of children and young adults as a social and spiritual category as much as a physical one.

To conclude this section, the discussion has embraced a number of different forms of life purpose, from those more orientated towards spirituality to volunteering and philanthropic concerns and a commitment to various activities, including personal wellbeing. The linear nature of writing means we foreground first one issue and then another. This is why these two films are important (Figs 8.1 and 8.2). In both cases it is clear that one particular activity, music or photography, has become sufficiently significant that it could certainly be regarded as a major contribution to that individual's life purpose.

However, these are not simply engaging activities. In both cases they involve service to the local community, whether through teaching, performing or creating work for public consumption. They are also retirement activities that speak to earlier interests and thereby help in some sense to tie loose ends of life together, whether it was playing music when young or re-engaging with the urban landscape of one's youth. Not surprisingly, when one finds an activity playing such a prominent role it is often because it speaks to the whole range of concerns discussed in the last two sections rather than to any one in particular.

Figure 8.1 Film: *Composing, uploading and playing music in retirement.* Available at http://bit.ly/musicinretirement.

Figure 8.2 Film: *Photography in retirement: Smartphones and analogue.* Available at http://bit.ly/retirementphotography.

Walking and pilgrimage

Juxtaposing frenetic activity with mindfulness implies that most people are seeking some of kind of balance, as would also be the case in the simultaneous pursuit of the spiritual and the commitment to physical activity. Although much of this is new, the activity that seemed to have proved most effective was one of the oldest established forms of leisure – walking. Early on in research, a local estate agent described retirees as:

> the empty nesters out enjoying themselves, fit as fiddles, travelling … walking by the sea, being by the sea, the sense of freedom, no matter how small your house is, you have all that space there.

The estate agent had found that walking in parks or near the sea is a major local attraction for potential residents. This is where people are most likely to bump into others, as in the case of the Thornhill Strollers described in chapter 4.

Walkers are often quite explicit about the increasing recognition by the medical profession of the psychosomatic value of exercise in healing. 'Walking is something everyone can do and it makes you feel good to be alive,' says one retired nurse. This participant recalled how Mental Health Ireland organises walking groups for people with depression. This may be at least juxtaposed with morality and religion. Veronica, aged 56, describes having lost a friend the previous June at the age of only 48, which 'makes you think'. Although she also declares that she has 'no interest in religion', she described her walking in an almost philosophical way.

> You should use every moment, [losing someone] makes you aware that life is precious. I think it is important to stay fit and be active. I'm not as brave as I was, I broke my shoulder a couple of years ago and would be more careful about the activities I do now.

People vary considerably in the degree to which their walking is deliberately casual or has become a more rigorous and purposeful activity. While older people generally reject bespoke mHealth apps,[16] as noted in chapter 5, the exception is the step-counter. A few of the younger participants may now sport Garmins and Fitbits and more elaborate self-tracking devices. Mark, a bank executive aged 58, explains how:

> MyFitnessPal allows me to log intake of food daily basis and record exercise and I have been using it for a month. You've got to be

honest. So last Tuesday I programmed my weight and my age and weight loss goal and it gives me an allowance of calories each day. Last Tuesday I had porridge with fruit for breakfast; it gave me the calories for it and there is some link that records your steps and I cycle to work each day … and it tells me I burned 800 calories. That day I took in 2,000 calories, and it tells me how much I would weigh in five months.

Mark wants to lose weight and promote health for retirement 'so I'm around for myself and my family,' he says. He is also a keen sportsman. He cycles to work every day and he used to play hurling and football when he was younger. But when he talks about retirement, he tells us mainly about the walks with his wife in the Ox mountains in Sligo. He also has an app (Walks.ie) which tracks the different stages of the walk; his ambition is to do the complete trail, plus take a good walk each week in the Dublin and Wicklow mountains.

For me, it's just being out in fresh air and away from the desk and the city. Every day has its charms. I'm not an overly spiritual person, but when I'm up there I do feel more spiritual. I did Croagh Patrick [a pilgrimage] there a few years ago on a beautiful April day. We were looking down on Clew Bay and I got this huge spiritual feeling of really being close to something and there has to be something behind this. The Ox mountains, funnily enough, are also called St Patrick's mountains because St Patrick did pilgrimages there around.

Mark is by no means typical. Many more people just have a simple step-counter which they do not take too seriously, though our evidence suggested that people are genuinely walking more to achieve the normative 10,000 steps, seeing their dogs as a major asset in that quest.

In Mark's narrative there is simply no conflict between his emphasis upon the rational pursuit of calorie loss alongside something more spiritual. He is not alone, since the topic that brings this final discussion full circle to the concerns with which this chapter began is pilgrimage. Newspaper articles suggest that walking as pilgrimage has 'increased dramatically in the last five years in Ireland'.[17] Ireland's National Pilgrim Paths Day was launched in 2014, with the Pilgrim Passport following in 2016. Walkers can now collect stamps after completing any of the five principal paths. Knock is one of the most visited places in Ireland, attracting upwards of one million pilgrims a year, while between 25,000 and 30,000 people climb Croagh Patrick on the last Sunday of July annually. More arduous, but still attracting between 18,000 and 20,000 pilgrims annually, is the retreat at Lough Derg, in Donegal.[18]

One woman, aged 77, had been to Lough Derg 21 times; for a while she worked there as a spiritual counsellor. She felt that she had experienced a miracle on her first visit and only stopped going when she became too ill. By contrast, a man observed the current popularity of pilgrimage sites with some disdain:

> I think it's always been there, but it's become a craze and I think it's the internet. People show each other. They all want to do that. And you hear a few famous people do it. The number of people who told me they went to Lough Derg to pass their school leaving certificate, and I thought good grief. Then I read more about it. I thought I'm not going there, it's quite awful. This to me is just anathema. That wouldn't be my kind of religion.

The pilgrimage sites seem to vary in relation to how far the motivation is religious. The most religious tend to visit Međugorje, a site in Bosnia and Herzegovina, where some miraculous apparitions are claimed, though it is not fully legitimated by the Church. Many people there see it as the most efficacious of the pilgrim sites and vouch for sacred experiences, though one visitor who broke her ankle on the way down was somewhat less enthused. There are regular organised trips to the site from Cuan. Lourdes is also a reasonably common destination where some people report finding a spiritual peace that they crave, though others find the site too crowded.

For the purposes of this chapter, however, it is the Camino de Santiago which is most important. It is by far the most commonly visited site, and the one that comes up frequently in everyday discussion. Many people watched a recent BBC series on walking the Camino and it featured in the film about Deirdre in chapter 3 (Fig. 3.1). A survey of 3,000 pilgrims found that only 28 per cent of respondents walked for religious or spiritual reasons. A further 28 per cent did it for the challenge, while a further 18 per cent did it to connect with nature and escape the daily routine.[19] One of the key conclusions to this chapter is that these reasons are not in opposition to one another. There has been a growing synergy between the physicality of walking, the separation from everyday life represented by holidays, the ideal of spirituality found in a more direct engagement with nature and an overall life purpose directed at a vague but significant ideal of wellbeing.

The Camino is likely to be popular in part because northern Spain has a much warmer climate than Ireland. It also suits those who have second homes in Spain and are learning Spanish. Much of the discussion of the Camino is around the physical challenge of the walk, which can be quite intense, though ending each evening in good food, wine and company. An advantage of the Camino is that it can take up quite a number of holidays, each one based in a different section of this 500-mile walk and ending in the Cathedral of Santiago de Compostela in Galicia. A few do cycle, and more elderly people might ride much of the way.

This synergy is very clear in the case of Brendan, the founder of the ukulele group in Cuan whom we discussed in chapter 2. A lifelong scientist who insists upon verification, he also wants to believe that there is more to life than what we see. For Brendan, the Camino offers the best of both worlds. Having walked the entire path over four holidays, he enjoyed the sun and landscape but mostly the camaraderie. He maintained a leisurely pace and did not mind sleeping in hostel dormitories, enjoying the three-course meal with a bottle of wine for €10 that they provide. Yet he initially went to come to terms with the death of a loved relative whose picture he left on a shrine. He would join in whatever prayer meetings were held in the evenings. Walking could include conversation with anyone who passed him and spoke English, but also at least an hour a day's silent contemplation, including thinking about what it means to suggest that each person had three aspects analogous to the Father, the Son and the Holy Spirit. However, Brendan retains his scepticism that the tourism industry is trying to cash in on the growth in holiday pilgrimage. At the end of the Camino he spotted a statue of St James where, at the base, petals have been used to cover over the depiction of Muslims being trampled beneath his horse. Yet he also regards the Camino as an effective means to re-engage with the search for spirituality and depth, and the complex issue of life purpose.

The synergy with the spiritual applies not just to Brendan, but also to his smartphone. The anthropologist who has carried out the most extensive research on the Camino is Nancy Frey,[20] who has been forthright about what she sees as the destructive effects of new media such as the smartphone.[21] Previously, the Camino represented a complete break with mundane life and she views that separation as central to its authenticity. Yet the evidence from Brendan and others seems to contradict her conclusions. Brendan is close friends with several other retirees who share his general ethos: at one level quite secular, but also strongly committed to the maintenance of some sense of the spiritual, albeit one that is quite vague. Yet on his belt Brendan has a device for measuring how far he had walked that day and his GPS is being followed by friends back in Cuan.

People such as Brendan seem to have no issue about the use of smartphones on the Camino. They generally see themselves as fortunate if they have the money and time to go on the pilgrimage and, as sociable and generous people, they want to share this experience. Their friends back in Cuan both follow Brendan on GPS and look forward to his daily accounts of the journey. They may then discuss this among themselves, thus vicariously sharing, at least to a degree, this separation from mundane life and focus upon the spiritual. The smartphone replicates the prior tradition of people, including pilgrims, walking on their own in their own thoughts for some of the time and engaging in long conversations with fellow travellers at others. The prior experience was more isolated because the technology did not exist. But there are grounds for thinking that for our participants this more sociable Camino with smartphones is at least as authentic as its predecessor.

Conclusion

The starting point of this chapter was a Catholic church that was not demarcated off as a thing called religion but rather a way of life; its cosmology incorporated any explicit concern with life purpose. The situation today with regard to life purpose is a good deal less explicit or clear cut. Rather than looking for something that has taken the 'place' of religion, however, it is better to extrapolate life purpose from the general pattern of people's lives. This chapter builds upon the previous chapters in this volume. Life purpose is strongly linked to the drive towards activities discussed in chapter 3 and the maintenance of strong social relations described in chapter 4, as well as the pursuit of good health and fitness described in chapter 6. Perhaps most surprisingly, it is also fully affirmed by the way in which people have integrated the smartphone into their lives, as discussed in chapter 5.

Walking the Camino is a good example of the journey the participants in this chapter have taken, from more explicit religious devotion to something that seems closer to keeping fit through extended walking: the journey from mass to wellbeing. By taking this route we can see how looking after oneself, whether through yoga, walking or healthy eating, retains a strong moral connotation of being a good person. Rather than avoiding sin, it makes morality more like an incentive to do something which can now be experienced as enjoyable in its own

Figure 8.3 'Darkness into Light' charity walk. Photo by Daniel Miller.

right. Keeping fit has become an activity which, alongside art classes and writing poetry, feels both virtuous and uplifting. Also virtuous is the linkage to philanthropy and the demonstration of concern for others. An event such as the 'Darkness into Light', a walk at dawn to raise money for awareness of teenage suicide, is hugely popular precisely because it fits this new configuration, with walking used as an instrument for charity (Fig. 8.3).

There is, however, considerable variation in the way individuals respond to this trajectory. Some ignore it, preferring to remain devoted to traditional religion, others because they find more relaxation and consolation in alcohol, television or just in the demands of their immediate family. Some feel bereft of purpose and have severe problems with depression, based partly on existential emptiness. Yet the two ethnographies suggest there is also a typical normative route that has led most people from a life dominated by religious belief and practice to one that returns to this book's motif of crafting. In this case, it is crafting their specific combination of looking after themselves and others. It follows in part from the initial finding in chapter 2 that it is frailty rather than age which impacts on life purpose. There is a preference for keeping fit through activities which are more generally uplifting, whether yoga and Pilates, sailing, power walking along the beach or enjoying the landscape from an arduous trek, whether within Ireland or along the Camino.

In a similar fashion, examples such as the Thornhill Strollers help to prevent any glib suggestion that this turn towards wellbeing through personal fitness is necessarily a retreat to individual pursuits at the expense of the wider social and moral concerns of religion. As previously noted, it is perfectly possible to walk by oneself, or with just a partner, but for most people walking is a social and community activity, expressing a shared commitment to the values that these represent. The smartphone, far from extending individualised narcissistic pursuits, is mainly a means of extending that sociality, including sharing the spirituality of the Camino.

The same issue applies to attitudes towards the state. Most people recognise that the state is trying to save money by shifting the burden of health care to an individual pursuit. There is some pride in an Irish cynicism about the motivation of politicians, especially those who have been in power for some time; such a cynicism says that they will not be fooled by those in power. At the same time this dominant ethos finds a genuine alignment with the many participants who worked in education, health and the civil service. They are persuaded that saving money for the health services is also a means of maintaining taxation at its current level, and the business of government is compromise. They associate *with* rather than against the reasoning of the state and, whether in their working life or retirement, see the value in this promotion of fitness and wellness.

Overall then, life purpose consists of crafting a balance that applies at every level – the way in which people craft their own lives, their relationship to social relations, their relationship to altruism, their relationship to the state and their relationship to ideas of spirituality. There is the legacy of older formal religion and the new crafting of their environmental ethics and practices. So while most people leave explicit discussions of the meaning of life to Monty Python, the normative pattern of their commitments, and the way they choose to spend their time, allow us to see clear paths emerging that can certainly be considered as life purpose today.

Notes

1. White 2010.
2. Indeed, the percentage of Catholics falls as settlement size rises: small towns of 9,999 or fewer persons have 80.7 per cent Catholics, while large towns of 10,000 or more have 72.1 per cent. Those with no religion were concentrated in urban areas, with just over three out of four in this group located in cities, towns or settlements of 1,500 or more persons. Dublin city and suburbs accounted for 23.6 per cent of Church of Ireland members, while 55.1 per cent are based in urban areas over all, compared with 44.9 per cent in rural areas. Muslims in Ireland are also highly concentrated in urban areas. Only 5.8 per cent lived in rural areas, while 43.5 per cent were in Dublin city and suburbs alone. See Central Statistics Office 2016b.
3. In twentieth-century Ireland the Catholic church played a central role in running industrial and reformatory schools for children. As Kenny argues, this situation suited both the religious orders and the impoverished state. The number of people affected is staggering: 29,500 children born after 1930 were committed to industrial or reform schools by courts or parents. See Kenny 2009, 64.

4. In 1983 67 per cent voted in favour of inserting an amendment into the Irish constitution recognising the equal right to life of both mother and unborn child, effectively prohibiting abortion in almost all cases. In 2018 almost the same number voted against these measures, with 66.4 per cent voting to repeal the amendment, leading the way for abortion legislation to be introduced.

5. Inglis argues that an emphasis on self-denial 'has been central to what makes Ireland different' (2007, 4). He calls it a surrender of the self to the wider group, a peculiar form of self-repression and surrender that lies at the heart of the idea of 'craic' (craic here means fun). This apparent shift from self-denial to greater openness to self-realisation poses questions that are central to this chapter.

6. See McWilliams 2018b.

7. Witoszek and Sheeran 1998, Taylor 1989, Graham 2016.

8. Ward et al. 2018.

9. Miller 2016, 187–92.

10. 'To shoot the breeze' means to have a good chat.

11. See Funchion and McHugh 2018.

12. The National Council for Curriculum and Assessment states 'In health promotion, health is about more than physical health and wellbeing. It is also concerned with social, emotional and spiritual health and wellbeing'. See National Council for Curriculum and Assessment 2011.

13. See Ireland Department of Health 2020.

14. See Ireland Department of Health 2013.

15. See Government of Ireland 2019.

16. Originally mHealth stood for mobile health, as in mobile phones and online mobile devices. Now, however, it increasingly designates the development of bespoke health apps for smartphones.

17. See O'Dwyer 2018.

18. McGarry 2016.

19. See Bradshaw 2017.

20. See Frey 1998.

21. See Frey 2017.

9
Conclusion

A good way of appreciating how much has been learned from a research project is simply to compare the original proposal to the description of the results. When this project began, it was a rather unwieldy combination of three elements: the study of ageing, of the smartphone and of mHealth, that is, the use of the smartphone for health purposes. The proposal identified its target age group as between 45 and 70 years old. It assumed that studying smartphones would be mainly based on investigating the individual apps with which smartphones are populated, and that mHealth consisted of the creation of bespoke smartphone apps for health purposes. However, all these proposals – and every one of these assumptions – has had to be substantially modified as a result of our actual research findings. We regard this as a testimony to what we have learned. The last of these modifications will not be discussed here since it will form the subject of another book. In brief, however, we found that our intention to focus on bespoke mHealth apps was almost completely replaced by a focus on the way in which people use non-specialist ubiquitous apps such as Google and WhatsApp for health purposes,[1] because this turned out to be far more consequential for their health.

The first relevant modification was to the age profile of this study. The decision to focus on people between 45 and 70 was premised on a critique of studies of ageing. These emphasise populations defined by age, that is either youth or the elderly. Yet the experience of ageing is obviously not confined to these two groups. Our reasoning was that by 45 people might no longer see themselves as young, while they may turn 70 before they considered themselves as elderly. It did not take long to realise that our premise failed to correspond to how people see themselves today. What we found instead was that people are increasingly distancing themselves from a self-perception based on any age at all. Instead of being between young and elderly, they are mostly static with regard to age. As long as people are in good health, there is today simply continuity from youth. On a Saturday night when a rock cover band plays songs from the 1960s or 1970s, people themselves in their sixties and seventies can get up and dance in the knowledge that this is their music and it remains current. The Who remains 'their generation', as do The Chieftains and The Beatles. True, they also kept anticipating that things would change at the next decennial birthday, when they turned 60, 70 or 80. But then they discovered that if they retained good health, life just continued. They could do most of what they did in their thirties, follow sports and the news, work for the community, go drinking in pubs and other similar activities.

This was a radical departure from the past, as our participants knew well from old photos of previous generations. Familiar to most are the sepia images of family patriarchs or matriarchs who were actually younger than they are now. It has not been all gain: the figures in those photographs might have been treated with more respect by contemporaries, not least for possessing wisdom garnered from experience. With the development of new technologies, however, digital skills are increasingly the property of the young and have rendered decades' worth of learning redundant. In response to this, our participants have developed a relationship based on consensus and equality in their daily interactions. Other people's perception of common sense carries more influence than seniority.

What is still indisputable is that an older person has lived through more history. For these middle-class suburban fieldsites, it has been quite a radical history. Most of our participants were born into relative poverty, within large families during a post-Independence political regime closely aligned with a deeply conservative Catholicism. Today, these fieldsites are deemed typical of a massive shift to liberal values that is particularly pronounced in middle-class suburban Dublin and associated regions, including Cuan. As popular journalist and economist David McWilliams puts it:

> In one generation, to use V S Naipaul's phrase about India, 'millions of little mutinies' had kicked off inside Irish heads.[2]

By and large, our participants' lives have followed this trajectory from poverty and conservative social values to affluence and a liberal pluralist modernity.[3] These are reflected in national legislation with regard to contraception (legalised in 1980), homosexuality (decriminalised in 1993), civil divorce (legalised in 1998), same-sex marriage (legalised in 2015) and abortion (legalised in 2018). Nor have these gone unnoticed internationally. *The New York Times*, for example, has acknowledged that this once deeply conservative population became the 'vanguard of social change' in being the first country to legalise same-sex marriage by popular vote.[4]

In Cuan and Thornhill, many of our participants positively associate with this vision of modernity. Of course this varies, and some will have voted against these changes. Older people may continue the routines of their youth, such as going to mass, but they are also fully aware that their children probably never will. They were often themselves unsure as to whether going to church was about routines or faith, while those involved in the church increasingly spoke about 'getting out into the community' and organising retreats, walks or choirs.

We conclude that it is the traditional category of age itself that has diminished, rather than older people. It has been replaced by something else, which is frailty. Eventually people succumb: with arthritis they cannot go on long walks, with acid reflux they cannot drink alcohol. Some may be housebound, others may have diabetes. These constraints may start in their forties and fifties, but we encountered quite a few sprightly 80- and even 90-year-olds still waiting for frailty to hit home. The final period seems to remain essentially the play of fate. They may have an aggressive cancer that still allows them to hold an intelligent conversation until they pass away. Many older people are more fearful of dementia, a condition in which cognitive capacities fade faster than physical ones.

These research participants were born into a society in which institutional religion played a dominant role in education and health; discussion of the afterlife was thus an important component of their world.[5] People were assured that death was not the end, though with less certainty as to the subsequent direction of travel. It might be thought that this provided some reassurance, a comforting promise of immortality to overcome the fear of death as oblivion. Yet for the majority of our research participants religious faith has largely disappeared and been replaced with ... nothing in particular. People are facing up to a scientific conception of their biological end. Some return to faith at that time. Others are reassured by a rather vague ideal of a humanistic or ecological return to nature, or see the continuity of their genes in their descendants. Instead of being concerned with the consequences of an action for the afterlife, the focus is now on enjoying life while it is being lived and confronting the moral and ethical challenges that life brings. Among these are people's sense of responsibility to themselves and the maintenance of good health.

While there is a kind of existential continuity with regard to who they basically are, people do experience steps in the ladder of time that are clearly marked and indicate change, if not rupture. For women the experience of menopause can be one of those, though this varies hugely from something barely noticed to a quite debilitating period affecting almost every aspect of their lives. There was also a striking difference between the meaning of retirement compared to many of the other ASSA fieldsites. Professional people may continue for a few years in some kind of consultancy position after they have retired, but they do not generally try to retain their workplace identity. Sometimes it is just not possible. One man who retired from a senior position in the civil service believed that he could have contributed to the Brexit negotiations; he felt frustrated that there was no provision for him to do so. Several men, especially those who had occupied senior management positions, commented on how their previous colleagues or employers never contacted them for advice after the moment of their retirement. Others establish walking or coffee groups who meet every month, but this is generally to keep in contact and to exercise in company rather than to reminisce.

However, the Irish ethnography mainly differed from others, such as that in Brazil, in the extent to which people relinquished an identity based on their previous occupation; instead they embraced the new opportunities and interests represented by retirement. At the Men's Shed, for example, it was generally impossible to tell what work people had once done, in part because this might challenge the larger ethos of egalitarianism, which seemed to be far more important to such activities than any prior status. In our Dublin fieldsites there was more a sense that retired people were now free to explore other things they could now be and do. Indeed, some participants felt a need to establish a series of interests and activities in advance of retirement, precisely for this reason.

As a result of all this, our initial age range soon became meaningless. In practice, we worked equally with people who were in their seventies and eighties, or sometimes even their nineties, as long as they did not appear to be especially frail or vulnerable. The reason is that while they did not conform to our original age bracket, which ended at 70, they manifested the underlying principle of people who saw themselves as neither young nor elderly. Our attention was then less on who they were and more on what they did. Around halfway through fieldwork we came up with the subtitle of this volume, 'When life becomes craft'.

When life becomes craft

The phrase 'When life becomes craft' does not refer to any evidence that people take up crafts, though this is certainly something they may do. Rather, it refers to the observation that as people age they become increasingly involved with one craft in particular, and the subject of that craft is themselves. They are themselves the cake that they are baking, based on their own gradually refined recipe. As in other crafts, they do this by careful points of addition and subtraction. This crafting was the subject of two central chapters which dealt with their activities and social lives; the idea of crafting applies equally to the way in which they construct sociality and fill up their time of retirement.

In Cuan Danny heard a claim so many times that it became something of a cliché – people said that this was the sort of place where, if someone came up with an idea for an activity, they would always find other people to make it happen. Equally often, he was told that the main reason people took part in any activity was to socialise and make friends. It is perfectly possible to walk in the countryside or to go cycling on one's own, but Pauline spent her time with knitting or walking groups because she much preferred to knit or walk in company; so did many others. Most participants, before retirement, had worked in places that were full of people. They recognised the need to be proactive in replacing the social engagements that they lost when they retired. Crafting in our sense is thus a social, not an individual, activity; it is not the work of an individual artisan, although it does also extend to the private domain. Rather than downsizing, the house becomes something of a project. People may choose to shift to a more modern house if they wish and can afford it, or take on DIY projects and gardening if they cannot. Or they may decide to compensate for a small garden by taking on an allotment.

The term crafting seems appropriate because people are 're-making themselves' from a wide variety of possible ingredients or raw materials. When retired people get up in the morning they want a sense of the day ahead and this means crafting routines: setting things to do on a Wednesday that make it different from a Tuesday. People want a sense of how much time they will give to looking after grandchildren, how often to go to yoga, whether to watch the new television series that other people are talking about, whether to take an adult education course, how much time they would volunteer to serve on a committee for a good cause, when to go walking in the countryside and how to ensure they did not neglect regular meetings with friends. At a higher level, the crafting consisted of how to make these pieces of life's jigsaw fit together in a manner that would not be too stressful. Another cliché expression was 'If you need something done, ask a busy woman'; many older people proudly informed us they had 'never been so busy'.

If ill-health and frailty have increasingly replaced biological age as to what constitutes the experience of ageing then, not surprisingly, chapter 5 showed how health issues become more of a hub around which other things are discussed and understood. At a time when complementary therapies are employing considerable numbers of people, we can see how this more holistic perception of health represents precisely such a movement towards crafting. Biomedical perspectives on health pertain to states that are not regarded as normal health. They are employed for the task of eliminating an often painful or debilitating distraction from life. By contrast, complementary therapies create linkages between family issues, stress, minor aches and pains as well as severe illnesses. Incorporating diet and keeping fit in general become what constitutes health, or what is now called wellbeing or wellness, a kind of ringmaster around which the rest of life can circulate.

For women, menopause may become the harbinger of this new sensibility. It is a condition that may impact on anything from the way in which women sleep or look after their bones to their emotions or a change in attitude to their relatives. Menopause seems to be evidence for the necessity of a more holistic understanding of wellbeing. This holistic approach to wellness often carries rather vague connotations of the spiritual, as in yoga, walking the Camino or some of the complementary health practices discussed in chapter 6. They may refer back to the memories of a kind of much-diluted version of Buddhism that many engaged with in the 1960s. This diffused spirituality also stems from individuals seeking meaning or solace – often in repudiation of what they saw as the highly authoritarian and collective practices of the Catholic church.

If anthropology was a natural science, then almost every statement in this volume would be wrong. There are always exceptions. Not everyone is crafting, or indeed is free to craft. Some have never truly been free of depression at any stage in their lives. There are those who nurse private tragedies, such as experiencing the death of a child, from which they will never recover. Many were born to families who could not afford for them to finish education and they never developed the self-confidence to embrace new technologies or new hobbies. There are still important class divides. So not everyone goes through a period of life where the word 'craft' would be appropriate. Equally, the life they craft may consist of developing the true vocation of the couch potato;

watching daytime television, especially sports, while downing at least a bottle of wine at home, alone. Yet it is still important to acknowledge the majority experience, in which people are astonished by the possibilities of a life they never ever expected.

An Irish ethos

What this crafting produces is not just an individual's life and routines; it is also the creation of Cuan and Thornhill as particular places that serve this age group. When creating our Social Prescription websites, it was possible to take a comprehensive view of the area as a locality for activities. At this time of life, particular sites come to the fore while others may fade. Cafés have become key localities, for instance, often at the expense of the pubs. There is the church, the community centre, some sports clubs, as well as particular venues where people walk their dogs or meet up with their friends. The public sphere is tremendously important in both fieldsites: the centre of Cuan was not the high street but the walk along the seafront, while the most populated part of Thornhill was often the park. These are not so much places redolent of a single entity to be called 'community' so much as age-based, layered and multiple communities. The town's geographies may look very different for children or young couples.

In some respects all of this can be represented and experienced as a return to more traditional values, or even some perceived notions of essential Irishness. Consensus and informality within group settings are highly valued by our research participants and closely tied to nostalgia surrounding claims of a companionate egalitarian collectivity in their youth. Often contemporary living is not portrayed as particularly egalitarian, particularly amid a two-tier health system and ongoing housing crisis. Yet this keen awareness of the injustices of contemporary life could again be read as a hallmark of a shared liberal ethos of equality. People make a point to register their unhappiness with the deprivations experienced by those less well off than themselves and often actively look for ways to 'give something back'.

Retirement is an ideal time for this ethos to flourish as the workplace is rarely an egalitarian space. People are organised into hierarchies of workers, managers, leaders and so forth; employees are designated senior and junior and are accorded high or low status. In this retirement space, however, the ethos and aspiration are resolutely egalitarian. People take on positions of authority, such as chairperson, as a dutiful obligation when it is their turn. This is again in marked contrast to some of our other fieldsites in the ASSA project, where every committee or activity becomes an opportunity of competing for status. Whether or not life really was so collective, generous and neighbourly in those dimly remembered days is beside the point. What matters is merely that it is believed to have been so, and that these traditions were central to what it should mean to be 'Irish'. Our evidence is that these are not just aspirations for our participants, but ideals that they often impressively realise. Consensus is highly valued, and finding agreement and working as a group was the basis of many of the activities we observed.

Consensus can have its burdens too; it may be difficult to disagree openly or strenuously. This became very apparent during the Covid-19 pandemic, when one or two participants left WhatsApp groups rather than disagree openly with each other on rules and recommendations. What was also striking was the active engagement of individuals who saw it as their citizen's duty strenuously to enforce the dictates of lockdown. On Facebook a typical posting might be:

> Don't mean to be a spoilsport BUT! – do parents realise that their teens are socialising in big groups walking around the town, hanging around on the beaches etc and there is absolutely NO social distancing going on? Please Parents, be aware of what your teenagers are doing and then they are coming home to you and the rest of the family. It is hard for them, I know but we all have been so good, let's not throw all that away with a new wave of Covid-19!

The sense that there might be some enjoyment in this policing of new norms was neatly encapsulated by a variety of memes (Figs 9.1, 9.2a and 9.2b) which – as in much of our project – show the fine line between care and surveillance.

More often the primary mechanism for maintaining a working consensus is a particular play of humour, which incorporates quite a powerful potential for insult. Wit and banter chop the legs off pretentiousness or claims to superiority. An egalitarian ethos by no means forecloses a powerful class divide, and it has been clear throughout that the focus of this volume is primarily a relatively affluent middle class. The social housing within Cuan was for many a world apart – one from which the middle class was distanced and occasionally denigrated as a place of crime and indolence. Parts of the north inner city of Dublin, as well as areas not far from Thornhill, are extremely disadvantaged and some participants assumed that research such as ours should focus on these

Figure 9.1 Memes also illustrate some of the mechanisms that are important in developing and policing this kind of community consensus.

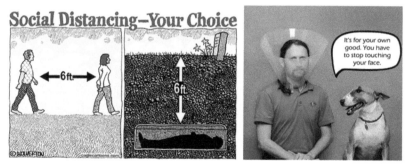

Figures 9.2a and 9.2b Two further examples of memes relating to community consensus.

areas they regard as problems, rather than on themselves as the taken for granted 'mainstream'. We are mindful therefore that a volume focused upon those populations, who have experienced disadvantage and disenfranchisement, would be entirely different. Yet it is the expansion of the middle class that has been a singular hallmark of the twentieth-century Irish Republic. It is therefore essential to research the experience of retirement, health and age among populations who would in most respects consider themselves the unexceptional face of contemporary Ireland[6] – a face that, one hopes, will be more representative of the country's future.

The smartphone

All of this leads directly to our understanding of the smartphone – both an icon of this craftsmanship and an object that has, with astonishing rapidity, become the single most important device in that crafting. The smartphone is iconic because it draws together all that has been said so far. For a while it seemed most likely to fit within more traditional categories of age, patrolling the borders between youth and the older population, destined only for the former. It is amazing how recently people were certain that smartphones would never be used by anyone over 40 and there remain extensive older populations not at all comfortable with the smartphone. We were made fully aware of this through our various attempts to become involved in teaching smartphone use. We saw how people struggled with a device that, contrary to the claims of many younger people, is not the least bit intuitive. The smartphone can create digital expulsion, intimidation and anxiety.[7] Nevertheless, for those who *do* master the smartphone it means that something seen until recently as essentially a youth technology is now their technology too. It then comes to mean the diametric opposite: no longer a device defining the controlled borders of age, but one that further facilitates the elimination of age itself.

The significance of smartphones is even greater than this. If the categorisation of age is being replaced by the distinction between frail and not yet frail, then smartphones are not just symbolically iconic but really useful. At no time do smartphones feel more essential than when one is immobile and housebound. Prior to this, immobility was inevitably accompanied by some form of social exclusion and probably also loneliness. With smartphones, however, one can be even more in social connectivity than when one had to drive a car or take a bus in order to visit another person.

WhatsApp was also hugely important to those looking after frail parents or parents with dementia. Just as people are losing physical capacities, they are gaining other capacities which sometimes, though by no means always, relate to those same desires and needs that were being otherwise reduced, such as keeping in touch with information and people. If this point needed further evidence, it was supplied shortly after the end of fieldwork with the arrival of the Covid-19 pandemic; in lockdown everybody shared some experience of social isolation. Certainly this made the limitations of online communication clear. Yet the mere thought about what lockdown might have been like without online communications and smartphones may well have taken the appreciation of their merits to a whole new level (Fig. 9.3).

Figure 9.3   Communicating during the Covid-19 lockdown. Photo by Claudia Luppino.

Equally, for older people who are not frail, the smartphone becomes a kind of control hub for crafting those busy lives with all their social interactions and activities. The key transformations discussed in this volume with respect to the changed experience of ageing and the idea of crafting one's life on retirement both predated the smartphone, which is clearly then not their cause. Yet the smartphone has insinuated itself into these transformations incredibly deeply and incredibly quickly – to the extent that those who organise their life around and through smartphones find themselves unable, within only a month or two, to imagine doing this without them.

Smartphones are mainly a change not so much in what is done or aspired to, but in the means by which – and the extent to which – something can be achieved. There are consequences, of course: social relations are more extensive and more immediate. The ability to co-ordinate family support for a frail parent is far more possible and effective thanks to WhatsApp. To a degree, the smartphone reverses the historical shift from the extended family to the nuclear family. But whereas the traditional extended family might be experienced as oppressive and a curtailment on freedom, the smartphone has resolved these historical dilemmas. Contact with the wider family is now more frequent and often more informal, such that people may feel once again more part of the family. But, since they are not living in the same place and can return a message at the time of their choosing, contact is also limited and controlled.

Crafting life is often experienced as a kind of juggling. Many of these retired people see themselves as extremely busy. They could help with the grandchildren – but then they are supposed to be at a meeting of a community group, there is the 'homework' to be supervised before the next choir practice, a friend who needs comforting after the loss of her husband, research to be done for the next holiday abroad, work to be done on improving their bridge skills and the need to finish reading that novel before the next meeting of the book club. This is why, within a short time, many older people just cannot imagine life without their iPhone or Samsung Galaxy. They help to keep their lists of tasks on track, prioritise their schedules, let people know about changes and allow them simultaneously to be seen to be paying attention to multiple relationships through WhatsApp. Smartphones can also help people find their way to a meeting in another town, or giving them a much-needed break from all these activities through playing Solitaire, Patience or Schubert.

Smartphones also provide an unprecedented intimacy. This can directly express the personality of an individual, whether a gruff descendent of fishermen's stock, disdainful of new technology, or a highly organised professional woman. As well as expressing an individual's character, it accords with traditional relationships in which the wife does the social connecting and the husband follows sports – but can be vice versa. It then extends to the wider sociality discussed in chapter 3, whether organising grandparenting or the community. If the smartphone reflects persons, then persons, in turn, will reflect Irish cultural practices and values.

The characterisation of the gruff male or the professional woman are cultural tropes – in other societies gender works differently. This can most clearly be seen by comparing this volume with others in the ASSA series. The smartphone becomes 'Irish' simply because it is more frequently used to organise practices relevant for Irish people, such as spending time with family members, attending funerals or plotting relationships with the Irish diaspora on ancestry.com.

Most of the discussion so far relates to what might be seen as positive consequences. Yet while participants generally liked to show off the new capacities of some particular app, older people tend to talk about the smartphone as a whole in disparaging terms that condemn many of its other consequences. They see it as time-wasting, a device that replaces social interaction with screen interaction, leading to a kind of screen addiction. Mainly they condemn smartphones because of what they see as their corrupting influence upon the next generation, rather than their own. If the smartphone has become an icon of this rapid shift to a new modernity, it is not surprising that some people are ambivalent about it and point out the way it has stripped them of respect for skills and knowledge accumulated over decades. Others worry about more direct ill effects on health, including the impact of some sort of radiation. Finally, many older people worry about what corporations will do with their private information, extrapolated as data.

There are clear negative consequences to smartphones.[8] Among others, the smartphone accentuates education and class differences. People who had worked in senior professional jobs flaunt their ability to incorporate the smartphone as part of everyday life with ease; they are creative in appropriating its possibilities to make this a key instrument in crafting life. By contrast, those with less education may feel intimidated by a very unfamiliar device that demands a kind of dexterity for which they feel mentally ill-equipped. They also see that it forms part of a pressure towards online literacy, complemented by an increasingly punitive treatment of those who are unable to use online services. These people find they pay more, take longer to get things done and are denigrated as technological illiterates.

A prime example of this observation was googling for health information. By and large well-educated people who are comfortable with using their search engines as research tools became still better informed, while the less well educated became more confused and anxious. Smartphones can equally accentuate the digital divide of age, as both companies and the state in effect disenfranchise those who do not know how to go online to fill out forms or make complaints. From booking a flight to online banking, people who are not fluent with digital technologies find themselves excluded from rudimentary tasks that they previously accomplished easily. The smartphone thus turns out to be equally proficient at standing for the ills and travails of modern life as for its benefits.

Many other conclusions regarding the nature of the contemporary smartphone are not detailed here because they appear in the final chapter of our collective and comparative book, *The Global Smartphone*.[9] In that volume you can read about our characterisation of the smartphone as the 'Transportal Home'. This expression suggests that, rather than seeing the smartphone as an external device, it feels more like something we live *within*. There are 'rooms' within the smartphone where we play games, do our shopping, store our photos and music. People discuss the way they tidy and delete in a manner analogous to our bricks and mortar home. For a young person who is still living with their parents, this may represent their private home within a home. For an older person who has declining mobility, they can portal to another person's smartphone rather than having to travel to visit them.

The smartphone creates a capacity for the 'Death of Proximity' to match the earlier 'Death of Distance'. This means that people may be physically present, even sitting next to you, but they might as well not be there since they have actually returned to their smartphone homes; there they are busy meeting other people, gathering information or being entertained. There is a more general shift in people's sensibility to the world which we describe as 'Perpetual Opportunism'. One can always take a picture the moment something interesting presents itself and share that immediately with the person it made you think of, or take a snap of a community noticeboard for future reference.

Other general conclusions that may be found in *The Global Smartphone* include 'Beyond Anthropomorphism', which was illustrated by the intimate relationship between individuals and their smartphones described on pages 121–2 through the example of Eleanor, as well as 'Care Transcending Distance'. These all apply to the evidence from Ireland. Rather than repeat them here, however, the reader is directed towards this comparative volume.

Becoming younger

The initial claim of this volume to be in part a study of how people become younger was clearly a provocation: it sounds like an impossibility. Yet, as just noted, once older people feel comfortable with smartphones, previously seen as a youth technology, precisely the fact that they are now associated with it may appear as a sprinkling of the fairy dust of youthfulness. People who use smartphones are young and contemporary – to the extent that an alternative title for this book might have been *Not Ageing with Smartphones*.

To make such a counterintuitive claim requires far more evidence than simply that which pertains to smartphones, however. It helps that the music with which this generation grew up became, and remains, the foundations of pop music thereafter and has now returned to them on Spotify. Even the fact that older people have made a general transition from the culture of the pub to that of coffee and café society, mostly for health reasons, has become conveniently aligned with this same modern movement, as opposed to the old-fashioned tea shop. But these are always generalisations and do not apply to everyone. Attending the Active Retirement group in Cuan or Thornhill is to experience a different world, where up to 70 people seem to prefer to relax into their ageing process. They are fierce in protecting their right to spend the afternoon playing bingo rather than having to deal with devices that connote modernity or cause anxiety, such as computers or smartphones.

Chapter 7 showed how the argument about getting younger applies as much to the traditional bricks and mortar of the family home as to the smartphone, the Transportal Home. There was a clear imperative to move from older, less efficient houses designed for large families to something more suitable and easier to maintain for a couple or single person, with an eye to the specialist changes that are required when people become frail. Yet downsizing proved less prevalent than might have been expected. The more symbolic aspects of housing remained important; in some ways, people exploited the house to express their continued youth by shifting to a more modern contemporary home. It helps that furnishing made from tubular steel and glass is still considered the modern look, even though it was established as the modern style back in the 1920s.

It is not just the practice of downsizing that is exploited as a means to become modern rather than elderly. The same chapter revealed how the need to relinquish possessions could be turned into an expression of older people's alignment with green ideals. Environmental causes are generally understood as an ideology that should appeal to youth, who have more to fear from long-term climate change and environmental degradation and whose most famous spokesperson during this period, Greta Thunberg, was aged 16. Yet it was often retired people who could afford the time to be active in their environmentalism, now expressed through Tidy Towns or campaigning to save some trees. In Dublin, as elsewhere, it is very likely that there are also status connotations of these ideals, which tend to denigrate those who fail to espouse what have become seen as quintessentially middle-class values.[10]

It is perhaps not surprising that older people feel positive about a goal called 'sustainability': the word pretty much sums up what we found in chapter 9 to be the central life purpose to which they now devote themselves. Whether by going on long walks or doing yoga, whether by keeping an eye on their diet or dabbling with complementary therapies, considerable attention is paid to self-crafting in the very immediate physical sense of keeping as healthy as possible. One of the complementary health practitioners discussed in chapter 6 was quite explicit about using the term 'sustainability' in her work with middle-aged people. She saw just how neatly this word acted to link the ideal of keeping older people fit and healthy, thereby adding to their longevity, with the political concerns about the longevity of the planet advocated by the Green Party. Devoting oneself to sustainability makes looking after the self not an individualistic but rather a collective pursuit, and one that could be admired. In turn, sustainability linked life purpose to a general sense of an afterlife. Several older people talked about ecological ways of disposing of their bodies after death or gave a philosophical view of death as the dispersal of one's atoms back to the wider universe where they remain immortal, linking with Buddhist and other anti-materialist ideologies. Under the banner of sustainability, even the afterlife has become green.

In all of these ways, this demographic has, in effect, sloughed off the crinkled skin that corresponds with traditional associations of ageing. Instead it has found ways of not just being associated with but often being in the vanguard of activities and projects associated with the young. Rather than being the left behind remnants of an Irish past, they can be the spokespeople and activists for the bright, green, sustainable wellbeing aspired to as the Irish future. The title *Ageing with Smartphones* indicates the potential simultaneity of these two processes: people can indeed become both older and younger.

The 'youth' that is being crafted for the sixty- and seventy-year-olds is something of a mélange. Embracing technology is one element, but older people have other resources too. It was curious how often references were made to their lives in the 1960s, the music, the drugs, the Eastern mysticism. An activity such as yoga and chanting 'OM' is partly a reminder of their first youth. Equally important are their financial assets. Life in retirement is not experienced as a gradual relinquishing. Rather, they are embracing trips abroad in the spirit of an extended gap year from university because they can afford to spend that time in the sun and escape the Irish winter. Older people may also remain quite 'sporty', with their cycling and very extensive walks, but they can also now afford to follow the Irish rugby team to Japan – something completely unimaginable in their youth. If men nurse their pint of Guinness and make it last the evening, this is more often for health reasons than poverty. They will, as will we all, eventually become frail and die – but what is astonishing is the degree to which older people increasingly spend their latter days becoming younger.

Notes

1. A good example of this may be found in our publication of a 150-page manual on how health services can use WhatsApp. Duque 2020.
2. See McWilliams's article on the Dún Laoghaire-isation of Ireland. McWilliams 2018b.
3. The main exception was the deep recession of the 1980s and after 2008, but during fieldwork there was a sense that these were now past.
4. See Hakim and Dalby 2015.
5. Religious orders are still heavily involved in education and health, but these connections are not uncontroversial. Two orders of nuns own some of the biggest hospitals in Dublin. The St Vincent's Healthcare Group is owned by the Sisters of Charity, while the Sisters of Mercy own the Mater Hospital, the Children's University Hospital at Temple Street and Cappagh Orthopaedic Hospital in Finglas.
6. Middle-income households – i.e. those with an income that is two-thirds to double the national median household income – had incomes of between €24,475 and €73,426 in 2010, the latest year for which data on the income distribution in Ireland was available. Lower-income households had incomes of less than €24,475 and upper-income households had incomes in excess of €73,426 (all figures computed for three-person households and expressed in 2010 prices). For more, see McWilliams 2019 on the expansion of the middle class in Ireland.
7. Many examples of what was learned from teaching smartphone use appear in *The Global Smartphone*. See Miller et al. 2021.
8. See Miller et al. 2021 for more in-depth discussion of this topic.
9. See Miller et al. 2021. It is possible to read *The Global Smartphone* here for free: https://www.uclpress.co.uk/products/171335.
10. Studies in the early years of the twenty-first century found that membership of environmental groups was low in Ireland; most engagement with environmental concerns was largely confined to recycling and the periodic signing of petitions. See Motherway et al. 2003, 46; Collinson 2015, 47. Similarly concerns over the environment 'were strongly related to the wealth of a household'. Motherway et al. 2003, 28; Collison 2015, 47.

Bibliography

Aguilar, Mario I., ed. 2007. *Rethinking Age in Africa: Colonial, post-colonial and contemporary interpretations of cultural representations*. Trenton, NJ: Africa World Press.

ALONE Charity Ireland. 2020. 'ALONE News'. ALONE Charity Ireland website. Accessed 26 May 2020. Available at: https://alone.ie.

Amárach Research, Ronan Lyons, Lorcan Sirr, Innovation Delivery and Keith Finglass. 2016. 'Housing for older people: Thinking ahead'. Commissioned by the Ireland Smart Ageing Exchange and the Housing Agency. Accessed 24 September 2020. Available at: http://www.housingagency.ie/sites/default/files/publications/35.%20Final-Report-Housing-for-Older-People-Dec-2016.pdf.

Andrews, Molly. 1999. 'The seductiveness of agelessness', *Ageing and Society* 19 (3): 301–18. https://doi.org/10.1017/S0144686X99007369.

Arber, Sara and Virpi Timonen, eds. 2012. *Contemporary Grandparenting: Changing family relationships in global contexts*. Bristol: Policy Press.

Arensberg, Conrad M. 1937. *The Irish Countryman*. London: Macmillan.

Arensberg, Conrad M. and Solon T. Kimball. 2001 [1940]. *Family and Community in Ireland*. 3rd ed. Clare: CLASP Press.

Barr, Rebecca A. 2019. 'Repealing the eighth: Abortion referendum was won by narrative', *The Irish Times*, 31 May 2019. Accessed 27 May 2020. Available at: https://www.irishtimes.com/culture/books/repealing-the-eighth-abortion-referendum-was-won-by-narrative-1.3909909.

Barrett, Alan, George Savva, Virpi Timonen and Rose A. Kenny. 2011. 'Fifty plus in Ireland 2011: First results from The Irish Longitudinal Study on Ageing (TILDA)'. Accessed 24 September 2020. Available at: http://www.tara.tcd.ie/handle/2262/55417.

Bealtaine festival website. 2020. 'Festival history'. Bealtaine festival website. Accessed 24 September 2020. Available at: http://bealtaine.ie/page/about_us/festival_history.

Birdwell-Pheasant, Donna. 1992. 'The early twentieth-century Irish stem family: A case study from County Kerry'. In *Approaching the Past: Historical anthropology through Irish case studies*, edited by Marilyn Silverman and Philip H. Gulliver, 305–47. New York: Columbia University Press.

Blaikie, Andrew. 1999. *Ageing and Popular Culture*. Cambridge: Cambridge University Press.

Bradshaw, Karl. 2017. '7 reasons why people walk the Camino de Santiago'. Caminoways.com. 23 May 2017. Accessed 24 September 2020. Available at: https://caminoways.com/7-reasons-why-people-walk-camino.

Breen, M. J. and C. Reynolds. 2011. 'The rise of secularism and the decline of religiosity in Ireland: The pattern of religious change in Europe', *The International Journal of Religion and Spirituality in Society* 1 (2): 195–212.

Brody, H. 1973. *Inishkillane: Change and decline in the west of Ireland*. London: Allan Lane.

Brody, J. 2016. 'The health benefits of knitting'. *New York Times Blog* (blog). 25 January 2016. Accessed 25 May 2020. Available at: https://well.blogs.nytimes.com/2016/01/25/the-health-benefits-of-knitting/.

Buch, Elana. 2015. 'Anthropology of aging and care', *Annual Review of Anthropology* 44: 277–93. https://doi.org/10.1146/annurev-anthro-102214-014254.

Burke, Sara, Sarah Barry, Rikke Siersbaek, Bridget Johnston, Maebh Ní Fhallúin and Steve Thomas. 2018. 'Sláintecare – A ten-year plan to achieve universal healthcare in Ireland', *Health Policy* 122 (12): 1278–82. https://doi.org/10.1016/j.healthpol.2018.05.006.

Byrne, Anne and Deirdre O'Mahony. 2012. 'Family and community: (Re)Telling our own story', *Journal of Family Issues* 33 (1): 52–75. https://doi.org/10.1177/0192513X11421121.

Byrne, Anne and Deirdre O'Mahony. 2013. 'Revisiting and reframing the anthropological archive: The Harvard-Irish Survey (1930–1936)', *Irish Journal of Anthropology* 16 (1): 9.

Campbell, D. 2018. 'NHS should expand "Social Prescribing", says Health Secretary', *The Guardian*, 6 September 2018. Accessed 27 May 2020. Available at: https://www.theguardian.com/society/2018/sep/06/nhs-should-expand-social-prescribing-says-health-secretary.

Canavan, John. 2012. 'Family and family change in Ireland: An overview', *Journal of Family Issues* 33 (1): 10–28. https://doi.org/10.1177/0192513X11420956.

Carey, D. et al. 2018. 'Wellbeing and health in Ireland's over 50s 2009–2016'. Wave 4. The Irish Longitudinal Study on Ageing (TILDA). Ireland: Trinity College Dublin. Accessed 25 September 2020. Available at: https://tilda.tcd.ie/publications/reports/pdf/w4-key-findings-report/Key%20Findings.pdf.

Carolan, Mary. 2000. 'Menopause: Irish women's voices', *Journal of Obstetric, Gynecologic & Neonatal Nursing* 29 (4): 397–404. https://doi.org/10.1111/j.1552-6909.2000.tb02062.x.

Carvill, Elizabeth. 2014. 'Retirement in Ireland: A survey report 2014'. Retirement Planning Council of Ireland. Accessed 25 September 2020. Available at: https://www.iapf.ie/_files/events/274/ElizabethCarvill_Presentation.pdf.

Central Statistics Office (CSO) Ireland. 2016a. 'Census of Population 2016 – Profile 4 households and families'. Central Statistics Office website. 2016. Accessed 25 September 2020. Available at: https://www.cso.ie/en/releasesandpublications/ep/p-cp4hf/cp4hf/ms/.

Central Statistics Office (CSO) Ireland. 2016b. 'Census of Population 2016 – Profile 8 Irish travellers, ethnicity and religion'. Census. 2016. Accessed 25 September 2020. Available at: https://www.cso.ie/en/releasesandpublications/ep/p-cp8iter/p8iter/p8rrc/.

Central Statistics Office (CSO) Ireland. 2016c. 'Figure 4.1 Percentage of population with a medical card by age group, 2007 and 2016'. Central Statistics Office website. 2016. Accessed 25 September 2020. Available at: https://data.gov.ie/dataset/figure-41-percentage-of-population-with-a-medical-card-by-age-group-2007-and-2016.

Chambers, Pat. 2018. *Older Widows and the Life Course: Multiple narratives of hidden lives*. Abingdon, Oxon; New York: Routledge.

Clark, Alex. 2019. 'Why is Irish literature thriving? Because its writers and publishers take risks', *The Guardian*, 30 July 2019. Accessed 25 May 2020. Available at: https://www.theguardian.com/commentisfree/2019/jul/30/irish-literature-thriving-risks-sally-rooney-edna-obrien.

Cohen, Lawrence. 1994. 'Old age: Cultural and critical perspectives', *Annual Review of Anthropology* 23 (1): 137–58. https://doi.org/10.1146/annurev.an.23.100194.001033.

Coleman, Steve. 2004. 'The nation, the state, and the neighbors: Personation in Irish-Language discourse', *Language & Communication* 24 (4): 381–411. https://doi.org/10.1016/j.langcom.2004.03.001.

Collins, C. and M. O'Riordan. 2015. 'The future of Irish general practice: ICGP member survey 2015'. Lenus – The Irish Health Repository. 2015. Accessed 27 May 2020. Available at: https://www.lenus.ie/handle/10147/614387.

Collins, Liam. 2018. 'Iron out a few details and Ross's "granny flat" grant is actually a pretty good idea', *The Irish Independent*, 3 October 2018. Accessed 25 May 2020. Available at: https://www.independent.ie/business/budget/iron-out-a-few-details-and-rosss-granny-flat-grant-is-actually-a-pretty-good-idea-37379363.html.

Collinson, P. 2015. 'Environmental attitudes, community development, and local politics in Ireland'. In *Alternative Countrysides*, 46–60. Manchester: Manchester University Press.

Commission for Communications Regulation (ComReg). 2018a. 'Annual report 2017–2018'. Accessed 25 September 2020. https://www.comreg.ie/media/2019/08/COMREG-AR-2018-Final-1.pdf.

Commission for Communications Regulation (ComReg). 2018b. 'Quarterly key data report – Q4 2018'. Accessed 25 September 2020. Available at: https://www.comreg.ie/publication/quarterly-key-data-report-q4-2018.

Condon, D. 2011. 'Being older in Ireland today'. Irishhealth.com. 8 September 2011. Accessed 25 May 2020. Available at: http://www.irishhealth.com/article.html?id=19722.

Connolly, Linda, ed. 2015a. *The 'Irish' Family*. London: Routledge.

Connolly, Linda. 2015b. 'Locating the Irish family: Towards plurality of family forms?' In *The 'Irish' Family*, edited by Linda Connolly, 10–38. London: Routledge.

Corcoran, Mary P. 2010. '"God's golden acre for children": Pastoralism and sense of place in new suburban communities', *Urban Studies* 47 (12): 2537–54. https://doi.org/10.1177/0042098009359031.

Corcoran, Mary P., J. Gray and M. Peillon. 2007. 'Ties that bind? The social fabric of daily life in new suburbs'. In *Best of Times? The social impact of the Celtic Tiger*, edited by T. Fahey, H. Russell and C. Whelan, 175–97. Dublin: Institute of Public Administration.

Corcoran, Mary P., J. Gray and M. Peillon. 2010. *Suburban Affiliations: Social relations in the Greater Dublin area*. Syracuse: Syracuse University Press.

Corcoran, Mary P. and Perry Share, eds. 2008. *Belongings: Shaping identity in Modern Ireland*. Vol. 6. Dublin: Institute of Public Administration.

Curtin, Chris, Hastings Donnan and Thomas M. Wilson. 1993. *Irish Urban Cultures*. Belfast: Institute of Irish Studies.

Curtin, Chris, Trutz Haase, Hilary Tovey and Combat Poverty Agency, eds. 1996. *Poverty in Rural Ireland: A political economy perspective*. Dublin: Combat Poverty Agency.

Daniels, Inge. 2010. *The Japanese Home*. London: Bloomsbury.

Degnen, Cathrine. 2007. 'Minding the gap: The construction of old age and oldness amongst peers', *Journal of Aging Studies* 21 (1): 69–80. Accessed 1 June 2020. https://doi.org/10.1016/j.jaging.2006.02.001.

Deloitte. 2019. 'Global mobile consumer survey 2019: The Irish cut'. Irish mobile consumer survey. Accessed 25 September 2020. Available at: https://www2.deloitte.com/ie/en/pages/technology-media-and-telecommunications/articles/global-mobile-consumer-survey.html.

Department of Health Ireland. 2019. 'Irish people are living longer, healthier lives, though access to healthcare remains an issue: Department of Health publishes "Health in Ireland – Key Trends 2019"'. Gov.ie. 27 December 2019. Accessed 25 September 2020. Available at: https://www.gov.ie/en/press-release/f0da4c-irish-people-are-living-longer-healthier-lives-though-access-to-heal/.

Drazin, Adam. 2018. 'The fitness of persons in the landscape: Isolation, belonging and emergent subjects in rural Ireland', *Social Anthropology* 26 (4): 535–49. https://doi.org/10.1111/1469-8676.12521.

Drążkiewicz, Elżbieta. 2019. 'Trust, Truth and Transparency: Conflicts over HPV and cervical check scandal in Ireland'. Royal College of Physicians of Ireland, Faculty of Public Health, Winter Scientific Meeting, 4 December 2019.

Drążkiewicz, Elżbieta. 2020. *Institutionalised Dreams: The art of managing foreign aid*. EASA Series 38. New York: Berghahn Books.

DuBois, Cora. 1941. 'Review of family and community in Ireland', *American Anthropologist* 1, 43 (3): 460–1.

Duque, Marília. 2020. *Learning from WhatsApp: Best practices for health. Communication protocols for hospitals and medical clinics*. London: ASSA.

Economic and Social Research Institute (ESRI). 2020. 'Irish tax system does most in Europe to reduce inequality'. 22 January 2020. Accessed 25 September 2020. Available at: https://www.esri.ie/news/irish-tax-system-does-most-in-europe-to-reduce-inequality.

Edmondson, Ricca. 2005. 'Wisdom in later life: Ethnographic approaches', *Ageing and Society* 25 (6): 339–56. https://doi.org/10.1017/S0144686X04003320.

Edwards, Elaine. 2018. 'Department seeks tender to monitor social media for "keywords"', *The Irish Times*, 27 August 2018. Accessed 25 September 2020. Available at: https://www.irishtimes.com/news/social-affairs/department-seeks-tender-to-monitor-social-media-for-keywords-1.3608275.

Egan, Keith M. and Fiona E. Murphy. 2015. 'Honored ancestors, difficult legacies: The stability, decline, and re-emergence of anthropologies in and of Ireland: World anthropology', *American Anthropologist* 117 (1): 134–41. https://doi.org/10.1111/aman.12174.

Egeraat, Chris van and Frank Barry. 2009. 'The Irish pharmaceutical industry over the boom period and beyond', *Irish Geography* 42 (1): 23–44. https://doi.org/10.1080/00750770902815604.

eHealth Ireland. 2020. 'Local Asset Mapping Project (LAMP) Introduction – the Local Asset Mapping Project (LAMP).' eHealth Ireland. 2020. Accessed 25 May 2020. Available at: https://www.ehealthireland.ie/Case%20Studies/Local-Asset-Mapping-Project-at-St-James-Hospital/.

European Innovation Partnership on Active and Healthy Ageing. 2012. 'The new agenda on ageing – To make Ireland the best country to grow old in'. European Commission website. 14 June 2012. Accessed 25 May 2020. Available at: https://ec.europa.eu/eip/ageing/library/new-agenda-ageing-make-ireland-best-country-grow-old_en.

Eurostat. 2018. 'Share of young people (aged 16–29 years) living with their parents, 2018'. European Commission website. 2018. Accessed 25 May 2020. Available at: https://ec.europa. eu/eurostat/statistics-explained/images/a/ac/Share_of_young_people_%28aged_16-29_ years%29_living_with_their_parents%2C_2018_%28%25%29-fig01.png.

Fahey, Tony. 2015. 'The family in Ireland in the new millennium'. In *The 'Irish' Family*, edited by Linda Connolly, 54–69. London: Routledge.

Fáilte Ireland. 2020. 'The gathering Ireland: Ireland welcomed the world in 2013'. Accessed 25 May 2020. Available at: https://www.discoverireland.ie/The-Gathering-Ireland.

Featherstone, M. and A. Wernick, eds. 1995. *Images of Aging: Cultural representations of later life*. London: Routledge.

Forsberg, Hannele and Virpi Timonen. 2018. 'The future of the family as envisioned by young adults in Ireland', *Journal of Youth Studies* 21 (6): 765–79. https://doi.org/10.1080/ 13676261.2017.1420761.

Fox, Kara. 2019. 'A scandal over cervical checks is a sign of a bigger problem in Ireland', CNN Edition. 5 October 2019. Accessed 25 May 2020. Available at: https://edition.cnn.com/2019/ 10/05/europe/ireland-cervical-check-scandal-intl/index.html.

Fox, Robin. 1978. *The Tory Islanders: A people of the Celtic fringe*. Cambridge: Cambridge University Press.

French, Brigittine M. 2015. 'Anthropologies in and of Ireland: Postcolonial subjectivities and institutional locations: world anthropology', *American Anthropologist* 117 (1): 143–44. https://doi.org/10.1111/aman.12176.

Frey, Nancy Louise. 1998. *Pilgrim Stories: On and off the road to Santiago*. Berkeley: University of California Press.

Frey, Nancy. 2017. 'Text: Pilgrimage in the internet age'. Talk, Annual General Meeting of the London Confraternity of St James, St Alban's Centre, London, September. Accessed 25 May 2020. Available at: https://www.walkingtopresence.com/home/research/text-pilgrimage-in-the-internet-age.

Funchion, K. and J. McHugh. 2018. 'Schools mental health strategies Dáil Éireann debate, Wednesday 28 November 2018 – Question 68'. Oireachtas.ie. 28 November 2018. Accessed 25 May 2020. Available at: https://www.oireachtas.ie/en/debates/question/2018-11-28/68/.

Gallagher, Carmel. 2012. 'Connectedness in the lives of older people in Ireland: A study of the communal participation of older people in two geographic localities', *Irish Journal of Sociology* 20 (1): 84–102. https://doi.org/10.7227/IJS.20.1.5.

Gallagher, J. 2016. 'Economic evaluations of clinical pharmacy services in Ireland, 2007–2015'. PhD thesis, University of Cork. Accessed 25 May 2020. https://cora.ucc.ie/handle/10468/ 3467.

Garattini, Chiara, Joseph Wherton and David Prendergast. 2012. 'Linking the lonely: An exploration of a communication technology designed to support social interaction among older adults', *Universal Access in the Information Society* 11 (2): 211–22. https://doi.org/ 10.1007/s10209-011-0235-y.

Garattini, Chiara and David Prendergast. 2015. 'Introduction: Critical reflections on ageing and technology in the twenty-first century'. In *Aging and the Digital Life Course*, edited by David Prendergast and Chiara Garattini, 1–15. New York: Berghahn Books.

Garvey, Pauline. 2018a. *Unpacking Ikea: Swedish design for the purchasing masses*. London; New York: Routledge.

Garvey, Pauline. 2018b. 'Neurochemical selves or Social Prescription?' *ASSA UCL Blog* (academic blog). 15 December 2018. Accessed 25 May 2020. Available at: https://blogs.ucl.ac.uk/assa/ 2018/12/15/neurochemical-selves-or-social-prescription/.

Gibbon, P. and C. Curtin. 1978. 'The stem family in Ireland', *Comparative Studies in Society and History* 20 (3): 429–53. https://doi.org/10.1017/S0010417500009075.

Giddens, Anthony. 1991. *Modernity and Self-identity: Self and society in the late modern age*. Stanford, CA: Stanford University Press.

Gilleard, Chris. 2016. 'The other Victorians: Age, sickness and poverty in 19th-century Ireland', *Ageing and Society* 36 (06): 1157–84. https://doi.org/10.1017/S0144686X15000240.

Gilleard, Chris and Paul Higgs. 2011. 'Frailty, disability and old age: A re-appraisal', *Health: An interdisciplinary journal for the social study of health, illness and medicine* 15 (5): 475–90. https://doi.org/10.1177/1363459310383595.

Gilleard, Chris and Paul Higgs. 2018. 'Unacknowledged distinctions: Corporeality versus embodiment in later life', *Journal of Aging Studies* 45 (June): 5–10. https://doi.org/10.1016/ j.jaging.2018.01.001.

Goodbody, W. 2018. '97% of Irish population have access to smartphone, survey finds'. RTÉ News website, 30 November 2018. Accessed 25 September 2020. Available at: https://www.rte.ie/news/2018/1120/1012041-smartphone_survey/.

Gorecki, Paul K. 2011. 'Do you believe in magic? Improving the quality of pharmacy services through restricting entry and aspirational contracts, the Irish experience', *The European Journal of Health Economics* 12 (6): 521–31. https://doi.org/10.1007/s10198-010-0264-0.

Government of Ireland. 2019. 'Wellbeing policy statement and framework for practice'. Accessed 25 September 2020. Available at: https://www.education.ie/en/Publications/Policy-Reports/wellbeing-policy-statement-and-framework-for-practice-2018%E2%80%932023.pdf.

Graham, Barbara. 2016. *Death, Materiality and Mediation: An ethnography of remembrance in Ireland*. New York: Berghahn Books.

Gratton, Lynda and Andrew Scott. 2017. *The 100-year Life: Living and working in an age of longevity*. Paperback edition. London: Bloomsbury Business.

Gray, Jane, Ruth Geraghty and David Ralph. 2016. *Family Rhythms: The changing textures of family life in Ireland*. Manchester: Manchester University Press.

Gullestad, Marianne. 1994. *The Art of Social Relations: Essays on culture, social action and everyday life in modern Norway*. Scandinavian Library. Oslo; New York: Scandinavian University Press.

Hagerty, Barbara Bradley. 2016. *Life Reimagined: The science, art, and opportunity of midlife*. New York: Riverhead Books.

Hakim, D. and D. Dalby. 2015. 'Ireland votes to approve gay marriage, putting country in vanguard', *New York Times*, 23 May 2015. Accessed 25 May 2020. Available at: https://www.nytimes.com/2015/05/24/world/europe/ireland-gay-marriage-referendum.html.

Hannan, Carmel. 2015. 'Marriage, fertility and social class in twentieth-century Ireland'. In *The 'Irish' Family*, edited by Linda Connolly, 39–54. London: Routledge.

Harris, R. 1988. 'Theory and evidence: The "Irish stem family" and field data', *Man (N.S.)* 23 (3): 417–34.

Hayes, Blanaid, Gillian Walsh and Lucia Prihodova. 2017. 'National study of wellbeing of hospital doctors in Ireland – Report on the 2014 National Survey'. Royal College of Physicians of Ireland. Accessed 25 September 2020. Available at: https://static.rasset.ie/documents/news/wellbeing-report-web.pdf.

Hazan, Haim. 1980. *The Limbo People: A study of the constitution of the time universe among the aged*. International Library of Anthropology. London: Routledge & Kegan Paul.

Hazan, Haim. 1994. *Old Age: Constructions and deconstructions*. Cambridge: Cambridge University Press.

Health Insurance Authority Ireland. 2016. '2016 Annual report and accounts'. Accessed 28 September 2020. Available at: https://www.hia.ie/sites/default/files/62580%20HIA%20Annual%20Report%20ENGLISH%20with%20Cover.pdf.

Health Insurance Authority Ireland. 2020. 'Private health insurance market continued to rise in 2019 but impact of Covid19 is yet to be quantified', www.hia.ie/. July 2020. Accessed 28 September 2020. Available at: https://www.hia.ie/sites/default/files/I%20HIA%20Annual%20Report%202019%20Release%20I%2030%20July%202019%20FINAL.pdf.

Health Service Executive Ireland. 2020a. 'What is dementia?' Health Service Executive Ireland. 2020. Accessed 25 September 2020. Available at: https://www.hse.ie/eng/services/list/4/olderpeople/dementia/about-dementia/what-is-dementia/.

Health Service Executive Ireland. 2020b. 'Social Prescribing'. Ireland's health services website. Accessed 25 September 2020. Available at: https://www.hse.ie/eng/health/hl/selfmanagement/donegal/programmes-services/social-prescribing/.

Heffernan, Emma, John McHale and Niamh Moore-Chery, eds. 2017. *Debating Austerity in Ireland: Crisis, experience and recovery*. Dublin: Royal Irish Academy.

Hickman, Mary. 2014. '2014 thinking about Ireland and the Irish diaspora'. In *Are the Irish Different?*, edited by Tom Inglis, 133–44. Manchester: Manchester University Press.

Higgs, Paul and Chris Gilleard. 2015. *Rethinking Old Age: Theorising the fourth age*. London: Palgrave Macmillan.

Hockey, Jenny and Alison James. 2002. *Social Identities Across the Life Course*. Basingstoke: Palgrave Macmillan.

Hodkinson, Paul and Andy Bennett, eds. 1999. *Ageing and Youth Cultures: Music, style and identity*. London: Berg.

Horgan, Mervyn. 2004. 'Anti-urbanism as a way of life: Disdain for Dublin in the nationalist imaginary', *The Canadian Journal of Irish Studies* 30 (2): 38. https://doi.org/10.2307/25515532.

Hunt, Stephen J. 2005. *The Life Course: A sociological introduction*. Basingstoke: Palgrave Macmillan.

Hurd Clarke, Laura, Lauren Currie and Erica V. Bennett. 2020. '"I don't want to be, feel old": Older Canadian men's perceptions and experiences of physical activity', *Ageing and Society* 40 (1): 126–43. https://doi.org/10.1017/S0144686X18000788.

Husk, Kerryn, Julian Elston, Felix Gradinger, Lynne Callaghan and Sheena Asthana. 2019. 'Social Prescribing: Where is the evidence?', *British Journal of General Practice* 69 (678): 6–7. https://doi.org/10.3399/bjgp19X700325.

Hyland, Lucy. 2013. '"Doing" separation in contemporary Ireland: The experiences of women who separate in midlife'. D.Soc.Sc thesis, University College Cork. Accessed 25 May 2020. Available at: https://cora.ucc.ie/bitstream/handle/10468/1179/HylandL_DSocSc2013.pdf?sequence=2&isAllowed=y.

Inglis, Tom. 1998. *Moral Monopoly: The rise and fall of the Catholic Church in modern Ireland*. 2nd ed. Dublin: University College Dublin Press.

Inglis, Tom. 2007. *Global Ireland: Same difference*. Globalizing Regions. New York: Routledge.

Inglis, Tom. 2015. 'Family and the meaning of life in contemporary Ireland'. In *The 'Irish' Family*, edited by Linda Connolly, 70–84. London: Routledge.

Inglis, Tom and Susie Donnelly. 2011. 'Local and national belonging in a globalised world', *Irish Journal of Sociology* 19 (2): 127–43. https://doi.org/10.7227/IJS.19.2.9.

Ireland Department of Foreign Affairs and Trade. 2017. 'Global Irish civic forum'. Accessed 25 May 2020. Available at: https://www.dfa.ie/global-irish/support-overseas/global-irish-civic-forum/.

Ireland Department of Health. 2013. 'Healthy Ireland – A framework for improved health and wellbeing 2013–2025'. Irish governmental report. Accessed 25 September 2020. Available at: https://assets.gov.ie/7555/62842eef4b13413494b13340fff9077d.pdf.

Ireland Department of Health. 2019. 'Ministers Jim Daly and Damien English launch policy statement: "Housing options for our ageing population" – Increased options and more choice for people as they age'. www.gov.ie, 7 June 2019. Accessed 25 September 2020. Available at: https://www.gov.ie/en/press-release/924a81-ministers-jim-daly-and-damien-english-launch-policy-statementhousing/.

Ireland Department of Health. 2020. 'Healthy Ireland'. Gov.ie. Accessed 25 September 2020. Available at: https://assets.gov.ie/7555/62842eef4b13413494b13340fff9077d.pdf.

Isenhour, C. 2012. 'On the challenges of signalling ethics without the stuff'. In *Ethical Consumption: Social value and economic practice*, edited by J. Carrier and P. Luetchford. London: Berghahn.

Kamiya, Y. and V. Timonen. 2011. '3 – Older people as members of their families and communities'. In *Fifty Plus in Ireland 2011: First results from the Irish Longitudinal Study on Ageing*, edited by A. Barrett, George Savva, V. Timonen and R. A. Kenny. Vol. 37. Accessed 25 September 2020. Available at: https://tilda.tcd.ie/publications/reports/pdf/w1-key-findings-report/Chapter3.pdf.

Keenan, Mary. 2014. 'Sexual abuse and the Catholic Church'. In *Are the Irish Different?*, edited by Tom Inglis, 99–110. Manchester: Manchester University Press.

Keith, Jennie, Christine L. Fry, Anthony P. Glascock, Charlotte Ikels, Jeanette Dickerson-Putnam, Henry C. Harpending and Patricia Draper. 2005. *The Aging Experience: Diversity and commonality across cultures*. Thousand Oaks, CA: SAGE.

Kenny, Colum. 2009. 'Significant television: Journalism, sex abuse and the Catholic Church in Ireland', *Irish Communications Review* 11. Accessed 25 May 2020. Available at: http://www.dit.ie/icr/media/diticr/documents/5%20Kenny%20ICR%2011.pdf.

Kenny, Gillian. 2018. 'My cousin has just put me in a WhatsApp group called "Funerals" – it will keep us abreast of all upcoming deaths and details (the aunties are getting quite old now). This may be the most Irish thing that's ever happened to me.' Twitter. 6 December 2018. Accessed 25 May 2020. Available at: https://twitter.com/medievalgill/status/1070771612784431104?s=20.

King-O'Riain, Rebecca Chiyoko. 2015. 'Emotional streaming and transconnectivity: Skype and emotion practices in transnational families in Ireland', *Global Networks* 15 (2): 256–73. https://doi.org/10.1111/glob.12072.

Kochhar, Rakesh. 2017. '1. The middle class is large in many Western European countries, but it is losing ground in places'. PEW Research Center. 2017. Accessed 25 September 2020. Available at: https://www.pewresearch.org/global/2017/04/24/the-middle-class-is-large-in-many-western-european-countries-but-it-is-losing-ground-in-places/.

Lee, Joseph. 2008. *The Modernisation of Irish Society 1848–1918*. Dublin: Gill and Macmillan. http://search.ebscohost.com/login.aspx?direct=true&scope=site&db=nlebk&db=nlabk&AN=1034693.

Leibing, Annette and Lawrence Cohen, eds. 2006. *Thinking about Dementia: Culture, loss, and the anthropology of senility*. New Brunswick, NJ: Rutgers University Press.

Lunn, Pete, Tony Fahey and Carmel Hannan. 2010. 'Family figures: Family dynamics and family types in Ireland, 1986–2006'. Economic and Social Research Institute and the Family Support Agency. https://researchrepository.ucd.ie/handle/10197/5602.

Lyons, Ronan. 2017. 'Lack of apartments hits home', *The Irish Independent*, 25 September 2017. Accessed 25 May 2020. Available at: https://www.independent.ie/life/home-garden/homes/lack-of-apartments-hits-home-36160557.html.

Lyons, Ronan. 2020. 'Irish rental report Q4 2019: Daft.ie'. Daft.ie. 6 February 2020. Accessed 25 May 2020. Available at: https://www.daft.ie/report/ronan-lyons-2019q4-daftrentalprice.

Maguire, Mark and Fiona A. Murphy. 2015. *Integration in Ireland: The everyday lives of African migrants*. Manchester: Manchester University Press.

Maguire, Mark and Fiona Murphy. 2015. 'Ontological (in)security and African Pentecostalism in Ireland', *Ethnos* 81 (5): 842–64. https://doi.org/10.1080/00141844.2014.1003315.

Malone, Patrick. 2019. 'Irish population health: Life expectancy and mortality', Public Policy Ireland. 2 September 2019. Accessed 25 May 2020. Available at: http://publicpolicy.ie/papers/irish-population-health-life-expectancy-and-mortality/.

Marcoux, J. S. 2001. 'The refurbishment of memory'. In *Home Possessions*, edited by D. Miller, 68–86. Oxford; New York: Berg.

McBride, Louise. 2018. 'Pay alternative therapy health bills with conventional plans', *The Irish Independent*, 22 April 2018. Accessed 25 May 2020. Available at: https://www.independent.ie/business/personal-finance/pay-alternative-therapy-health-bills-with-conventional-plans-36830112.html.

McCullagh, Ciaran and Jo Campling. 2012. *Media Power: A sociological introduction*. Basingstoke; New York: Palgrave Macmillan.

McGarrigle, Christine and Rose Anne Kenny. 2013. 'Profile of the sandwich generation and intergenerational transfers in Ireland'. 1. The Irish Longitudinal Study on Ageing, Trinity College Dublin. TILDA. Accessed 25 September 2020. Available at: https://tilda.tcd.ie/publications/reports/pdf/Report_SandwichGeneration.pdf.

McGarrigle, Christine, Orna Donoghue, Siobhan Scarlett and Rose A. Kenny, eds. 2017. 'Health and wellbeing: Active ageing for older adults in Ireland. Evidence from The Irish Longitudinal Study on Ageing'. In TILDA (The Longitudinal Study on Ageing). Ireland: Trinity College Dublin. Accessed 25 September 2020. https://tilda.tcd.ie/publications/reports/pdf/w3-key-findings-report/TILDA%20Wave%203%20Key%20Findings%20report.pdf.

McGarrigle, Christine A., Virpi Timonen and Richard Layte. 2018. 'Choice and constraint in the negotiation of the grandparent role: A mixed-methods study', *Gerontology and Geriatric Medicine* 4 (January). https://doi.org/10.1177/2333721417750944.

McGarry, Patsy. 2016. 'Popularity of pilgrimages endure despite drop in mass attendance', *The Irish Times*, 7 June 2016. Accessed 25 September 2020. Available at: https://www.irishtimes.com/news/social-affairs/religion-and-beliefs/popularity-of-pilgrimages-endure-despite-drop-in-mass-attendance-1.2675471.

McNally, S., M. Share and A. Murray. 2014. 'Prevalence and predictors of grandparent childcare in Ireland: Findings from a nationally representative sample of infants and their families', *Child Care In Practice* 20 (2): 182–93. https://doi.org/10.1080/13575279.2013.859566.

McWilliams, David. 2018a. *Renaissance Nation: How the Pope's children rewrote the rules for Ireland*. Dublin: Gill Books. https://search.ebscohost.com/login.aspx?direct=true&scope=site&db=nlebk&db=nlabk&AN=1920972.

McWilliams, David. 2018b. 'We have witnessed the Dún Laoghaire-Isation of Ireland', *The Irish Times*, 27 October 2018. Accessed 25 September 2020. Available at: https://www.irishtimes.com/opinion/david-mcwilliams-we-have-witnessed-the-d%C3%BAn-laoghaire-isation-of-ireland-1.3674049.

McWilliams, David. 2019. 'Expansion of the middle class is Ireland's biggest feat', *The Irish Times*, 20 April 2019. Accessed 25 September 2020. Available at: https://www.irishtimes.com/opinion/david-mcwilliams-expansion-of-the-middle-class-is-ireland-s-biggest-feat-1.3865046.

Meaney, Gerardine. 1994. *Sex and Nation: Women in Irish culture and politics*. LIP pamphlets. Dublin: Attic Press.

Miller, Daniel, ed. 2001. *Home Possessions*. Oxford; New York: Berg.

Miller, Daniel. 2008. *The Comfort of Things*. Cambridge, UK; Malden: MA: Polity Press.

Miller, Daniel. 2016. *Social Media in an English Village: Or how to keep people at just the right distance*. London: UCL Press.

Miller, Daniel. 2017a. *The Comfort of People*. Cambridge, UK; Medford, MA: Polity Press.

Miller, Daniel. 2017b. 'The ideology of friendship in the era of Facebook', *HAU: Journal of Ethnographic Theory* 7 (1): 377–95. https://doi.org/10.14318/hau7.1.025.

Miller, Daniel. 2020. 'Brexit and the decolonization of Ireland', *HAU: Journal of Ethnographic Theory* 10 (2): 356–60. https://doi.org/10.1086/709797.

Miller, Daniel, Laila Abed Rabho, Patrick Awondo, Maya de Vries, Marília Duque, Pauline Garvey, Laura Haapio-Kirk, Charlotte Hawkins, Alfonso Otaegui, Shireen Walton, Xinyuan Wang. 2021. *The Global Smartphone: Beyond a youth technology*. London: UCL Press.

Money Guide Ireland. 2020. 'Inheritance tax in Ireland', 2 May 2020. Accessed 25 September 2020. Available at: https://www.moneyguideireland.com/inheritance-tax-in-ireland.html.

Motherway, B., M. Kelly, P. Faughnan and H. Tovey. 2003. *Trends in Irish Environmental Attitudes between 1993 and 2002*. First Report from the Research Programme on Environmental Attitudes, Values and Behaviour in Ireland. Department of Sociology, University College Dublin, Dublin, Ireland. Available at: http://www. ucd. ie/environ/home. htm.

Murphy, Fiona. 2017. 'Austerity Ireland, the new thrift culture and sustainable consumption', *Journal of Business Anthropology* 6 (2): 158. https://doi.org/10.22439/jba.v6i2.5410.

Murphy, Fiona. 2019. 'Friend or foe?: A reflection on the ethno-politics of friendship and ethnographic writing in anthropological practice', *Etnofoor* 31 (1): 11–28.

National Council for Curriculum and Assessment (NCAA). 2011. 'Social, personal and health education: Curriculum framework'. National Council for Curriculum and Assessment (NCAA). Accessed 25 May 2020. Available at: https://curriculumonline.ie/getmedia/007175e5-7bb7-44c0-86cb-ba7cd54be53a/SCSEC_SPHE_Framework_English.pdf.

NHBC Foundation. 2017. 'Moving insights from the over-55s: What homes do they buy?' Accessed 24 September 2020. Available at: https://www.nhbcfoundation.org/publication/moving-insights-from-the-over-55s-what-homes-do-they-buy/.

NHS (National Health Service). 2020. 'Social Prescribing'. NHS website, 2020. Accessed 28 September 2020. Available at: https://www.england.nhs.uk/personalisedcare/social-prescribing/.

Ní Léime, Áine and Debra Street. 2019. 'Working later in the USA and Ireland: Implications for precariously and securely employed women', *Ageing and Society* 39 (10): 2194–2218. https://doi.org/10.1017/S0144686X18000508.

Norgaard, Kari Marie. 2011. *Living in Denial: Climate change, emotions, and everyday life*. Cambridge, MA: MIT Press.

Norris, Michelle. 2017. 'The rise and fall of Ireland's property-based welfare state: home-ownership rates, policies and meanings in a historical perspective'. In *Housing, Wealth and Welfare*, edited by Caroline Dewilde and Richard Ronald, 37–59. Cheltenham, Glos; Northampton, MA: Edward Elgar Publishing.

Norris, Michelle. 2020. 'Unmaking home: Making homes for shelter or for investment?' 'Davis now lectures: Making home' series. rte.ie. 4 February 2020. Accessed 25 May 2020. Available at: https://www.rte.ie/culture/2020/0131/1112298-davis-now-lectures-making-homes-for-shelter-or-for-investment/.

Norris, Michelle and Aideen Hayden. 2018. 'The future of council housing: An analysis of the financial sustainability of local authority provided social housing'. Report for the Community Foundation of Ireland, p.4.

Nussbaum, Martha Craven. 2017. 'Our bodies ourselves: Ageing, stigma and disgust'. In *Aging Thoughtfully*, edited by Martha Craven Nussbaum and Saul Levmore. Oxford: Oxford University Press.

Ó Crualaoich, Gearóid. 2003. *The Book of the Cailleach: Stories of the wise-woman healer*. Cork: Cork University Press.

Ó Giolláin, Diarmuid. 2000. *Locating Irish Folklore: Tradition, modernity, identity*. Sterling, VA: Cork University Press.

Ó Laoire, Lillis. 2005. *On a Rock in the Middle of the Ocean: Song and singers in Tory Island.* Conamara: Cló Iar-Chonnachta.

O'Doherty, Colm and Ashling Jackson, eds. 2015. *Learning on the Job: Parenting in modern Ireland.* Dublin: Oak Tree Press.

O'Dwyer, J. G. 2018. 'Interest in country's pilgrim walks continues to flourish', *The Irish Examiner*, 26 March 2018. Accessed 25 May 2020. Available at: https://www.pressreader.com/ireland/irish-examiner/20180326/281779924670958.

O'Halloran, Marie. 2018. '"Lots of us did": Varadkar says he was among housebuyers who got deposit from parents', *The Irish Times*, 23 January 2018. Accessed 25 September 2020. Available at: https://www.irishtimes.com/news/politics/oireachtas/lots-of-us-did-varadkar-says-he-was-among-housebuyers-who-got-deposit-from-parents-1.3366241.

O'Halloran, Marie. 2019. '"Humiliation, disrespect, deceit": Taoiseach apologises for cervical check controversy', *The Irish Times*, 22 October 2019. Accessed 25 September 2020. Available at: https://www.irishtimes.com/news/health/humiliation-disrespect-deceit-taoiseach-apologises-for-cervicalcheck-controversy-1.4058892.

O'Riain, Sean. 2014. *The Rise and Fall of Ireland's Celtic Tiger: Liberalism, boom and bust.* Cambridge: Cambridge University Press.

Ortner, Sherry. 1992. *High Religion: A cultural and political history of Sherpa Buddhism.* Delhi: Motilal Banarsidass Publishers Private Ltd.

O'Shea, Eamon and Áine Ní Léime. 2012. 'The impact of the Bealtaine Arts Programme on the quality of life, wellbeing and social interaction of older people in Ireland', *Ageing and Society* 32 (5): 851–72. https://doi.org/10.1017/S0144686X11000717.

Peace, Adrian. 1989. 'From Arcadia to Anomie: Critical notes on the constitution of Irish society as an anthropological object', *Critique of Anthropology* 9 (1): 89–111. https://doi.org/10.1177/0308275X8900900107.

Peace, Adrian. 2001. *A World of Fine Difference – The social architecture of a modern Irish village.* Dublin: University College Dublin Press.

Peillon, Michael and Mary P. Corcoran, eds. 2002. *Ireland Unbound: A turn of the century chronicle.* Vol. 3. Dublin: Institute of Public Administration.

Pierse, Tom, Luke Barry, Liam Glynn, Diarmuid Quinlan, Andrew Murphy and Ciaran O'Neill. 2019. 'A pilot study of the duration of GP consultations in Ireland', *Pilot and Feasibility Studies* 5 (1): 142. https://doi.org/10.1186/s40814-019-0532-4.

Pope, Conor and Ronan McGreevy. 2020. 'Coronavirus: Ringsend residents invent balcony bingo to keep entertained', *The Irish Times*, 21 March 2020. Accessed 24 September 2020. Available at: https://www.irishtimes.com/news/ireland/irish-news/coronavirus-ringsend-residents-invent-balcony-bingo-to-keep-entertained-1.4209098.

Prendergast, David and Chiara Garattini, eds. 2015. *Aging and the Digital Life Course.* New York: Berghahn Books.

Raidió Teilifís Éireann (RTÉ). 2018. 'RTÉ Investigates – Public v private: the battle for care'. News website. Raidió Teilifís Éireann (RTÉ), 1 February 2018. Accessed 24 September 2020. Available at: https://www.rte.ie/news/investigations-unit/2017/1122/922105-rte-investigates-public-v-private-the-battle-for-care/.

Ramirez, Michelle. 2006. 'Manufacturing heterosexuality: Hormone replacement therapy and menopause in urban Oaxaca', *Culture, Health & Sexuality* 8 (6): 545–58. https://doi.org/10.1080/13691050600891909.

Reddan, Fiona. 2017. 'The new retirement: "My big fear is being old and poor"', *The Irish Times*, 29 July 2017. Accessed 28 September 2020. Available at: https://www.irishtimes.com/life-and-style/people/the-new-retirement-my-big-fear-is-being-old-and-poor-1.3168564.

Reuters Institute and OII (Oxford Internet Institute). 2019.'Digital News Report – Ireland', Digital News Report (annual). Accessed 26 May 2020. Available at: http://www.digitalnewsreport.org/survey/analysis-by-country/2019/ireland-2019/.

RTÉ News. 2018. 'Referendum results: At a glance'. RTÉ News, 26 May 2018. Accessed 25 September 2020. Available at: https://www.rte.ie/news/newslens/2018/0526/966234-referendum-results-at-a-glance/.

RTÉ Radio 1. 'News at One', 15 January 2020. Accessed 25 September 2020. Available online at: www.rte.ie/radio/radioplayer/html5/#/radio1/11140162.

Saris, A. Jamie. 2008. 'An uncertain dominion: Irish psychiatry, methadone, and the treatment of opiate abuse', *Culture, Medicine, and Psychiatry* 32 (2): 259–77. https://doi.org/10.1007/s11013-008-9089-z.

Saris, A. Jamie and Brendan Bartley. 2002. 'Icon and structural violence in a Dublin "underclass" housing estate', *Anthropology Today* 18 (4): 14–19. https://doi.org/10.1111/1467-8322.00139.

Scharf, Thomas, Virpi Timonen, Gemma Carney, Catherine Conlon, Irish Centre for Social Gerontology, Trinity College Dublin and Social Policy and Ageing Research Centre. 2013. *Changing Generations: Findings from new research on intergenerational relations in Ireland.* NUI Galway: Irish Centre for Social Gerontology.

Scheper-Hughes, Nancy. 2000. 'Ire in Ireland', *Ethnography* 1 (1): 117–40. https://doi.org/10.1177/14661380022230660.

Scheper-Hughes, Nancy. 2001 [1979]. *Saints, Scholars, and Schizophrenics: Mental illness in rural Ireland.* 20th anniversary ed., rev. and expanded. Berkeley: University of California Press.

Settersten, Richard A. 2018. *Invitation to the Life Course: Toward new understandings of later life.* New York: Routledge.

Seward, Rudy Ray. 2017. 'Jane Gray, Ruth Geraghty, and David Ralph, family rhythms: The changing textures of family life in Ireland', *Irish Journal of Sociology* 25 (3): 334–38. https://doi.org/10.1177/0791603517711566.

Share, Michelle and Liz Kerrins. 2009. 'The role of grandparents in childcare in Ireland: Towards a research agenda', *Irish Journal of Applied Social Studies* 9 (1), Article 5. https://doi.org/10.21427/D7NQ8C.

Share, Perry, Hilary Tovey and Mary P. Corcoran. 2007. *A Sociology of Ireland.* Dublin: Gill and Macmillan.

Sokolovsky, Jay, ed. 2020. *The Cultural Context of Ageing.* Santa Barbara, CA: Praeger.

South, Jane, Tracy J. Higgins, James Woodall and Simon M. White. 2008. 'Can social prescribing provide the missing link?', *Primary Health Care Research & Development* 9 (04): 310. https://doi.org/10.1017/S146342360800087X.

Spencer, Paul, ed. 1990. *Anthropology and the Riddle of the Sphinx: Paradoxes of change in the life course.* London; New York: Routledge.

Stafford, Philip B., ed. 2019. *The Global Age-Friendly Community Movement: A critical appraisal.* New York: Berghahn Books.

Statista. 2020. 'Number of smartphone users in Ireland from 2018 to 2024 (in Millions)*', Statistics aggregator. 21 April 2020. Accessed 24 September 2020. Available at: https://www.statista.com/statistics/494649/smartphone-users-in-ireland/.

Steadman, Lyle B., Craig T. Palmer and Christopher F. Tilley. 1996. 'The universality of ancestor worship', *Ethnology* 35 (1): 63. https://doi.org/10.2307/3774025.

Taylor, Lawrence. 1989. 'Bás InEirinn: Cultural constructions of death in Ireland', *Anthropological Quarterly* 62 (4): 175–87.

Taylor, Lawrence J. 1995. *Occasions of Faith: An anthropology of Irish Catholics.* Series in Contemporary Ethnography. Philadelphia: University of Pennsylvania Press.

Taylor, Lawrence. 1996. 'There are two things that people don't like to hear about themselves: The anthropology of Ireland and the Irish view of anthropology', *South Atlantic Quarterly* 95 (1): 213–66.

The Economist. 2017. 'Retirement is out, new portfolio careers are in', *The Economist*, 6 July 2017. Accessed 24 September 2020. Available at: https://www.economist.com/special-report/2017/07/06/retirement-is-out-new-portfolio-careers-are-in.

The Economist. 2019. 'Graphic detail: Tax and inequality', *The Economist*, 13 April 2019.

The Irish Longitudinal Study on Ageing (TILDA). 2017. 'New TILDA report on ageing in Ireland launched today', The Irish Longitudinal Study on Ageing (TILDA), 7 March 2017. Accessed 25 September 2020. https://tilda.tcd.ie/news-events/2017/1702-w3-key-findings/.

The Irish Longitudinal Study on Ageing (TILDA). 2020. 'The Irish Longitudinal Study on Ageing (TILDA)', Trinity College Dublin – TILDA Study. https://tilda.tcd.ie/.

The Pensions Authority. 2020. 'State pensions: State pension age'. The Pensions Authority webpage. 2020. Accessed 25 September 2020. Available at: https://www.pensionsauthority.ie/en/lifecycle/state_pensions/state_pension_age/.

Turkle, S. 2011. *Alone Together: Why we expect more from technology and less from each other.* New York: Basic Books.

Wall, Martin. 2019a. 'Costs of free GP care for all could increase "exponentially"', *The Irish Times*, 8 October 2019. Accessed 25 September 2020. Available at: https://www.irishtimes.com/news/health/costs-of-free-gp-care-for-all-could-increase-exponentially-1.4044258.

Wall, Martin. 2019b. 'Doctors abused and bullied in health service, Medical Council warns', *The Irish Times*, 9 October 2019. Accessed 24 September 2020. Available at: https://www.irishtimes.com/news/ireland/irish-news/doctors-abused-and-bullied-in-health-service-medical-council-warns-1.4045353.

Wall, Martin and J. Horgan-Jones. 2019. 'The old country: Get ready for an ageing Ireland', *The Irish Times*, 24 August 2019. Accessed 24 September 2020. Available at: https://www.irishtimes.com/life-and-style/health-family/the-old-country-get-ready-for-an-ageing-ireland-1.3993009.

Walsh, John. 2017. 'Ireland leads EU in expansion of middle class', *The Times*, 26 April 2017. Accessed 24 September 2020. Available at: https://www.thetimes.co.uk/article/ireland-leads-eu-in-expansion-of-middle-class-qhmmc6cbg.

Ward, K. 2003. 'An ethnographic study of internet consumption in Ireland: Between domesticity and the public participation'. Dublin: COMTEC Research Centre, Dublin City University. Accessed 24 May 2020. Available at: http://www.lse.ac.uk/media@lse/research/EMTEL/reports/ward_2003_emtel.pdf.

Ward, Mark, Sarah Gibney and Irene Mosca. 2018. '4 – Volunteering and social partication'. In *Wellbeing and Health in Ireland's Over 50s – 2009–2016*. Wave 4. Accessed 24 September 2020. Available at: https://tilda.tcd.ie/publications/reports/pdf/w4-key-findings-report/TILDA-Wave4-Key-Findings-report.pdf.

Ward, Mark, Richard Layte and Rose Anne Kenny. 2019. 'Loneliness, social isolation, and their discordance among older adults', The Irish Longitudinal Study on Ageing (TILDA). Ireland: Trinity College Dublin. Accessed 24 May 2020. Available at: https://tilda.tcd.ie/publications/reports/pdf/Report_Loneliness.pdf.

Wels, Jacques. 2020. 'Assessing the impact of partial early retirement on self-perceived health, depression level and quality of life in Belgium: A longitudinal perspective using the survey of health, ageing and retirement in Europe (SHARE)', *Ageing and Society* 40 (3): 512–36. https://doi.org/10.1017/S0144686X18001149.

Weston, C. 2018. 'Revealed: How much we spend visiting the doctor each year', *The Irish Independent*, 13 March 2018. Accessed 25 May 2020. Available at: https://www.independent.ie/business/personal-finance/revealed-how-much-we-spend-visiting-the-doctor-each-year-36699145.html.

White, Timothy J. 2010. 'The impact of British colonialism on Irish Catholicism and national identity: Repression, reemergence, and divergence', *Études Irlandaises*, no. 35–1 (June): 21–37. https://doi.org/10.4000/etudesirlandaises.1743.

Wills, Clair. 2001. 'Women, domesticity and the family: Recent feminist work in Irish cultural studies', *Cultural Studies* 15 (1): 33–57. https://doi.org/10.1080/09502380010006745.

Wilson, Thomas M. 1984. 'From Clare to the Common Market: Perspectives in Irish ethnography', *Anthropological Quarterly* 57 (1): 1–15.

Wilson, Thomas M. 1997. 'Themes in the anthropology of Ireland'. In *Europe in the Anthropological Imagination*, edited by Susan Parman, 107–17. Englewood Cliffs, NJ: Prentice Hall.

Wilson, Thomas M. and Hastings Donnan. 2006. *The Anthropology of Ireland*. Oxford: Berg.

Witoszek, Nina and P. F. Sheeran. 1998. *Talking to the Dead: A study of Irish funerary traditions*. Vol. 117. Amsterdam and Atlanta, GA: Rodopi.

Wulff, Helena. 2007. *Dancing at the Crossroads: Memory and mobility in Ireland*. New York: Berghahn Books.

Wulff, Helena. 2015. 'Ireland in the world, the world in Ireland: World anthropology', *American Anthropologist* 117 (1): 142. https://doi.org/10.1111/aman.12175.

Wulff, Helena. 2017. *Rhythms of Writing: An anthropology of Irish literature*. London; New York: Bloomsbury Academic.

Yeats, William B. 1968. *Selected Poetry*. Edited by Alexander Norman Jeffares. London: Macmillan.

Zamorano Llena, Carmen. 2019. 'Looking very old age in the eye: A nuanced approach to the fourth age in contemporary Irish fiction: A case study', *The Gerontologist* 59 (5): 956–63. https://doi.org/10.1093/geront/gny035.

Index

Lightning Source UK Ltd.
Milton Keynes UK
UKHW021828050521
383183UK00002B/22